under the sun

under the sun

CAROLINE CONRAN'S
FRENCH COUNTRY COOKING

PHOTOGRAPHS BY GILLES DE CHABANEIX

LAUREL
GLEN

San Diego, California

Contents

A Personal Journey Through Southern France

My obsession with southern France began, as it did for many others, with a trip to St. Tropez. In the sixties, everyone who loved food and eating shared the open secret that it took no more effort to get across the English Channel than driving to Lydd's tiny airport, with its planes designed to take three or four cars. These planes did a noisy, wallowing trundle from English sand and sea to French sea and sand, and soon you were leaving Le Touquet and heading south for golden Provence, with a bookmaker's sandwich (steak pressed overnight in a loaf of bread) burning a hole in the picnic basket.

The best routes took one along lengthy, straight green roads, avoiding Paris completely. They were lined with sycamores, all but traffic-free, and once the muddy beet fields of northern France were left behind, the eye was revived with a feast of wildflowers, forests, meadows, Charolais cattle, and a string of pearl-like villages, built first from dark granite and then warm limestone.

It was not necessary to reserve a hotel, since every small town had hotels with rooms, some rather stylish and bourgeois, smelling comfortably of *sauce hollandaise*, others in hidden back streets. If the chosen hotel was full, and if it was already getting dark, there was a *frisson* of anxiety. But there was always a place to stay, and even the simplest provided fresh *crudités* followed by *steak frites* or the *plat du jour*—stewed rabbit, *navarin* of lamb, or *coq au vin*. The following day, having followed the old Roman trade route through Burgundy and down the Rhône, you were in the Var.

In St. Tropez we came upon a restaurant called Chez Fifine, one of those rare places with a Woman-Genius in the kitchen. Fifine herself cooked and served *soupe au pistou* in yellow pottery bowls, with enough basil and garlic floating in it to diffuse your whole body with a rose-colored glow. The next day we were on the beach . . . and the next suffering the agonies of scorched shoulders. After a week of looking for, and finding, the best local restaurants in the Var, high in the hills away from the burning sands of Pampelonne and a Mediterranean iridescent with suntan oil, it was obvious that the South, or more specifically, the region known as the Midi, offered something far more seductive, even, than lying in the sun. It was the food.

The French Midi is defined in the *Grande Larousse de la Langue Française* as "the southern part of the country." It is just that, but for the sake of clarity one can say that it lies south of the 45° meridian. Valence and Brive la Gaillarde are regarded as "gateways" to the Midi. Bordeaux is near the line too. Daudet, the author of *Lettres de mon Moulin*, lived at Fontvieille, just a few miles from Arles, and was the greatest chronicler and aficionado of the Midi. He was infatuated with it and its people. In his novel *Numa Roumestan*, which illustrates the heterogeneous nature of the Midi, he refers to the enormous Café Malmus, in the rue du Four St. Germain in Paris, smelling of garlicky stews and stinking mountain cheeses, frequented by the students from all over the South. He tells us, "The whole of the French Midi blossomed, here in the café, in all its shades of diversity: Midi gascon, Midi provençal, people from Bordeaux, from Toulouse, from Marseille, Midi périgourdin, Auvergnat, Ariégeois, Ardèchois, Pyrénéen." But despite its diversity, you can feel a change of atmosphere, a sense of relaxation, as you enter the Midi, which has a spirit quite separate from and different to the rest of France.

Large plane trees in village squares shade the markets and cafés, where people meet to shop, drink coffee and *kir*, or *pastis*, or to eat. Water, being scarce, is the favorite sight and sound; fountains and cisterns spout and splash. In the long summer afternoons, shuttered streets stand baking in flat light, empty of people. Shops close inconveniently and only the occasional dog or drunkard stays outdoors. As the late afternoon shadows give the streets their character back, outdoor social life revives.

There is a casual flow to this life, and when you eat, the food seems more casual too. You may look for a dark local café with check cloths, where everyone eats the same simple *plats du jour*, and local wine is placed on the table in blackish, open bottles, which serve as carafes, and which are replaced as often as they are empty. Or you may prefer a restaurant serving marvelous Michelin-starred food, but even here you are generally spared intimidating pompous service.

Southern food is warm and generous in feeling—it looks good, it is mainly olive-oil based, and most of it is not outrageously rich. Butter and cream are luxuries here. The Southwest is, it is true, overflowing with foie gras and Armagnac, but *le paradoxe français* is that the inhabitants live longer than their fat-fearful critics. Statistics show that the people of Gascony, for example, are outstanding for their health and longevity. Cooking with goose fat is considered healthier than cooking with butter, and gives a crisp and gooey caramelized finish and a deep, satisfying taste. If you drink red wine and eat lots of garlic with it, your heart will rejoice, it seems.

At its best everyday level, the food from the South is simple to make and relies on a harmony of flavors rather than a lot of decoration or extravagant ingredients to make it appetizing. The French call it *cuisine du terroir*—country cooking—and there can be few things on earth more conducive to comfort and well-being, a comfort much needed by those who work on and live from the land. For life can be hard here; in winter, the Mistral or some other wind cuts you in half and strips the soil to its bones, and too much rainfall comes all at once and floods everything. In summer, alongside the vines, blue lavender, and sunflowers are harsh, rocky, marginal territories, home only to lizards, and dotted with stumpy bushes of thyme, juniper, rosemary, and thorny thistles. But olives and grapes get their strength and sweetness from the sun and develop more concentrated flavors when water is scarce. And when the familiar, earthy scent of the herb-covered terrain of the *garrigue* and repetitive sounds of cicadas saturate the atmosphere, life seems sweet. At lunchtime, the taste of the rose-pink or red wine, and the elemental flavor of food eaten outdoors, bring a different sense of well-being, which the French describe as feeling at home in your skin—*bien dans la peau*. In the evening, a fast but magical dusk precedes an appreciable cooling of the air and with a sense of relief one can light the mosquito coils and eat outdoors by candlelight.

Due to southern France's borders with Italy and Spain, and its historic connections with the Greeks, the Romans, and North Africa, the food of the Midi is vibrant, unendingly interesting, and thoroughly rewarding for the cook. Pasta, particularly ravioli, has crept over the border from Italy and has become a traditional and beautifully made local food in the Alpes Maritimes (although they claim that raviolis were a French invention, coming from the Vercors). In the Lot, many villages celebrate their fête with a *méchoui*—a lamb cooked in a pit, Moroccan-style, and basted with a mop dipped in salty water. The North African influence is also noticeable in Arles, where vendors sells couscous, harissa (a paste of chilies and tomato flavored with cumin), spices, huge bunches of fresh mint and coriander (cilantro), and great heaps of lemons, both fresh and preserved. Spanish paella is cooked on the streets on fête days and the pastry shops sell crescent-shaped pastries and sweets, a Muslim crescent moon symbol. Shocking pink, a color that sweeps across the Middle East to India, is a favorite for *dragées* and other candies. In the Pays Basque, the colors are the scarlet of peppers, the black of squid ink, and the warm yellow of saffron; tortilla, chorizo, piquillos, and a Spanish black sausage give menus here a Hispanic flourish, while salt cod is on every menu and the most refined art of chocolate-making is at home in Bayonne, brought across the Pyrenees by Jews fleeing persecution in Spain.

For those fortunate enough to live in the Midi, it is always *notre Midi*. For those who don't live there but often wish they did, one of the best ways I know of keeping hold of treasured memories is to smell and taste in your own kitchen the distinctive flavors of southern France. Anyone can get into the kitchen and chop and slice and pound away, making saffron-scented fish soups, grilled squid with fresh lemons, vegetable dishes cooked with olive oil and plenty of garlic, or grilled fish with aromatic herbs such as fennel. The kitchen air fills with the comforting smell of sliced onions frying, of cut lemons, of bruised mint and basil. Such scents evoke a certain sensual atmosphere, just as flavors can revive past experiences with great intensity.

Because of the rich diversity of the cooking of the South, I have felt it unnecessary to stick to the perceived notion of what French food should be, or once was, and I have taken some liberties. I hope that this simple, easygoing version of southern French country cooking, infused with the characteristic essences of sun, earth, and garlic, will give enjoyment to those who love the Midi, bringing back memories of, or perhaps instilling a new enthusiasm for, the food of the warm South.

Impressions of the South

THE LOT AND THE DORDOGNE

In the mid-seventies, I began cooking in a small French kitchen whose blue-shuttered windows look out on the river Dordogne, below Souillac. This is a land of deep-cut, fertile valleys and high limestone plateaus known as *causses*. It has many exceptional country markets, so the first thing I did was to pin up, on the plate cupboard, a list of them and which day they were held. The two favorite places were, and still are, the hilltop town of Gourdon, whose stalls are beside or inside the elegant entrance of a massively buttressed fourteenth-century church at the top of the old town, and Martel, with its seven spectacular stone towers.

Martel's old streets, built of crumbly limestone, enclose a comfortable central marketplace. Under the little open-sided market building, and clustered around it, are stalls where you can still find all the fruits and produce of the local farms and gardens. In spring it is all red, white, and green—the season of peas, asparagus, artichokes, and wild strawberries—and in the fall, brown, gold, and orange—fungi, pumpkins, and dahlias. Equally inviting are the cheese stalls. In spring and summer, goat farmers preside over mounds of fresh white goat's cheeses called *cabécous*, tasting of thyme, which harden and turn ivory-colored with age. As the leaves turn bright yellow, bags of shelled fresh walnuts, white as teeth, for which this town is a trading center, accompany the cheeses. Later, the new season's walnut oil, which is particularly sweet for bitter winter salads, makes its appearance with the cabbages and pumpkins. The seasons all bring new tastes, new ingredients for dishes that suit the weather. There is always a mix of flowers, fruit, vegetables, cheeses, pâtés, and poultry, the things that make living in the Midi so agreeable.

In summer, making lunch is not difficult in this part of the world, with an abundance of local terrines, locally cured hams, nobbly tomatoes, Cavaillon melons, and good bread to choose from. I must have bought hundreds of chickens and guinea fowl, roasting them in my tin Calor gas oven, and I cannot recall ever having been disappointed. Eating in a meadow that is a tangle of wild mint and marjoram, blue scabious, and purple vetch, shaded by a tree loaded with greengages, may have something to do with it. At one time, across this meadow came Madame Malbec with her vast loaves of homemade sourdough bread, risen in baskets in the sun and cooked in an outdoor wood oven. Locally baked bread, in large rounds, with a holey, chewy, satisfying interior is still just as good and is tough enough to keep for at least a week.

Because of the proximity of the Dordogne river, the pleasure local people take in fishing, and the distance from the sea, menus tend to favor river fish: a whole pike on a white oval dish, quickly fried trout, or rustling plates of tiny fried fish (*la friture de la Dordogne*) are all regular features.

In order to sell their produce, many of the local farmers have opened tiny shops in barns or cellars offering their best pâté, foie gras, pork fillets in aspic, and confit of duck or goose. Others sell their own lavender honey and homemade *pruneaux*—plums dried on special drying racks called *claies*, which are also used for drying goat's cheeses, ceps, apples, apricots, and pears, and, a new activity, tomatoes. The *Reine Claude* greengages are an important crop locally, and traditionally a street market dedicated to them takes place at Carennac, beneath the walls of Fénelon's (a seventeenth-century poet and writer) château, when the wholesalers and jam-makers arrive. They are eaten as a dessert, preserved in eau-de-vie or Armagnac, but best of all they are turned into *La Vieille Prune*, a delectable *digestif*, which warms and mellows the spirit; too bad if you feel ghastly the next day.

BORDEAUX, THE LANDES, AND THE GERS

All around Bordeaux is "Vine Country"; to the west of the Gironde lies the gravelly Médoc, where many of the most eminent red wines, and some not so glorious, are made. Here the landscape is neat, conservative, and prosperous, covered in vineyards and geared toward the making, keeping, selling, and drinking of wine. Beneath the streets of Bordeaux, below the old Quays, lie extensive cellars, some of which are so vast that they have to be crossed by bicycle. Even the food in this region tends to be chosen for its compatibility with the wine, for while it is rich and sensuous, there are few strident flavors.

For a taste of the vineyards, have lunch in St. Emilion, a gem of a village, and buy some of the supreme almond macaroons made locally. The afternoon, or indeed the whole day, or a week, or a lifetime, can be spent around the châteaux of the area (the most admired is Château Cheval Blanc), tasting wine until the horizon begins to tilt. Beware the late purchase, when palate and judgment may be overexcited or blurred. Sometimes with a wine tasting, there comes a tipping-point and it has to stop; my antidote is to head southwest from Bordeaux, toward the west coast and Arcachon, where vines give way to the pine trees of the Landes. Then comes the sea.

The Bassin d'Arcachon, with its linear blue, green, and white seascape, is a vast tidal basin, separated from the Atlantic by a long peninsula covered in pine forests and, toward the tip, holiday houses; at the sandy mouth of the basin lies Cap Ferret. Twice a day the beach is covered by the tide, when all you can see are boats and rows of dark sticks emerging from the water. These mark out the oyster beds, which are uncovered to the changing sky as the tide streams out to sea. Working in rhythm with the tides are the oyster harvesters. As the morning tide drops, there are stooping figures in the silver water. They grab the flat mesh bags of oysters from their racks and swish them about to wash off the seaweed, before lifting them onto tractors or placing in rustic-looking barges that take them to Arcachon, on their way to seafood restaurants all over France. A few of the old, tarred oyster cabins are left in this area of sandy inlets, although several are new. Approached by paths of crushed oyster shells, they sell oysters, opened and placed on beds of ice and seaweed on huge Styrofoam platters, with lemons. In restaurants, and at the great summer street fair, the deep *creuses* oysters, called *Portugaises*, are served with grilled pork sausages, which you eat in mouthfuls alternately with the icy oysters, washed down with chilled white wine.

If, instead of going to the seaside, you head directly south from Bordeaux, you will drive through the main part of the Parc Regional des Landes de Gascogne. This flat land has a strange, hypnotic atmosphere. You see the same landscape—receding rows of vertical pines, followed by heath, followed by cornfields, followed by receding rows of pines again—repeated like a sophisticated exercise in perspective. In the past, it belonged to the shepherds, who used to wear wooden clogs, pancake-shaped berets, and big shaggy capes of unshorn sheep hides, with the wool on the outside. They did their shepherding on stilts, in order to see the sheep across the sandy flats. In old photographs they look charming and bizarre, making omelettes on a little bonfire for an Easter feast in the open air, with a small, black frying pan whose handle is about a yard long, presumably so they can cook with stilts on. This Easter omelette traditionally contains black pudding or tripe sausage and some highly seasoned pork sausage cut in slices. Other omelettes are made with garlic shoots or little fish called *pesquits*. Once, after a morning's walk through the countryside, I relished a Gascon omelette of *pibales*, the tiny white eel-fry, fried with chili flakes and sliced garlic.

A little farther south, in the Gers, several walks in April through orchards and rolling meadows have been cut short by sudden rainfall. For although on a level with Nice and Monte Carlo, this region has some capricious weather sweeping in from the Atlantic and swirling off the Pyrenees. It also has what is well-described as *douceur de vie*, where life is sweet.

THE PAYS BASQUE

Follow the straight roads south, and you will find yourself in the land of the berets—the Basque country. The first stopping place is Bayonne, where the land of bullfights starts. It is a cathedral town, center of chocolate-making and the main marketplace for the regional hams, with a special *Foire aux Jambons de Bayonne* on the Thursday before Easter, which takes place next to the covered market on the quay by the river Nive.

The French Basques have sea and mountains in their bones. They love poetry, songs, and dancing. Exploring their country, the Pays Basque, you can go rapidly from eating chili-hot fish stew and drinking Sangria in the little resort of St.-Jean-de-Luz, seated in the sun by the wind-chopped Bay of Biscay, to

following the pilgrim route to Santiago into St.-Jean-Pied-de-Port, high up in the Pyrenees, a handsome market town on the river Nive with timbered, flower-bedecked medieval houses.

The mountain people of the Pyrénées-Atlantiques, whose lines of communication have until recently been restricted, continue with their traditional trades and skills. One of these is making sheep's cheeses, the *fromage de brebis*, called *Ardi Gassna*, a strong, salty, stinging mountain cheese rather like pecorino.

It is hard to imagine a better breakfast than this fromage de brebis served with black cherry jam. Or, a more satisfying finish to a meal than a slice of white sheep's cheese accompanied by juicy homemade quince jelly and fresh golden raisin bread. To buy one of these cheeses you can either go to a farm in the Vallée d'Ossau, or to the market in the main street of St.-Jean-Pied-de-Port (where they have a cheese fair in August). Or try the Quais on the river Nive in Bayonne, where local farmers sell their versions of the delicious cheese, together with huge bunches of arum lilies and their own chestnut or acacia honey, which is eaten with *les Caills*, a fresh white ewe's milk curd cheese.

Perhaps the most important local work, though, is making charcuterie, not only the local ham cured with the local red chili (*piment d'Espelette*), but *lomo* (cured pork loin) chorizo, and a mountain sausage *Jens Basque*, black puddings, and lots of game *saucissons*, including wild boar.

PYRÉNÉES-MEDITERRANÉE AND THE PAYS-CATALAN

Like the Basques, the Catalans have feet on both sides of the French-Spanish border, with a combination of mountains and sea, this time the Mediterranean. Collioure, near the Spanish border, is a steep village descending to a fishing port of monumental architecture, including the grand Château Royal, surrounded by gigantic fig trees giving off a divine scent. The quayside walk is covered in a carpet of dried figs and bathed in sulphur-golden light. Up in the town there are palms and magnolias, and outside the Hôtel de Limmonnier, big bushy lemon trees grow profusely. Behind lie vineyards and the lower slopes of what eventually become the Pyrenees.

At one time practically everybody in this appealing town was involved either with trading pearls, silk, and spices with the East, or with *le poisson bleu*—the anchovy. The Catalans like strong flavors, strong spices (particularly saffron), strong contrasts; their cuisine is based on the trio, so well known in the Mediterranean, of olive oil, garlic, and onions, plus tomatoes. They start most of their dishes by making a *sofrito*—onions very slowly fried in oil to which is added tomato, garlic, and other ingredients, all reduced to a soft, oily jam. A *samfaina* is the same but with eggplant and peppers. Food here, with its Spanish and Moorish influences, has its own identity, often playing on sweet and salty, or sweet and sour opposites—anchovies with grilled peppers, spinach and pine nuts, lamb with chestnut honey, aubergines (eggplants) with cumin and honey, or pork cooked with raisins, pine nuts, apricots, and vinegar. Like the Spanish, from whom they took the habit, they like *tapas*, and they excel at cooking salt cod, squid, and other seafood. A special dish, *Llagostada*, a *civet* or stew of crawfish or lobster made with local Banyuls wine, is cooked over burning vine stumps on August 15, fête day. Then there are snails, special fresh onions that are eaten roasted, kid, hams and black puddings, and *saucissons* made with blueberries or with tripe.

Sweet cherries, the first of the year, ready in early May or even late April, come from Céret, a short drive above Collioure, set in the foothills of the Pyrenees and surrounded by mimosa and cherry blossom, and the distant snow peaks of Canigou. So important are cherries to this delightful little town that, at Easter, a bough of cherry blossom is given to the figure of Christ in the local church. Throughout the year you will find cherry cakes, cherry liqueur, cherry jam, and cherry chocolates in abundance in Céret. This small town, with its oversized trees and grand houses, was taken up by Picasso in 1911, which was quite early in his Cubist period; it was here that he often painted one of his favorite subjects, that of musicians. He turned the town briefly into an artist's colony, while Dérain and Matisse, in 1905, were both picking up on and expressing the vivid reds, blues, and yellows of the fishing fleet in Collioure in their art. Both towns still retain their raffish, arty charm.

THE LANGUEDOC AND THE CAMARGUE

A drive eastward through Languedoc, taking a scenic inland route, leads one through the vast, empty, Cathar country and the vineyards of Corbières and the Minervois. Great mountains provide a bluish backdrop for the dry, vine-planted plains and rocky, occasionally castle-topped, hills. In late summer, or in the fall for the higher vineyards, where the *vendange* comes later, the small roads buzz with tractors pulling trailers dripping with piles of black grapes. The streets of the small villages are stained deep purple and the smell of fermenting grape juice charges the sun-burned air. Wine writers have recently become enthusiastic about the dense, herby red wines of the Languedoc: Modern methods and improvements mean that Corbières and the Minervois, once the home of coarse *vins de table*, are more interesting and certainly better value than some of the big names farther north.

The Mediterranean and the light of the Midi have magnetized many artists who visited this region. In 1888, Van Gogh wrote about his visit to the Camargue, a few hours west of Collioure: "The Mediterranean has the color of mackerel, changeable I mean. You don't always know if it is green or violet, you can't even say it's blue, because the next moment the changing reflection has taken on a tinge of rose or gray."

If you approach the flat, windy Camargue from the west, you may be lulled into a false sense of security by the drive through well-ordered orchards of peach and apricot, and lightly sloping vineyards, but in the distance lie, like a mirage, large areas of sky on the ground. As the dry farms peter out into a world of water, where the river Rhône loses itself and runs out to sea, you will find yourself in a wild place with gray scrub, pools, rustling rushes, and waterbirds—flocks of pink flamingoes, heads down in the water. There are herds of white, semiwild horses and black bulls bred for bullfighting, which, along with the local wild boar, provide the ingredients for the famous *saucisson d'Arles*. Then comes the sea, vast, scoured sands, and salt-edged pools (there is a thriving salt industry). In the winter these lands can be freezing and hostile.

THE BÔUCHES-DU-RHÔNE AND PROVENCE

From the Camargue, it is a short drive through paddy fields to Arles, one of the Midi's loveliest Roman towns. It is near Arles that I had my last French kitchen, and, in the garden, a fireplace with a grill, built into the old *dependance*, where rabbits and poultry had lived before. Grilling outside is a natural and aromatic process in this region. Wood is plentiful because the Mistral, which is supposed to blow for sixty days a year, but actually sometimes blows for ninety, flings the branches off the trees, and quite regularly blows one down. Herbs grow profusely around here; the Alpilles, a small range of sculptured limestone rocks running through the area, have skirts of wild thyme or *farigoule*, savory, rosemary, fennel, marjoram, and hardy miniature wild mint. Bay trees, once established, proliferate into huge clumps.

From Arles, head northeast toward Cavaillon, celebrated for its tiny, sweet-fleshed melons, which make such a good marriage to *jambon cru*, as do small purple summer figs. Beyond lies the Lubéron, an area of vines, orchards, and lavender, where the rolling countryside throws up little hilltop towns whose medieval and renaissance houses, beautiful churches, and village squares look across the plains to the mountains, a vast national park, ideal for walking. At Lourmarin you can find the best *gibassiers*, and *fougasses*, flattish breads made with pork fat or olive oil, in an oval leaf-shape slashed with holes (like Matisse's paper cutouts), and sprinkled with herbs, or seeds, or pieces of frizzled pork fat. You will find good bakers here and in Bonnieux, where there is also a baking museum whose wood ovens date from 1844.

The farther east you travel, the more prosperous and built upon the cultivated parts of the countryside become and the more refined becomes the food. And, when you reach Nice, the presentation and quality of the ingredients surpasses anything I have seen, even in Paris. But I do not underrate the more earthy quality of the food of the Southwest, with its strong flavors; the Midi as a whole has everything to give, and gives it generously to those who go there to find it.

Specialties of the South

This chapter introduces some of the special foods of the Midi and the Southwest, together with *les trucs et les astuces*, tricks of the trade and clever ideas. It attempts to make it easy to identify, and use, some of the gloriously inspiring ingredients and products, whether you are buying them in the region, or have ordered them from specialty stores, mail-order companies, or websites such as those listed at the end of this book. Since it is impossible to cover everything in these pages, I have simply introduced some things to look out for and have tried to give a glimpse of the seductive and sun-filled produce that makes southern French food so good.

BEANS AND OTHER LEGUMES

Beans and legumes are an essential part of French cooking. Some fresh, others dried, they are used as accompaniments to meat or fish dishes, with a sprinkling of olive oil or in soups and *cassoulets*, providing substance, texture, and flavor.

Butter and Lima Beans (*Haricots Beurres, Soissons, Judia*)
In the Pays Basque, the flat, dried butter bean (closely related to the slightly smaller lima bean and not to be confused with the yellow wax bean, also sometimes called *haricot beurre*), reminiscent of institutions, makes an appearance in a totally different guise. After soaking and cooking (some varieties are poisonous raw), they are eaten cold as a salad, or cooked with splendid things like pig's ears and pimento-laden sausage. Another flat white bean from the Béarn, *le Tarbais*, is traditionally called *le haricot-maïs* (the corn-bean), because it is trained up the stalks of corn, a clever way of growing two crops at once. These are often used in the famous Béarnaise *garbure* instead of *haricots blancs sec* (dried haricot beans).

Chickpeas (*Pois Chiches, Pois Pointus, Chichourles*)
Chickpeas (garbanzo beans) can be grown in limited and mild areas of the Mediterranean, but in the Languedoc are highly prized, those from Carlencas, in the Hérault, being considered the most tender and easy to cook. They are eaten in salads, especially on Good Friday, with *brandade de morue* (salt cod puree) or soup, or in couscous (see p. 178). They must be soaked thoroughly overnight, preferably with a pinch of baking soda to soften the water, and they will take up to four hours boiling in unsalted water, with more baking soda, to become tender. Cooked carefully, they are nuttier than those in cans, which lack flavor and texture.

A pancake, made from chickpea flour, olive oil, water, and salt and called *socca*, is a street-food speciality of the Alpes-Maritimes, and in particular Nice. *Panisses*, sold in parts of Provence, and also in Corsica, are made from a kind of chickpea polenta, which is traditionally stirred with a twig from a bay tree as it cooks. It is poured into little molds, cooled, deep-fried, and served hot with salt and grated cheese, or sugar.

Fava Beans (*Fèves, Fava*)
One of the favorite *primeurs* or "spring vegetables" in the Pays Basque and the Languedoc is the fava bean, venerably ancient, and massively predating haricot beans in Europe. They are eaten raw, with *apéritifs*, straight out of their velvet-lined pods, or cooked, when their flavor is freshened with mint or mellowed with savory, or perhaps intensified with ham and garlic. In the Pyrenees they make a fine gratin with fresh, cooked broad beans, grated sheep's cheese, and breadcrumbs, baked in the oven, or they put them in a tortilla. They also stew the beans with chorizo, ham, and bacon, and a few leaves of lettuce. Fava beans can be dried for winter bean stews. These russet-brown beans have a warm, earthy flavor and are particularly good with chorizo, but are best skinned after soaking, and before cooking.

French (green) Beans and Haricot Beans
(*Haricots Verts, Haricots Blancs Frais, Haricots Blancs Sec*)
French (green) beans are grown profusely throughout the summer in the South, the very best coming from Toulouse. They are eaten at three different stages; first of all farmers, who spend the long summer evenings working in their kitchen gardens or potagers, pick the *haricots verts*, which we know as French beans or green beans, in their infancy. Others are left to ripen until August or September, when the beans have matured in their pods, and are picked and podded and eaten as *haricots frais à écosser* or *haricots grains*. Lastly, for the winter pantry, the remaining plants, with beans still on them, are pulled up by the roots and hung up in an airy barn to dry. When the beans are really hard and dry, they are shelled and stored—these dried haricot beans, *haricots secs*, will keep for a year, but are best within a few months.

In general, dwarf bean varieties (*haricots nains*) are the best for eating green, and climbing varieties (*haricots à rames*), which are grown up poles, are the ones for eating mature or dried. The very best fresh white beans, *haricots blancs frais*, are the round *cocos de Pamiers*, also known as *mongettes*; there are also various beautiful colored varieties such as *rose coco* or *coco de Prague* (cranberry or pinto beans), found at the markets in late summer and autumn. Both also sold dried. The *haricot lingot* is perfect for *cassoulets*.

Shell and cook or freeze the *haricots frais* soon after you buy them, and do not leave them in plastic bags as they quickly go moldy. They make the very best soups and stews, particularly cabbage soup (*garbure*). They are excellent cooked with a little chopped ham, garlic, and parsley as a side dish.

Haricots grains (fresh beans) need no soaking and will cook in thirty to forty-five minutes. *Haricots demi-sec* (partly dried beans), which still have a fairly high moisture content, will also cook without being soaked, but will take from forty-five minutes to an hour.

Once they have dried, and make a clicking noise when shaken together, the new season's beans must be soaked for at least an hour and a half, and for older beans up to twelve hours. Very old beans that have been lurking in the back of a cupboard should be thrown out.

There is a time-honored way of degassing beans to make them more digestible, and I find it works fairly well. Simply put them into a saucepan of cold, unsalted water, enough to cover by one inch, and bring to a boil. Cook for five minutes, remove from the heat, cover the pan, and leave for five more minutes. Drain the beans, return them to the pan, cover by one inch of stock, water, or water and wine (but if wine or any other acid, such as vinegar, is used the beans will take longer to cook). Do not add salt, but do add herbs or other flavoring that you like, and cook until the beans are tender, when their skins curl up if lifted out of the liquid.

Pole beans *(Phenomène à Rames)*
The French tend to cultivate these favorites only for their scarlet flowers, although they do favor one variety called *phenomène à rames*, which is tender when green and gives a splendid haricot (navy) bean when dried. However, any pole bean can be left to form proper beans inside its pod. Mature pole beans are a glorious shocking pink, darkening to purple with indigo spots and then to a dark blue as they harden; when they are cooked they turn a warm brown and give a good, thick texture to soups or stews when mashed.

CHEESE
A look at the selection of cheeses in a southern restaurant will reveal that most of the cheeses made locally are made with sheep or goat's milk, which may be covered with herbs or with chestnut leaves, or rolled in wood ash, while the rich, runny cheeses and the hard cheeses made with cow's milk are mainly imported from the North. In the South, the dry climate makes it hard to feed cows enough grass and hay to produce the rich milk needed for cheesemaking. The making of cheese in the South thus relies mainly on sheep and goat's milk, and I have written about some of the more important ones.

Cow's Milk Cheeses *(Fromages de Vache)*
Aligot and cantal are often found in the market stalls of the Lot, although they are made farther northeast, in the Auvergne. The nearest thing outside France to *aligot*, a melting, ivory-white cow's milk cheese from the Rouergue district, is mozzarella; aligot is soft and supple and should be eaten fresh. One of the most sumptuous local dishes is called *aligot* after the cheese, and consists of a super-rich mixture of pureed potatoes, melted cheese, garlic, butter, and cream; it is often served at weddings and, because it is such heavy work to stir in quantity, is generally made by men.

The Mont-Dore, where the river Dordogne rises, is full of dairy farms, which specialize in making Saint-Nectaire, Bleu d'Auvergne, another blue cheese, Fourme d'Ambert, and hard, cylindrical cheeses of a *tome* type. Those made in the winter are called Cantal, but between the first of May and thirty-first of October, the cows are taken to graze in the high, lush volcanic pastures of the Monts du Cantal and the superb cheeses made from this rich milk are called *Salers*. They are stored and turned for up to two years, and mature to a golden-yellow color; if they are white, they may only have passed through the town of Salers and are not the real thing.

A visit to one of the cantal cheesemakers at the *Ferme de Besse*, in Ytrac, on the *Route du Fromage* will show how the cheese is made, in handcrafted *jerles*, vats of chestnut, oak, or acacia wood, the only wooden utensil allowed in making cheese by the EC. The cheeses are salted, pressed, and kept on a shelf in a cool store, great gray-brown cylinders weighing one hundred pounds each. It is these that the cheesemaker brings to Martel and other markets.

Curd *(La Brousse)*
La brousse is fresh curd produced from the whey left after milk has been curdled and strained for cheesemaking. It can be made from cow's milk, but in Roquefort country, in the Aveyron, the whey from sheep's milk is thick, yellow, and creamy and makes the finest *brousse*, which is eaten with bread and honey. Mixed with egg, it makes a kind of cheese-cake tart, often flavored with orange flower water or peel.

Goat's Milk Cheeses *(Fromages de Chèvre)*
On the cheese stalls of most southern markets you will find stacks of tiny, flat, disk-shaped goat's milk cheeses. There are so many artisan makers of goat's cheese it is impossible to define them all; some make hard cheeses and some soft, fresh cheeses, which are only available in the summer, when the goats produce plenty of rich milk. So in summer you may find Pélardons, white and fresh, made in the Rhône area of the Languedoc, and in the Ardèche, from May until the grass loses its goodness in November (it is sold in winter preserved in olive oil and eau-de-vie). Or, you may see little Cabécous, a word that comes from the Oc dialect and means "little goat"; firm and nutty, these are made in the *causses* of Rouergue and in Rocamadour, and may also be made with sheep's milk or with a mixture of goat's and cow's milk. The small cheeses covered with savory and wrapped in chestnut leaves may be Provençal Banons, sweet, nutty, and cured with a fermentation

process that involves either brandy or white wine. Poivre d'âne, another rustic Provençal cheese, is sprinkled with rosemary and savory to give it an evocative taste of the *garrigue* (the Midi's wild herb–covered scrubland). Picodon, a softer, small, round golden or reddish disk with a nutty taste, made in the Rhône Valley, is a delicious *casse-croûte* (snack) with a glass of wine—white, rosé, or red Côtes-du-Rhône.

Sheep's Milk Cheeses (*Fromages de Brebis*)

Shepherding has always been an important part of Basque life, both culturally and economically. Patrolled by eagles, covered in fields of asphodel, the upper slopes of the Pyrénées-Atlantiques are dotted with flocks in the summer, little dainty sheep with pointed horns and long, slender legs, some with reddish heads, the *manech tête rousse*, and some with black, *manech tête noir*. These are the milking sheep whose milk is made into piquant *fromage de brebis*, strong, stinging, salty, and full of the flavor of meadow flowers. Sometimes the shepherds stay with the sheep in the mountains all summer, milking them there and making the cheeses on the spot. In winter—from autumn to May or June—the flocks are brought down to the farm, bedded down on ferns, and fed on hay, alfalfa, and corn.

The sheep are milked twice a day for cheese, each sheep giving about one and three-quarter pints a day. It takes ten and a half pints of milk to make one large cheese, which is kept for at least three months, but usually from six months to a year, before it is ready to eat.

The fromage de brebis is traditionally eaten for breakfast or at lunch, and is often accompanied by *pâte de coing* (quince paste) or black cherry jam. It is a splendid cheese for eating with a salad of lettuce hearts and walnuts, can be used like pecorino or Parmesan for cooking, and keeps extremely well. To buy a well-made cheese, go to one of the farms on the Ossau-Iraty *Route du Fromage* in the Vallée d'Ossau where they make Basque Ardi Gasna, or to one of the outdoor market stalls on the river Quay in Bayonne, where the local farmers sell their own versions of pale sheep's cheese, and soft white curd cheeses called *Mamia*. If you buy a large cheese to take home, you can keep it in a cool, dry place for a month or so; brush it occasionally to remove any mold from the outside, and use it rather in the same way that you would pecorino.

Prehistoric geological activity formed the airy, underground caves that provide perfect conditions for making Roquefort cheese—that rare, tingling combination of sweet and salty craved by all who enjoy complex flavors. Its provenance is the beautiful, but threadbare-looking limestone *causse* of the Aveyron, south of the Massif Central and east of the beautiful Gorges du Tarn, a land that supports little, other than the leggy Lacaune sheep, whose surprisingly rich milk makes the succulent, ivory-colored, blue-and-green-veined cheese. Driving

through limestone gorges you come to the area around Roquefort-sur-Soulzon, which stands on the collapsed mountain of Combalou. Here, as rainwater ran through the limestone, a vast underground reservoir collected, eventually undermining a whole mountain; the mountain collapsed inwards, cracks formed, and underground, cool caves were left. It is only here, in the center of Combalou, that ripening ewe's milk cheeses, doctored with small amounts of powdered, moldy rye bread (or now with a liquid culture), ripen and acquire their greenish veins and unique flavor.

Modest local village stores sell three or four different types of the local cheese. They all taste particularly sweet; there is less salt in the cheeses for local consumption than those for export.

Eat crumbly Roquefort at room temperature with salads or with juicy pears. Nut or raisin breads go well with this cheese, and with the other southern blue cheeses such as Bleu des Causses, from the Rouergue, a cheese similarly made in caves, but with cow's milk, and Bleu de Quercy, at its best with a glass of red wine from Cahors.

FISH, SHELLFISH, AND SEAFOOD

One of the most exciting experiences for me is shopping for fish in southern France. The passion with which people approach their fish and shellfish purchasing is a revelation—the market fish vans and fish shops in small towns everywhere put our fanciest and most expensive city fish shops in the shade. Inevitably, they offer boxes of fish like hoards of silver, bronze, and iridescent Lalique, shrimp and *langoustines* like bouquets of pink flowers, mackerel and sardines like blue butterfly wings, lobsters flaming like flamingoes . . . all sorts of sea creatures come from the Mediterranean, Atlantic, and the great estuary of the Gironde.

Anchovies (*Les Anchois, le Poisson Bleu*)

Fresh anchovies, *anchois*, narrow blue-and-silver fish with large eyes, can be eaten raw. Fillet them by removing the guts with the heads, opening them along the spine to remove the backbone, and then sprinkling with lemon, salt, garlic, and parsley and perhaps some finely sliced chili. Eat them with bread and butter *en apéritif* (as an appetizer).

Of the cured anchovies, the favorites are those packed in salt, carefully placed inside little glass jars. These can be washed to remove the salt, gutted, and filleted like fresh anchovies; taste one to see if it is too salty and, if so, soak them for half an hour in milk and water. The finest anchovies come from Collioure, a small, handsome Catalan fishing port and painters' retreat west of Perpignan. Buy them direct from the workshops where the fishing families, in spite of cheap Moroccan imports, still catch the fish from May to October, salting them, maturing them for three to six months, then hammering them flat and packing them in glass jars and cans.

The particularly classy fish they catch, *engraulis encrasicolus*, have a dark stripe along the spine and are deep in color. They are less oily and more tasty than the Atlantic anchovy and are packed in salt, oil, or tomato sauce, or made into *anchoïade*.

Caviar of Aquitane (Le Caviar d'Aquitane)

During the 1920s and the 1930s, caviar was taken from sturgeon caught in the Gironde estuary. Today, it is back on Médoquin tables. Caviar *l'or noir* is made at Biganos, at the Moulin de Casadotte on the Bassin d'Arcachon, where a huge, tidal fish farm, with lagoons, allows the sturgeon to thrive.

Clams (Coquillages)

Venus clams *(les Praires)* are smoothly ridged, cream and gray, and up to two and a half inches across. They must be thoroughly washed before cooking, and use only those that are closed. They are eaten raw; open them gently by holding the shell in the hollow of your left hand, the hinge toward your fingers. Insert the tip of a knife, held flat, in between the shell next to the hinge, closing your fingers over the shell and pushing the blade inward. Separate the two halves of the shell, detach the clam with the tip of your knife, sprinkle with lemon, and eat like an oyster. Venus clams can also be stuffed with a mixture of butter, fennel or parsley, garlic or shallots, and breadcrumbs, and baked in a hot oven for fifteen minutes. Another type are the smooth, shiny *vernis*.

Carpet-shell clams *(les Palourdes, Clovisses, Amandes)* are handsomely striped and barred in ivory and brown, and can be eaten in the same way as *praires*, in a pilaf (see *Pilau aux Palourdes* on p. 139) or steamed and eaten with cream.

Wedge-shell clams *(les Tellines, Tenilles, Olives de Mer)* are small (about one inch across), shaped like a haricot bean, smooth and shiny, with beautiful markings. These are the most delicate clams, and are best simply sautéed in olive oil with parsley and garlic, and perhaps hot, red pepper flakes.

Razor clams *(les Coûteaux, Pieds-de-Coûteaux)* are found in tidal beaches and look like an old-fashioned razor, long and thin, usually gray and cream, or cream and brown. They are generally dug by amateurs at low tide, who dig furiously with a metal spoon to catch the clam before it burrows its way down to safety. Once steamed or frozen open, it can be chopped up and fried like any other clam, or eaten raw.

Cockles (Les Coques, Rigadeaux)

Why is it that French cockles seem so much bigger and juicier than others? They are up to one and a half inches across and, after degorging in clean, salty water to remove the sand, can be eaten raw either on their own or on a *plâteau de fruits de mer* (seafood platter). They can also be cooked like mussels, and eaten with a vinaigrette, cooked in a pilaf, or sautéed in olive oil with parsley and garlic.

Cuttlefish (Seiches, Supions, Chipirons)

Cuttlefish, or *seiches*, are less delicate, thicker and whiter than squid. *Seiches* have lots of ink and a thick, calcareous bone but the best from a culinary point of view are *supions*, little cuttlefish about one to two inches long, which are often sold on Provençal market stalls. They look like little flowers with their frilly legs, ready-prepared, cleaned and white, asking to be shaken in seasoned flour, or not, and sautéed in olive oil, perhaps with some chopped garlic. They have a lovely chewy texture, but will become tough if cooked for more than ten minutes. Serve simply with wedges of lemon and plenty of leafy salad. Alternatively, *supions* can be stewed for about forty-five minutes, when they will be soft and tender. Buy extra, up to 9 ounces per person, as they shrink in cooking.

If you can get hold of the ink, which is sold separately in little bags (some fishmongers sell it), you can use this with white or red wine to make a much stronger-flavored stew, or an ink sauce such as that for Salt Cod Stuffed Bell Peppers with Squid Ink Sauce (see p. 130).

Crabs (Le Tourteau, L'Araignée, Etrilles)

Le Tourteau and *le Crabe* are ordinary large, orange-red crabs. They are often served simply boiled for fifteen to twenty-five minutes, according to the size. They can grow to more than eight inches across.

Choose female crabs, if possible, for their red coral; identify them by the broad, tongue-shaped flap underneath the shell. A male has a narrower, more pointed flap. They are usually served with mayonnaise, simply cut in half, with lobster picks and pincers to crack the shells and extract the meat.

Spider crabs (*l'Araignée, l'Araignée de Mer, Txangurro, Squinado*) are large and spiny, with spiderlike legs and little blunt spikes all over their orange or brick-red carapaces. They have finer, juicier white meat than normal crabs, but rather less of it, since there are no large claws. It is easier to pick than the common crab.

They are boiled in salted water for about twelve minutes according to their size, which can be up to eight inches across, and make a good salad, either with potatoes, eggs, and mayonnaise, or with mayonnaise flavored with chopped, fresh mint. In Toulouse, they are stuffed with mussels, paprika, and breadcrumbs and baked in their shells.

On the Atlantic coast, the small, dark-green shore crabs (*étrilles, crabes-chèvres*), usually about two inches wide, are picked out of the sea or from the rocks and collected in buckets, usually by amateurs—they are not much sold commercially. Some people wear gloves to avoid being nipped. They are usually boiled for about eight minutes and eaten with bread and butter and salt, or made into a *bisque*.

The small Mediterranean angry crabs (*cranquettes, crabes enragés*), dark brown or gray in color, are said to blush with anger, going a reddish color when threatened. They are boiled for one minute and then sautéed in olive oil with tomatoes and garlic, and perhaps some floury potatoes to thicken the delicious *ragoût*. There is not much meat on them—the whole crabs are crunched up and sucked and the shells are spit out.

Elvers or Eel Fry *(Pibales, Pibalas, Civelles)*
Pibales, or eel fry, were once fished in huge quantities. Today some fishermen still spend seven days a week during the winter months catching what they call "white gold." From the Gironde, right down through the Landes and the Gers, and into the Pays Basque and Spain, *pibales* are fanatically popular, particularly with the Basques, who eat them at Christmas or on New Year's Day. A recent scarcity has made them horribly expensive, but they can still be found.

Pibales are transparent when raw, white and almost spaghetti-like when cooked, although the little black eyes give away their fishy origins. They are usually sold ready-cooked, boiled or steamed for a minute with whole heads of garlic. They are eaten sautéed in olive oil with garlic and hot peppers or chilli flakes for five minutes. They are also made into omelettes, particularly at Easter. They can be bought in cans from Spanish suppliers.

Goosenecked Barnacle *(Le Pousse-Pied, Pouce-Pied)*
Most people's reaction to the goosenecked barnacle is one of dislike. Not so, however, in the Pays Catalan. They relish this rubbery cylinder, dark brown and covered in reptilian and slightly shiny scales. It has, at the extremities, knobs embedded with what look like bluish, chalky mussel shells or barnacles of different sizes. To cook this strange-looking seafood, bring some salted water to a boil with a bay leaf, throw in the *pousse-pieds*, and boil for five minutes. Be careful when opening them, as they tend to squirt red liquid over you. Hold the knob in one hand and carefully pull back the skin from the cylindrical stump, first breaking it at the base of the knob. Eat the delicious, sea-scented flesh inside the stump; you can also eat the inside of the knob.

Hake Cheeks *(Kokotxas, Kokoxtas de Colin)*
Kokotxas are a Basque delicacy and are, in fact, the chins of hake, or rather the soft part of the lower jaw. They can be cooked, like hake, in green sauce with clams (see p. 121), or they can be floured and fried.

Limpets *(Les Berniques)*
Limpets, tough little survivors during storms, are removed from their rocks by tapping the top of the pointed shell with a small hammer. They remain pretty tough even when cooked. In Southwest France, they are baked in a hot oven for fifteen minutes and then eaten with lemon, and bread and butter.

Lobsters, Sea-crickets, Crawfish, and Fresh Water Crayfish
(Homards, Cigales de Mer, Langoustes, Écrevisses)
Lobsters (*homards*) are plentiful on the Atlantic coast, reaching enormous sizes. They are best bought live, and should weigh heavy for their size—those kept in tanks for some days will waste and go soft. In the Mediterranean they are scarce, preferring colder water. Speckled navy-blue to black when raw, and a lively, bright carnation-red to orange when cooked, lobsters are boiled by plunging into boiling sea or well-salted water; they should be simmered fairly gently or they may cast their claws. A one-pound lobster takes about twelve minutes, Just over two pounds takes twenty minutes, and a real giant up to thirty minutes. Boiled lobster is generally eaten with mayonnaise.

Alternatively, for broiling, they can be cut in half, which kills them instantly. To do this, spread the tail out on a board, hold the front of the head with a dish towel, plunge the knife into the middle of the head, cut through the head shell where it connects with the tail, and continue to cut the tail in half lengthwise. Then finish by cutting the head in half. Keep the blackish stuff in the head, which is delicious tomalley liver and will change to orange when cooked.

When eating half a boiled or broiled lobster in the shell, it is a good idea to crack the big claws with the flat blade of a cleaver, and to provide special crackers or pliers and picks to extract the meat from the claws and legs.

Of all the lobster dishes that I have eaten, nothing has been as good as a Provençal lobster *au pistou*; it consisted of a rich soup of beans, tomatoes, potatoes, and lobster, with a strong *pistou* (see p. 279) of basil, garlic, pine nuts, and olive oil.

Flat lobster, or cricket of the sea (*grande cigale, cigale de mer*), is a magnificent and prehistoric-looking flattish lobster, brick-red with small, bright yellow-and-garnet stripes behind its head, and purple patches below. The creature has no claws, a thick shell, and frilly flaps on the front of its blunt head. It is named "cricket" because it makes a snapping sound under water.

Found in the Mediterranean, the *cigale de mer* is cooked like lobster or crawfish, and like them must never be overcooked as the flesh will toughen. It makes an excellent, but costly, component of bouillabaisse (see p. 104), or can be served cold with aïoli (see p. 279) or a Romesco sauce, containing hot red peppers, ground almonds, and garlic, tempered

The various kitchens featured in this chapter offer a selection that I have discovered and fallen in love with in the South of France. They belong to friends and family, each with its own atmosphere and homely essence of French country cooking.

with sweet tomatoes and acidulated with vinegar. The *petite cigale* is a small version of the same thing.

Langouste or crawfish, sometimes called crayfish, but a totally distinct species from the small, freshwater crayfish or *écrevisse*, are much tougher than lobsters, but they do have a good flavor, and are plentiful in the Mediterranean, where lobsters are scarce. You can tell them apart because they do not have the lobster's large, magnificent claws. They are reddish brown when raw, with handsome, long whiskers. They can be cooked in the same way as lobster, but in the Roussillon they have a special liking for a *ragoût* with wine, chopped ham, and tomatoes, flamed in Cognac, called *civet de Langouste, Llagostada*, which they eat on August 15.

Freshwater crayfish, *écrevisses*, are not strictly seafood, since they live in freshwater chalk streams. They look like little dark-brown lobsters when raw, bright, cardinal-red when cooked, and they have the most sweet and delicate flesh. They are frequently cooked in a *court-bouillon* until a good red color, about ten minutes, and then piled up in a pyramid, *en buisson*, and served with melted butter. They are also superb in a gratin, with a little *mousseline* sauce, which is lightly whisked hollandaise.

Mussels *(Moules)*
Moules de bouchot, mussels grown on posts stuck into the seabed just below the tide-line, are perhaps the finest, cleanest, sweetest mussels you can get. However, there is a huge cultivation of mussels called *moules de Bouzigues* in Languedoc-Roussillon, and all around the saltwater lagoon of the Bassin de Thau are sheds and bars where mussels are eaten in vast amounts by travelers to and from Spain. These are grown in mesh containers, and are either small (good for *moules marinières*) or large, for stuffing. On the Mediterranean, mussels are cooked in *mouclade*, with saffron (see p. 109), or with finely chopped ham.

Octopus *(Poulpe, Pieuvre, Poufre)*
Octopus, *poulpe*, can vary in size from two inches long up to almost ten feet. It has a pouch-shaped head, beautiful golden eyes, and eight tentacles with round suckers. The skin is usually speckled brown or purple. Octopus is best bought ready-prepared. If it is not, see page 133 for instructions on how to prepare it. Once cooked, its beautiful, pinky-brown meat offers a wonderful concentration of flavor. Baby octopus, if you can buy them already cleaned, make a superb *daube* or seafood salad. Sète, a charming fishing town in Languedoc-Rousillon, is a good place to try the small pie called *la tielle*, which is made of pastry shaped like a little patty pan with frilly edges, filled with chopped octopus and tomato-flavored oil.

Oysters *(Huîtres)*
The beach at Cap Ferret is the place to watch oyster harvesters collecting their precious catch, when the tide is out and the oyster beds uncovered. These oysters, raised on sand rather than mud, are delicious. The shells are slightly greenish on the outside, white, pink, purple, and pearly inside, the scarce Arcachon *(ostrea edulis)* being a round, flat-shelled *(belon or plate)* oyster and the Portugaise a deep-shelled oyster, *huître creuse* or just *creuse (Crassostrea angulata)* the shells frilly as ballerinas. The Banc d'Arguin oysters, nutty, sparkling, sweet, and salty, but not too salty, are the best. In restaurants, oysters are served with burning-hot grilled pork sausages or with *crépinettes* (see p. 190), which you eat in mouthfuls alternately with the icy oysters.

Pressed Mullet's Roe *(Poutargue)*
Poutargue is cured, pressed mullet's roe, sometimes smoked, encased in wax, and once a specialty of Martigues (which is now a huge oil refinery). Away from the Mediterranean coast, it can be bought in Italian delicatessens under the name of *bottarga*. In Provence, it is eaten finely sliced, sprinkled with oil and lemon juice and lots of pepper, but no salt.

Salt Cod *(Morue)*
It was the Basques, with their salt deposits and dry, windy climate, who developed salt cod; by the year 1000 they could travel huge distances by sea and bring back their fish, salted, to trade. They sailed west to Newfoundland, where the great cod shoals lay, and thousands of their boats landed there long before 1497 when it was "discovered" by Cabot and claimed for the British. But because of the cod, they had kept their discovery secret.

Morue, dried salted cod, has a long history. For centuries it was an essential staple for inland Catholics who could not get fresh sea fish for their obligatory fast days and Lent, and it was also the food that "fueled" slaves on the sugar plantations. Mainly fished and cured by Basques at sea, it was brought into France through Bordeaux, the Basque coast, and Sète, where, along with Nîmes, the manufacture of *brandade de morue*, that garlicky, satisfying puree of salt cod, olive oil, and milk, is still big business.

In the Pays Basque, salt cod is still popular today. At markets and in fish shops, it hangs huge and stiff, like fish-shaped blankets. Buy the thicker pieces.

There are several methods of soaking salt cod; some favor running water, others suggest changing the water several times. I have found the following method to be the best. It takes twenty-four hours.

Place the cod on a rack, in a large bowl of cold water, for eleven hours. Change the water and soak in cold water for eleven hours more. Change the water once more, this time

using warm water, and soak for another two hours. The cod should have swollen and softened all the way through and be ready for gentle poaching. It can then be used in several ways.

Sardines (Sardines)

Sardines, blue, silver, and mother-of-pearl, with shiny, coppery eyes, are in season from June to October. They are a vital element in the cuisine of the Midi, particularly in summer when they are fattest and cheapest, and when they can be cooked outside—the smell of broiling sardines indoors can be overwhelming. If they are fresh they do not really need gutting, and the scales are best left on. Rub them with bay leaves and grill for two to three minutes on each side, then eat them with bread and salty butter.

On the northern side of the Gironde, sardines are eaten raw—the smaller ones are best—scaled, gutted, and boned, and sprinkled inside and out with salt and a squeeze of lemon at the last minute.

Poutine or *poutina* is sardine and anchovy fry, eaten in soup and fritters in Nice, early in spring. These are also used to make *pissalat*, a cured fish-paste, often on a *pissaladière* (see p. 243). Other small fry are *nonnats* and *melet*; they may be eaten in omelettes or bound with a light batter into *beignets*—fritters—and served with quarters of lemon.

Sea Anemones (Orties de Mer, Ourtigo)

Sea anemones are eaten by a few aficionados in the South of France. Remembering their beauty, the blooms of childhood rock pools, but alive, I am reluctant to join in. However, they are said to be excellent. To prepare them, wash, clean them of sand, drain, and dip in flour. Fry them all over in hot olive oil, sprinkle with salt, and serve with slices of lemon. Or throw them, nicely fried, into an omelette.

Sea Bass and Channel Bass (Bar, Loubine, Loup de Mer, Maigre)

Slender, silver, delicately white-fleshed, the sea bass feeds cleanly in estuaries and is the most classically perfect fish to cook. Bass has different names in different places; in the Mediterranean it is known as *loup de mer*, in the Southwest as *loubine*, and on the Atlantic coast as *bar*.

Bar à la ligne is line-caught bass, and is the best, far better than those farmed in huge numbers, and penned in like salmon. *Bars mouchetés* or *brigues* are spotted sea bass, and are cooked like ordinary sea bass.

Maigre, a large look-alike, is Channel bass, meagre or red drum. It grows up to about three feet long, is good quality with delicate white flesh, and is highly prized in the Médoc. In summer it is caught in the Gironde and the Bassin d'Arcachon, and is less than half the price of bass.

Sea Lamprey (La Lamproie)

The estuary of the Gironde is blessed with unusual and generally interesting fish that flourish in a combination of salt and fresh water, such as shad, smelts, mullet, meagre or Channel bass (see above), and lampreys. The people of the Gironde think that they are showing their strength and innate heroism in eating this abominable creature from "the slimy waters of memory," as one official Bordelaise handbook describes it (although, in fact, it likes a stony or gravely habitat and has delicate flesh). Cooked in its own blood, lamprey has become a symbol to them of their own uniqueness; sad, then, that it is now so scarce that it costs as much as fillet steak, and so is actually rarely eaten. Sea Lamprey, sometimes known as lamprey eel, mottled, yellowish, with holes in the side of its head, has a sucker instead of a mouth, which it fastens onto its prey. Sea lamprey can be cooked like eel, and benefits from being marinated before cooking; it can be cooked in sweet Sauternes, but is often served in the Gironde *à la Bordelaise*, stewed in red wine, mixed with its blood.

Sea Urchins (Les Oursins, Châtaignes de Mer)

Sea urchins are covered in black or dark brown, brittle spines, and look far from edible. If you run into one while swimming, it is not fun extracting the spines from your flesh; however, they are keenly sought by snorkelers, who relish them. To open them, cut a round, skullcap-shaped piece from around the beak. Turn the urchin over, and tap it to expel the liquid, then use a small spoon to remove the little crescents of succulent, creamy coral-colored to golden-yellow roe, the iodiny essence of the sea. It is eaten raw, either right there by the rocks or at home, with bread and butter, and can be used in omelettes or as a sauce for sole.

Shrimp, Prawns, and Scampi (Langoustines, Crevettes, Gambas)

Langoustines are Dublin Bay prawns (scampi). They are smaller than lobsters, about four to eight inches in length, and they have long, spiny angular claws and pale orange or clear rose-pink shells. They are sold live or cooked, and since they don't change color when they are cooked, it is just as well to check. Cook them in boiling water up to 2 pounds at a time—with larger quantities, the longer the water takes to come back to the boil, the more likely it is that the flesh will go soft.

Langoustines are delectable; they are often boiled and eaten with mayonnaise, preferably still warm, and the shells are opened by hand, which is messy but enjoyable. A pair of lobster crackers and a pick are useful for larger langoustines, which have good meat in their claws. They can be sold as shelled tails, which are cooked in butter with a *persillade* (see p. 281) or grilled and served with aïoli (see p. 279).

Prawns and shrimps (*crevette roses, bouquets, gambas, camarons*) have a transparent, carnation-pink shell, covered with fine, penciled markings, and a dragonlike crest. This makes the *crevette rose* or *bouquet* one of the most beautiful creatures from the sea. It turns out to be the common shrimp, called *camaron* on the Atlantic coast of the Midi, *gamba* on the Mediterranean; but who has ever seen common shrimp five inches long? They are juicy, tender, and just as sweet and fine-fleshed as their smaller relatives. Try them grilled on the barbecue, or fried with parsley, garlic, and chili.

Shrimps start to be at their best in April, after they have lost their eggs. Tiny brown shrimps (*crevettes grises*) are cooked by plunging a quantity into boiling, salted water; when the water comes back to a boil, they are drained and sprinkled with salt, and wrapped in a cloth to cool. Eat with a squeeze of lemon and a glass of white Bordeaux as an appetizer.

Strange, ghostly looking white shrimps (*crevettes blanches*), a pale ivory color but otherwise identical to brown shrimps, are cooked in the same way, but the cooking water is flavored with fennel. They are also eaten as an appetizer.

Snails (*Escargots, Escargots de Vigne, Cagaraous, Cagarols, Cagouilles*)

Le grand aïoli is one of the most popular southern dishes featuring snails; vast platters of salt cod are surrounded with small snails, red carrots, and yellow potatoes, accompanied by large mortars of aïoli (see p. 279). Another ritual snail food, enjoyed by the Catalans, is the *cargolada*, often cooked at family gatherings, or on Easter Sunday. Here, snails are simply grilled over a wood fire. First the shells of the snails (collected a week or so earlier) are scrubbed and purged to remove any poisons, then they are laid in concentric circles or a spiral on a round, fine-meshed grill, with their openings uppermost. A little pork fat is put in each and they are grilled over a fire of vine prunings. As they start to spit and bubble, the snail-lovers pick them up and slurp them straight from the shells. With them, they eat huge slices of bread, generously spread with aïoli. It is said that some people can eat one hundred and fifty to two hundred snails. It makes our little plates of six or twelve *escargots de Bourgogne* look rather timid.

The best time to go snail-hunting is after rain, when every now and then you find small brown and gray *petits gris*, and, rarely, a stripy cream and brown monster, an *escargot de Bourgogne*, which I believe were brought over by the Romans, and generally live among vines. I do feel, though, that it is a pity to eat these grand creatures, when the smaller, less flamboyant snails actually taste better.

Squid (*Calamars, Calmars, Chipirons, Petits Encornets*)

Calamars or *calmars* are squid, and *encornet* is another word used (*petits encornets* are smaller squid). These dainty,

streamlined creatures, elegantly speckled with tiny purple dots, are enormously popular and, like *seiches*, they are cooked either briefly or for much longer in a liquid, for example in a savory stew or *marmitako* that is perfect with *millas* (see p. 82), the superb Basque version of polenta. Larger squid are often cut into rings before cooking, and poached for a salad or fried in a crisp coating of batter, flour, or cornmeal. Squid are generally sold whole and require cleaning, which is done by grasping the body in one hand and the head and legs in the other, and pulling gently; the body is then emptied, either by inserting your finger or by turning it inside out, after the removal of the supple, transparent backbone. The head, which contains eyes and a beak, must be cut away from the legs. The legs and bodies may need to be washed briefly to remove sand (the less water the better when cleaning any sea creature), then the thin, pink-speckled skin can be removed by rubbing and pulling it gently. If you look carefully just inside the squid, beneath the head, you will find a little silvery bag. This is the ink sac, which can be kept and used to make a rich, dark pilaf, sauce, or stew. Put it into a small bowl with a little water or red wine, mash it up well, and strain the black, inky liquid before you use it.

Small- to medium-sized squid can be stuffed before stewing or braising. The larger ones are best cut into rings, while the real babies may in fact be *chipirons*, little cuttlefish or *supions* (*sepiola rondoleti*). With their pink, pearly flesh, these small cephalopods are great in a seafood salad or simply fried in olive oil for ten minutes.

(*Le Violet, Figue de Mer*)

In Provence, this oddity, which has no English name, blessed with wrinkled gray skin and barnacle-like extremities, is a great delicacy and can be found on market fish stalls. The *violet* is cut in half and the yellow part inside is eaten raw, usually with a glass of chilled white wine.

Whelks (*Les Bulots, Les Buccins*)

Whelks are large whitish to gray to chestnut-colored spiral sea snails, which are eaten boiled like winkles, but allowed to cook for five to ten minutes before they are removed from the heat. They are eaten with mayonnaise or vinaigrette, or as part of a *plâteau de fruits de mer* (seafood platter), and are popular in seafood restaurants all over France. I have never been able to understand why; it may be something to do with their chewy texture, since they do not have much of a flavor.

Winkles (*Les Bigorneaux, Bigorneaux Noirs, Bioux, Vigneaux*)

Winkles are common, but they are good. The familiar black or gray curly little snail is washed, brought to a boil in salt water, removed from the heat, and allowed to rest for two minutes, then drained and eaten *en apéritif*, warm or cold, with rye

bread and butter. They are simply placed on the table in small white dishes with a cork into which are stuck a number of pins to extract them from their shells. When eating winkles, discard the little disk that covers the snail, and also the curly intestine at the inner end, although it can be eaten.

FRUITS OF THE COUNTRYSIDE

Anyone driving into southern France during the first flush of sap in spring will be dazzled by flowering fruit trees, by ghost-pale apricot blooms, then white cherry blossoms, then peaches, apples, and pears, even scarlet pomegranate flowers here and there, and fields of gaudy melon flowers, although most of these are grown under plastic these days. Of course grapes, figs, and mulberries are more modest and scarcely show their flowers, but if you move far enough south you may see orange and lemon trees flowering away at the same time as they show ripe fruit, one of the sights that make it certain you are very close to the Mediterranean coast.

Apricots, Peaches, and Nectarines (Abricots, Pêches, Brugnons)

In spring, after the almond-blossom and wild plum in February, come the apricots; the countryside around les Alpilles is covered with ghostly flowers the color of ash, on dark branches. Then come the peaches and nectarines, brash crimson twigs and bright pink flowers. From May through to August, the orchards of the South are covered with red and orange apricots, wine-colored vine peaches, flat peaches, yellow peaches, white peaches, nectarines with vermilion cheeks and white flesh, or scarlet with golden flesh.

At the sides of the roads, in markets and supermarkets, people buy whole boxes of fruit and gorge themselves. These fruits are not the hard, raw-potato-like specimens we are offered farther north. They are picked ripe and are saturated with perfumed juices.

New varieties are being developed all the time, not always as well flavored as the old ones. But, as a rule of thumb, the white varieties of peach and nectarine are finer-textured than the yellow, and in my experience they also have a superior perfume.

Cherries (Cerises)

The first cherries of the year to come from Céret, in the Pyrenees, are sent to the French president in May. This town is devoted to cherries, and has its own favorite varieties, burlat, la reverchon, la van, and summit, colored from purple to crimson-red to vermilion, with white or rose-colored flesh. They are picked by hand and sold mainly for eating fresh, or turned into fantastic liqueur chocolates, and jam.

Figs (Figues)

The Languedoc is a great fig-growing area, with an astonishing variety under cultivation in fig orchards. First there are summer figs, figues-fleurs, and then the autumn figs, which are smaller and sweeter. The names of the early "flower-figs" sound like an artist's paint colors; there is la boule d'or, la rouge d'Argenteuil, la violette-dauphine. All these are large, violet-colored figs with sweet and juicy rose-red flesh. A variety called Smyrne is large with stripy-green skin, and is usually dried. The noir de Caromb is early and large, la grise de la St-Jean, also called celestine, cotignon, or grisette, which grows around Montpellier, has particularly sweet fruits that taste of honey. Among the autumn figs there is the violette de Sollies, also called bougasotte noir, and the barnisott, both violet- to black-skinned with pomegranate-red flesh.

Melons of Cavaillon (Melons de Cavaillon)

Melons are grown all over the South, the best coming early in the season, around July; the later melons seem to grow coarser and less delicate in flavor. The most renowned are the small, sweet, orange-fleshed melons of Cavaillon. To see if they are ripe and sweet, sniff them at the flower end for a strong fragrance, or if you have the nerve to do it, press lightly with your thumb to see if they feel gently resilient but not hard, and not squashy. Another test is to look at the stalk and see if it is lightly cracking away from the melon. If so, the melon should be ripe. In the South, melons are usually eaten at the beginning of a meal, often with jambon cru, or chilled and cut in half, and served with a sweet wine, such as Banyuls, poured into the cavity.

Mulberries (Mûres)

Mulberry trees are abundant in Provence, once providing food for silk worms, now pruned into living umbrellas for shading terraces. The berries produce the most excellent jam; make it exactly as you would strawberry or raspberry jam.

Incidentally, mûre sauvage or mûre de ronce means "blackberry," another fruit that abounds in Provence, hanging in great swathes from the rows of cyprus trees, but they are not as juicy as ordinary blackberries.

Plums, Prunes, and Greengages (Prunes, Pruneaux, Reine-Claudes)

The Lot-et-Garonne, a rolling, gentle, unspoiled region, is the heart of the plum-growing country. These purple, blue-bloomed beauties, a variety called Ente, are destined to be prunes; they are ideally suited to being dried or half-dried prunes, mi-cuit, the latter a process reserved for the sweetest and juiciest of them. Occasionally they are dried over a wood-fired dryer, giving a smoky, luscious flavor. Most, however, are dried with more modern sources of heat, so they lose that

smoky taste. Fully dried prunes will keep longer than *mi-cuit*, but now that the latter come vacuum-packed, I intend to use more of them. In the Lot-et-Garonne, prunes are eaten with meat, especially rabbit, roast pork, goose, and game. Try them soaked in Armagnac (see p. 264) or instead of raisins in a bread and butter pudding (see p. 262).

Farther east, around Carennac in the Dordogne, greengages grow in riverside orchards, and here they hold an annual greengage market, around the feet of the turreted priory and château where the writer and poet Fénelon lived and worked. These golden-green fruits, with their attractive blue bloom, are the most delicious plums of all to eat raw. They make wonderful jam, and are best preserved in jars of eau-de-vie, and served in small glasses as a dessert, to bring a bit of summer to a winter meal. In Collonges-les-Rouges, I saw a distillery on wheels working at full blast. The locals brought their greengages, which are made into potent *eau-de-vie-de-prune*. A similar one is sold commercially in blackish bottles, sometimes mysteriously covered in sand, as *La Vieille Prune*.

MEAT AND GAME

Charcuterie in southern France is the obvious basis of most picnics and outdoor meals, although you will probably not see many pigs, unless you go to the Pays Basque and walk in the forests of the Pyrenees, where you will be rewarded with the sight of little black-striped, pink pigs rooting for acorns under the oak trees, fattening up for the artisan ham-makers and *charcutiers*. Hams are also made in the mountains from venison and wild boar. In the Pays Catalan, farther south, they specialize in making *saucissons* (salamis) using prime pork shoulder meat, and introducing such flavorings as juniper, bilberries, or paprika. It would be possible to write a whole book on the different varieties of stuffed tongue sausages, black and white puddings, pâtés, cured horse, bull, and donkey saucissons, and salted pigs' ears to be found in the South, and there is no space for this here, but I have discussed a few specialties below.

As for game, shooting is every man's right in the Midi and the hunters are out twice a week at least throughout the autumn and winter season. My neighbor in the Minervois, with his small village syndicate, had already shot fifty wild boar by the beginning of December last year; hunting game is no minor sport.

Bacon (*Ventrêche, Poitrine Fumée, Lardons*)

One of the best ways of curing pork belly is to dry-salt and air-dry it like a ham; *ventrêche*, made in this way and reminiscent of *pancetta*, is sold rolled or flat, and is much fattier than usual bacon. The inside is sometimes spiced with pepper and other spices. In many dishes, the meat is cut into *lardons* and fried to release the fat, which adds a wonderful flavor to any dish.

Bayonne Ham and Country Ham (*Jambon de Bayonne, Jambon du Pays*)

For once, free-range means what it says; some pigs really are allowed to run wild in the chestnut and oak forests of the Pyrénées-Atlantiques. You can see large pigs and small trotting out on their little feet to forage for nuts and roots in the undergrowth and returning home contentedly, if somewhat unwisely, to the barns where they live and are fed regularly. Not all local pigs are so lucky. Many *pie noir* or *pied noir*, the favorite breed, live a more enclosed life. Whatever their conditions, they are nearly all bred for the ham-makers.

Pigs, to qualify as Bayonne ham, must be reared in the Pyrénées-Atlantiques, Hautes-Pyrénées, or the Gers. The proximity of the underground saltwater spring at Saliés de Béarn, which yields a particularly fine rock salt, perfect for curing, helps form the character of these local hams.

The best *charcutier* in St. Etienne de Baïgorry in the Pyrenees makes hams year-round. He starts curing the hams with dry salt on Saturdays, and when they are ready he hangs them in his drying shed in an upper chamber, with shutters on all four sides, which allows the clean, dry mountain air to blow through, evaporating the moisture by degrees. By the time the curing is finished, they have lost up to forty-five percent of their original weight, and will keep uncut for a year.

Once cured, the hams are thickly rubbed on the inner side with *piment rouge d'Espelette* (see p. 49) to keep off mold and flies. If you buy a whole ham, ask for a muslin (cheesecloth) bag to keep it in, and hang it in a cool, dry, airy place.

One or two large, flat slices of *jambon cru*, cut by machine, and served spread out on a plate, is only one way it is eaten. At home, and in some restaurants, it is cut by hand into shavings and served with bread and a bottle of chilled Clairet, the deep rose-tinted wine of Bordeaux, as an appetizer.

Locally, ham is eaten, either raw or cooked, with almost everything. The end of the ham bone is valued for cooking beans and bean soups. Good restaurants offer the best Bayonne ham, wonderful served with *crème fraîche* mixed with crumbled fresh sheep's cheese, seasoned with chives, sherry vinegar, and salt. You may also be offered a Spanish ham, either *jamon serrano* or the sensuous, sought-after *Iberico* or *pata negra* ham, which is served at (warm) room temperature, with the fat glistening and soft, almost as if it had been anointed with oil.

The French hams tend to be a touch drier than the Spanish, but both are particularly good. One wonders why the British don't make more cured ham to be eaten raw. Top-quality Bayonne ham is expensive and most people are happy with the excellent *jambon du pays* from a local farm or charcutier, which is cured in the same way, but does not have quite such exacting controls and is less expensive as a result.

Raw jambon du pays cooked the Basque way is cut into large shavings and lightly fried, then placed over the top of fried eggs, omelettes, or *pipérade* (see p. 221).

One of the best places to buy genuine Bayonne ham is the covered market in Bayonne. Inside there are rows of *charcuterie* stands festooned with reddish orange, pimento-flavored saucissons. These stalls also sell whole hams and large pieces, or the ham can be sliced for you. I am always torn between the more authentic-looking artisanale stalls, with rougher homemade produce, and a knife or a rickety hand-slicer for cutting, and the stalls with efficient, modern, electric slicing machines. Cutting by hand is fine if you want thick, chewy slices, but many prefer it sliced thinly. Also, the hams on smaller stalls may look a little lopsided, or unusual, but often the meat is the real thing, compared to the factory-made examples sometimes sold on the more prosperous-looking stalls. It would be disastrous if small producers disappeared, and we end up with nothing but factory-made food, so I tend to go for the local artisan with the freshest-looking produce, avoiding anything that looks as if pink dye has been used.

If you decide to buy a whole ham, choose a boned ham, as it is usually easier to carve than one on the bone. If the ham is boned, it must be stored in the refrigerator crisper drawer, wrapped in a clean dish towel. As you carve shavings or slices from the ham, you can prevent it from drying out by coating the cut surface lightly with olive oil before it is stored again.

Cured Meats *(Charcuterie)*
Southern France, like the rest of the country, has a whole repertoire of charcuterie, all based on the preservation of different parts of the pig. Look on the market stalls and in the small artisan butchers and charcutiers for those fatty, coarse-grained *pâtés de foie de porc* made from the liver and all the scraps. They are sold in gargantuan slices and often turn out to be delicious, served with cornichons and toasted bread.

Other specialties include: *boudins noir* or *boutifarres* (types of black sausage) made from the blood (a particularly good one is made with rice); *lomos*, cured pork loin; *andouille pimentée* or *andouille béarnaise*, a sausage made of pig's intestines spiced with hot, red pepper from Espelette, garlic, and parsley; *hure* or *fromage de cochon*, a kind of pâté made from the head; *gayettes* or *fricandeaux*, balls of liver and the fat of the pig's intestine, spiced, garlicked, and wrapped in the lacy *crépine* or caul, then baked and served cold; *bougnettes*, similar, but made with a high proportion of bread and eggs; *fetge*, or *foie sec* from the Languedoc, salted, dried pig's liver (sometimes smoked), eaten sliced and fried with radishes, or raw with artichokes or snails; *oreilles séches*, salted, dried pig's ears, which are served stuffed, poached, and eaten with beans or cabbage and potatoes; *saucisses*, seriously good, pure pork fresh sausages made from a combination of lean and fattier parts of the pig; *embotis*, a rustic sausage seasoned only with salt and pepper and eaten fresh and cooked, or dried; saucissons, dried, salami-type sausage for eating raw; *pieds de porcs*, the gelatinous feet; *petit salé*, salt pork; *poitrine fumeé*, bacon; and of course, the prized *jambon cuit*, cooked ham, and *jambon cru*, *jambon sec*, or if it comes from the mountains of the Cerdagne, *gambajo*, cured ham, eaten raw or used for cooking.

In the Médoc, there is a splendid sausage called *grenier*, made from pig's stomach and well-peppered. It looks like an *andouillette* but is eaten sliced on a plate of charcuterie.

Lamb *(L'Agneau)*
The deep sand dunes of the Gironde and the Landes, windswept and continually changing under the huge currents and breakers of the Atlantic, seem an unlikely spot for rearing lambs. Until the late nineteenth century, however, when everything was newly planted with pine trees, these dunes, and the woodlands and scrub behind them, provided a sort of common, where in the summer wild horses, fierce bulls, herds of sharp-horned cows, and huge flocks of sheep were turned out to graze, wandering freely and sleeping under the stars. During the winter, though, the sheep were taken north to graze in the sheltered but stony pastures and vineyards of the Médoc. (At that time there were plenty of nourishing wildflowers and herbs growing between the vines.)

The owners of these Médoc farms and vineyards were rewarded with milk and manure and, at Easter, with lamb. There are still Pauillac lambs (named after the small town on the banks of the Gironde), whose mother's milk is enriched by its green meadows, although until 1999 any old lamb could be called Pauillac. Now they are regulated, and the great Pauillac lamb fair at the beginning of May celebrates their new status.

Authentic Pauillac lambs are eaten *sous la mère* at a few weeks old, when milk is still their only food, while a *broutard* (a browser) is a slightly less delicate lamb whose diet includes grass. You can eat every bit of a milk-fed lamb; the kidneys and liver are exquisite. When roasting the lamb, test it with a knitting needle or skewer: when the juice runs out, it is ready.

In Provence, the Gard, and the Languedoc, lamb and mutton have always dominated the menu, and the best come from around Sisteron, Nîmes, and the Cathar country in the Haut Languedoc. Traditionally, milk-fed lamb, *agneau sous la mère* or *viande blanche d'agneau*, is particularly eaten at Easter, at christenings, and sometimes at Christmas.

Lard *(Lard, Saindoux, Lardons)*
Confusingly, *lard* and *lard maigre* refer, respectively, to pork back fat and cured, unsmoked belly of pork, while *saindoux* refers to rendered pork fat or lard. Lard maigre can be cut up

and used to make *daubes*, salads, and any dish which calls for lardons. The best substitute is either a fatty dry-cured, unsmoked (green) bacon, or pancetta.

Sheep's Tripe and Feet in the Marseillais Way *(Pieds, Paquets Marseillais)*

This lamb dish embodies the essence of the sheep-cropped hillsides, a dish packed with herbs and reeking cheaply of old blankets and excessive amounts of garlic. *Pieds et paquets* is a complex, but basic, Provençal workingman's dish of sheep's tripe, made into little parcels enclosing chopped tripe and salt pork, parsley, and garlic, and plenty of black pepper. These parcels are braised slowly to a melting richness in a hermetically sealed earthenware pot, or *tripière*, together with more garlic, sheep's trotters, and perhaps a veal bone, leeks, onions, tomatoes, and carrots, all flavored with cloves and bay leaves, and moistened with white wine. You have to like tripe to enjoy this dish; I do, and I buy these *paquets*, ready to cook, in the market at Fontvieille.

Smoked Bacon *(Poitrine Fumée)*

Belly of pork, salted and smoked, is commonly known as *poitrine fumée*. This is also used in all sorts of dishes from omelettes to daubes, but has a more insistent smoky flavor than the *ventréche* or lard maigre.

Venison, Hare, and Wild Goat *(Chevreuil, Lièvre, Izard)*

Venison is eaten when it is available, which is frequently; as Christian Coulin says in his remarkable *Le Cuisinier Médoquin*, animals that once seemed on the point of extinction, such as deer and rabbits, are now becoming almost a nuisance, and the freezers of the Médoc are stuffed with an assortment of legs and haunches. In the Pyrenees, as well as venison (which is made into saucisson or eaten braised in red wine, perhaps with a quince puree) and hares (usually cooked *en civet*, a stew thickened with the animal's blood), there are *izards*, wild mountain goats, elusive and rarely bagged. If you see izard on a menu, try it; I have never managed to find it, but it is supposed to be extremely good.

Wild Boar *(Marcassin, Sanglier)*

There are an astonishing 200,000 or so wild boar in southern France; the Lot, although it does not hide as many boars as the Midi Méditerranée, has the best organized hunting and rearing programs. Elsewhere, *la chasse au sanglier* (the boar hunt) is somewhat anarchic. The *chasseurs méridionaux* are serious, tough romantics, and to them hunting the wild boar has some aspects of a noble quest, while the boar remains a noble and prestigious beast, representing spiritual authority, as he has since ancient times.

Called in the Midi, *singlar*, *goret*, or *le cochon*, wild boars have different names at different stages of their lives. The striped yellow-and-ginger piglets are called *marcassins*; younger beasts, russet in color, are *bêtes rousses*; and they then become *bêtes noires*. A male who lives to seven years becomes, like a grand old man, a *grand vieux sanglier*.

I saw my only really wild boar in the salt marshes of the Camargue, splashing along through brambles and reeds at a great speed, with its tail stuck straight in the air. But the woods and *garrigue* (the Midi's wild herb–covered scrubland) in almost any densely forested part of southern France show signs of them, they root about on farms, damaging crops and searching for windfalls in the apple orchards each autumn. Boar pens are used to rear animals for release into the wild, or for making charcuterie. A huge, black, hairy leg hanging up outside a butcher's shop may be either wild or farmed *sanglier*, but it will always taste gamy, since the boar pens cover enormous tracts of forest, and the inmates are almost wild. The meat can be dry, and in need of marinating. It is best in a *civet* (a stew) with juniper, Armagnac, red wine, and ceps; in the Languedoc it is served with aïoli (see p. 279), to which a puree of cooked quince has been added.

OIL AND VINEGAR

Throughout the low-lying areas of Languedoc and Provence, and reaching far up the Rhône valley, the tarnished silver of olive trees and the geometry of rows of vines have been an integral part of the landscape since the Romans brought irrigation to this water-starved land. Essential to the soul of the Mediterranean diet, olives and grapes helped to establish a cuisine based on olive oil, wine, and, to a lesser extent, on cooling *vin-aigre* (literally, sour wine) or vinegar, a by-product of the basic industry of wine-making and a major industry in the Gard.

Olive oil is healthy and a perfect cooking medium as well as being the best oil to make a little refreshing salad with, but the South produces other oils, and flavored oils too, as well as flavored vinegars, and I have covered a few of the regional specialties here.

Olive Oil *(l'Huile d'Olive)*

French olive oil is delicate, fruity, and varies in color from a pale straw color, to gold, to a greenish amber. The yellow-golden oils are sweeter, since they are made from fully ripe black olives. The greenish oils are fruitier and stronger. The golden oil from Nice is fine and delicate, perfect for light-flavored dishes, shellfish salads, and mayonnaise. The amber-gold oil from the Vallée des Baux is more robust and ideal for crudités, salads, and aïoli. Both have an exceptional aroma and well-balanced flavor. The other great olive oil center is Nyons, in the south of the Drôme, where the oil is beautifully fruity.

Olive trees have been in decline in Languedoc, once an

important olive oil–producing region, but new plantings are starting to yield again, and the oils, the sweetest and most delicate from the Hérault, the most robust from the Gard and the Aude, are just beginning to flow again. In the Vallée des Baux, the olive trees are predominantly the *picholine* variety, which make delicious cracked green olives as well as strong, nutty oil.

By the end of November some olives are ready for picking—at the start of the harvest some are still green, others striped with brown or purple; by the time the picking, which is done by hand, is over, most have ripened to black.

Everyone takes their own olives to the local mill, some in trailerfuls, others in a few plastic buckets in the back of the car. The mill at Maussane in the Vallée des Baux is a good place to meet your neighbors as over a thousand farms bring their olives here. Each lot of olives is weighed, and the cost of crushing thus worked out—the mill is paid in olive oil for its services. In most mills, they are washed, crushed, and cold-pressed and the oil is allowed to settle until it clears, when olive growers can pick it up in plastic five-liter *bidons*, or sell it all to the mill.

The currently fashionable flavored oils, from extravagant black truffle oil to oil scented with crushed lemons, can be made easily at home. Simply add dried chilies, twigs of fennel, bay leaves, and sprigs of thyme to the oil for extra aroma and flavor.

Verjuice (Verjus)
Made from green grapes before they start to change their color, this adds a sour element to cooking, somewhere between lemon juice and vinegar. *Verjus* fell out of favor, probably when lemons and commercially made vinegar became widely available, but it is still used in cooking in some parts of southern France. It is said that, unlike vinegar or lemon juice, it harmonizes with wine; use it in salad dressing when you open a really good bottle of wine.

To make verjuice, see p. 279.

Vinegar (Vinaigre)
Vinegar has been made in the South of France since Roman times, and even today about a quarter of all the vinegar made in France comes from Nîmes. Although the main production is white and red wine vinegars, there are others flavored with all sorts of things. *Vinaigre de framboise*, raspberry vinegar, supposed to be good for pregnant women, was a great favorite with the chefs of the Gers in the seventies. It is somewhat sweet, and too scented for my taste. *Vinaigre à l'estragon*, tarragon vinegar, is essential, with its sweet, haylike flavor, for making Béarnaise sauce, but beware; it can go off, so keep it in the refrigerator. Truffle vinegar appears on the markets at Christmas, for the truffle-flavored salad of endive or *frisée*,

which goes so happily with foie gras.

Vinegar from Banyuls *(vinaigre de Banyuls)* is a mature, elegant vinegar, aged for six years in storerooms that are warmed in winter to develop the flavor. It is then aged for a further six months in oak barrels. This vinegar is made from the sweet coastal wine of Banyuls, and makes a great alternative to sherry vinegar, having about the same density. It is less sticky and sweet than Italian balsamic vinegar, and is excellent for salads and for cooking.

Walnut Oil (Huile de Noix)
My first experience of walnut oil was a big disappointment and I expect that this may happen to lots of willing purchasers. I bought a can of it, and made a salad, and it tasted bitter, with a horrid, lingering aftertaste. It had gone rancid, and must have been stored in a warm place. Thick, amber walnut oil must be kept rather cool and eaten fairly quickly. When fresh, it has a sweet, nutty flavor that lifts bitter winter salad and bathes a summer lettuce in pure perfume, particularly a salad of *gésiers confits* (preserved duck giblets). Walnut oil can be used for cooking, but this is often considered a waste, as it is expensive, and, if warmed, loses some of its bouquet. However, I use it for frying, particularly artichokes, as it contrasts nicely with the bitter flavor.

POULTRY, FOIE GRAS, AND FEATHERED GAME
The southwest of France is one of the most renowned areas in the world as far as poultry-rearing is concerned, and they specialize in foie gras, with ducks now predominating over geese, as ducks stand up better to summer heat—which means duck, duck, and duck again on local menus. However, quite apart from the foie gras trade, the rearing of good chickens is considered an art form here, and guinea fowl, quail, and farmed squab are all raised by hand to extend the cook's repertoire. The traditional rearing, which means that birds are fed on grain and to an older age than they are elsewhere, means the birds are tender but not soft and have time to develop plenty of flavor. The yellow, corn-fed chickens are particularly good for frying and the black-legged, pearly white-fleshed birds are perfect for recipes that require poaching or boiling.

Alicot (Alicot)
One of the forgotten flavors today is the rich taste of poultry giblets; in southern France these have always been eaten with real pleasure, particularly in the Gers and the Landes. The fresh giblets of turkeys, ducks, geese, or chickens, which can include necks, wings, hearts, gizzards (carefully trimmed), and even feet (boiled and peeled), are cooked together in a succulent *alicot* or *alycuit* (a little ragout or stew), sometimes

with the addition of chestnuts or ceps. Alternatively, the gizzards may be preserved in goose fat to make *confit de gesiers*. They are eaten fried in a little goose fat and served on a salad of curly endive, hot from the frying pan, with a handful of fresh white walnut halves thrown on top and dressing made by deglazing the pan with vinegar.

Fattened Goose or Duck Liver (Foie Gras)

The ancient Egyptians first observed that wild geese started to stuff themselves with large quantities of food before embarking on their migration north, preparing themselves for the long journey ahead by acquiring reserves of fat in their livers. I emphasize this because it seems that this is a natural urge on the part of the geese, which makes the fattening process required to make the foie gras seem less of an imposition on their constitutions. The livers, of course, were best when the geese were fattest, and so naturally *le gavage* (feeding with extra food) followed, as the Egyptians quite successfully tried to imitate and outdo nature.

At various times geese have been fed with dried figs, cracked wheat soaked in water, and, toward the end of the nineteenth century, a special strain of white corn. Today, there are more ducks than geese in foie gras production and they are corn-fed, much of this process being mechanized.

However, there is a great respect for tradition in the Landes and the Gers, the largest French producers of fattened geese and ducks, with many small producers still hand-rearing *mulard* (Muscovy-cross) and *barbarie* (Barbary) ducks and local geese called *grise de sud-ouest* (southwestern gray).

The main markets for their luxurious foie gras in the Gers are Seissan, Samatan, Gimont, Fleurance, and Eauze, but there is foie gras for sale in markets throughout southern France before Christmas, including the Lot, the Dordogne, and Provence. At the beginning of January, there is a Foie Gras Fair in Brive, where you can buy foie gras raw, and pick it up four hours later in a jar, already conserved.

Experts debate over which is better, a goose foie gras, which can weigh up to 4½ lb., or a duck foie gras, which can weigh up to 1 lb. 5 oz. I prefer duck because it has more flavor, and because it is smaller and less prohibitively expensive. In the region, foie gras is eaten cooked, as a terrine, with toasted *pain de campagne* (country bread) or *brioche*, and a glass of Barsac, Sauternes, Rivesaltes, or Banyuls. Or it is sliced, fried, and served *en salade*. For details on how to prepare foie gras, see page 282.

Guinea Fowl (Pintade, Pintadeau)

A live guinea fowl, always flapping around in a panic, covered in the most exquisite spots, with a scrawny neck and Egyptian head, could not look more different to its chicken neighbors. It tastes different too, being more subtly gamy, although the texture can be on the dry side. So roast it carefully, turning and basting it every ten minutes in plenty of butter, and with a tasty stuffing to keep it juicy, or simply a bunch of tarragon, some lemon, and plenty of butter inside.

Other Feathered Game (Les Petits Oiseaux)

Larks (*alouettes*), buntings (*ortolans*), blackbirds (*merles*), and thrushes (*grives*) are scarce nowadays, as are plovers (*vanneaux*). In any case, it is illegal to sell larks and ortolans, although the blackbirds and thrushes that feed off grapes are still fair game in the South and in Corsica. Here they are either roasted over a fire of juniper bushes and flambéed with eau-de-vie or *marc* (a white grape spirit), or cooked in a Gascon fashion, by dripping sizzling pork fat over them through a conical metal funnel with a handle, heated up on the fire. They are also made into pâté flavored with juniper. In Gascony, woodcock (*bécasses*) and snipe, which today are also protected in some areas, are grilled, with their innards still in place, over a fire of vine prunings, and served on a piece of country bread, to mop up the juices.

Partridge (Perdrix, Perdreau)

Red-legged partridge are the only kind you will see in southern France. Known sometimes as the French infantry (who wore red britches), they are a little larger than gray partridges, and supposedly a little coarser in flavor. I roast them, in a Provençal way, by wrapping them in vine leaves or bacon, and serving them with wild mushrooms, or occasionally stuffing them as they do in the Pays Catalan, with roasted almonds pounded with garlic and bread fried in olive oil.

Pigeon (Ramier, Pigeon)

Pigeons, wild or tame, are considered a table bird; many old *bastides* (fortified farms) and *châteaux* have large and beautiful *pigeonniers* in the farmyards, often on stilts to keep out rats and foxes, where generations of pigeons stretching back for hundreds of years added to the cook's repertoire. Today, every poultry shop or butcher, and even supermarkets, sell oven-ready pigeons with fat breasts. These birds are delicious flavored with basil and roasted, cooked with green peas, or spatchcocked and grilled. Wild pigeons—wood pigeons, ringdoves, and rock pigeons—are all eaten, but the favorites for the table are the migratory or turtle doves, *tourterelles* or *palombes*.

These are caught (*la chasse à la palombe*) on their passage from the Black Forest to Africa in October. The local *chasseurs* (hunters) conceal themselves in makeshift hides or tree houses, and wave white sheets attached to poles to head the flocks toward the hunters. Tame doves, tied to the tops of trees, then lure them down to the ground, where they are netted. When caught, they are made into a *salmis*, a kind of stew, cooked in goose fat as confit, or in the local way, *rôtie à la goutte de sang*, extremely rare, and flambéed in Armagnac.

Poultry (Les Volailles)
The happy sight of hens, ducks, and geese pottering around a farm is a common sight in the South, particularly in the Dordogne, the Landes, and the Gers. Hens provide eggs for daily use, and for a family anniversary or Sunday lunch, a chicken from the local farm, rather than a joint of meat, makes the point of the meal. This is frequently served juicily stuffed and poached as *poule au pot* rather than roasted, while in restaurants today it is duck, duck, and more duck.

Foie gras (see p. 44) from geese and ducks can provide a significant source of income, with ducks now playing the more important part. One by-product of making foie gras is duck breasts, usually called *magrets* or *filets de canard*, similar in size and texture to a fine-grained steak, and now common everyday food. Duck hearts are also eaten, grilled on skewers, *en brochette*, while the *croupions* or *demoiselles*, the parson's nose and underside of the duck, are similarly grilled and served sprinkled with garlic and parsley. The duck carcasses (*carcasses*) are used to make soup, and the necks (*cous*) are stuffed with a delicate pâté to make *cou de canard farci*. The thighs (*cuisses*), wings (*ailes*), and giblets (*gésiers*) are all lightly salted and cooked in their own fat to make delicious confit (see p. 168). The white-golden fat is great for cooking, particularly frying, as it heats to a high temperature before burning—480°F as opposed to butter (265°F) and lard (390°F).

Quails (Cailles)
Quails are pretty little things, much appreciated in the Landes, where they do still live in the wild, often in the cornfields. Wrapped in vine leaves and roasted on skewers, or stuffed with raisins soaked in Armagnac, roasted, and served on a dish lined with vine leaves, they make a delicious meal.

REGIONAL VEGETABLES
Everyone who loves southern France loves the market experience, a morning in the Garden of Eden, provided it is not raining. The market stalls sell fast, there are hands everywhere, you fill your basket with thin-skinned tomatoes, eggplants, and bunches of basil. You catch the stallholder's attention, he or she weighs and adds up, and it costs almost nothing. Given a fair amount of water, vegetables are easy to grow in the sun and they are cheap; what is more, they taste of something. Sadly, mass-farmed, chemically enhanced vegetables are appearing on the markets, so for the best flavor, look to the stalls with local produce.

Asparagus (Asperges)
Wild asparagus, *asperge sauvage*, grows all along the Mediterranean, through the Languedoc and Provence. It is pale, thin, and somewhat bitter, and people have a great passion for its young shoots when they first appear early in the year, eating them mainly in omelettes.

In April and May, the cultivated varieties appear, one of the best being from the Lauragais. Although there has always been asparagus described as *violet*, until recently this was a tinge rather than a color. Now, though, you can find dark violet asparagus, which is supposed to be unusually sweet. It really is dark purple, almost black, when raw, but once cooked, it goes a disappointingly normal green.

Asparagus is always expensive and kept for special meals, when it is eaten with vinaigrette, especially the white variety, or melted butter. Sometimes it is eaten in omelettes (see p. 68), with scrambled eggs, or as tips with *morilles*—morels, and in restaurants it is overused as a garnish.

Black Truffles (Diamants Noirs)
If you love the mysterious, elusive black truffle, this is the country for you. The season starts in December and continues until February, and the truffles are sold on the markets, each truffle hunter with a small basket, lined with a white napkin, which is placed in the middle of a trestle table covered with a white cloth. You have to be beady-eyed, as the truffle sellers are crafty. Choose a specimen that has a little coat of earth to keep it fresh, but does not have large patches of clay stuck on it; this weighs heavy and can cover small insect holes. Inhale the glorious perfume; if it smells strong enough, you are in luck.

Despite their luxurious appeal, truffles seem more common in the places in which it is found, bringing pleasure, interest, and income to many in the middle of winter. Anybody with well-drained, limestone-based land can try to grow truffles, by planting the already-inoculated saplings of oak, evergreen oak, or hazel, sold in bundles like leeks in the winter market.

In Périgord and the Lot, particularly around Cahors, in Provence, the Vaucluse, and the Luberon, there are truffles everywhere; there are markets at Sauzy and Lalbenque; Aups has a truffle market every Thursday in winter; and there is a Grande Marché de Truffes et Gastronome before Christmas at Rognes, north of Aix-en-Provence.

The simplest approach to cooking with truffles is the best. For example, bake some potatoes, cut them in half, and serve with a sauce of hot cream and olive oil, and a thick layer of sliced truffles over the top. Or, leave the truffle overnight in a jar with some eggs, and then scramble these with some finely chopped truffle, and again serve with sliced truffle over the top. Jars of eggs with a truffle in the middle, ready for your Christmas party, are just one of the ways of selling truffles at the Grand Marché—you will also find truffle vinegar, truffle mustard, and a paste charmingly called *Truffelette* for making truffle omelettes.

Fresh truffles can be preserved and are excellent for pâté and for stuffing poultry. I learned from a charcutier, who made truffled *cervelas* sausages to sell for *Reveillon* (Christmas or New Year's Eve). All you have to do is to wash and brush the truffle clean of dirt, eat half of it fresh, put the rest into a small glass jar, and cover it with Armagnac or brandy. If you decide to peel it, the peel itself can be dried and powdered to use as a flavoring, or put under brandy. The brandy is permeated with the truffle smell and taste, and a little, with a little truffle, will flavor a pâté or stuffed, roast chicken.

Cabbage Shoots (*Broutes de Choux, Broutix, Broutos*)
Until recently, one of the essential, everyday winter vegetables in the Southwest, particularly in the making of cabbage soup (*garbure*, p. 93), were the tender green cabbage shoots, which appear from the stalk of the cabbage after it is cut. These were also frequently used to add flavor to soups made with dried haricot beans or dried fava beans, and were also eaten boiled like asparagus. The name *broutes* is also applied to a number of other shoots, such as kohlrabi, turnip, swede, and rutabaga, and the young shoots of mustard-related plants that appear in May, such as rape—these can also be eaten cooked like spinach, with a little oil and garlic. The somewhat bitter, earthy character of these vegetables is splendid and valuable. In Spain and Italy, greens such as these are still highly prized, and they deserve to keep their place in the southern French kitchen, particularly at a time when food is becoming increasingly uniform and bland.

Ceps and Other Boletus (*Cèpes et Autres Bolets*)
The greatest fungus of the oak and chestnut woods of southern France, and essential to the local cuisine, is the *cèpe* (cep). If it rains and thunders in August, the locals are not disappointed; it means a flush of wild fungi, ready to fry up with "a little garlic and a little parsley." There are over a hundred varieties of *bolets* in the South, the best being the firm, white-fleshed varieties, such as *boletus aureus* (*tête de nègre* or *cèpe bronzé*), with dark brown shiny caps and the *boletus edulis* (*cèpe de Bordeaux*), paler with suedelike skin and bulging white stems.

Then there is the *boletus pinicola* (*cèpe des pins* or *cèpe acajou*), a chestnut-colored variety found in pinewoods, the early *boletus aestivalis* (*cèpe d'été*), snuff-brown and covered in small cracks in dry weather, and the *cèpe de châtaignier*, which grows on the cool north slopes of chestnut woods. Sweet, nutty-tasting ceps, like peppery *chanterelles* and the exotic *morilles* that appear in spring, have always been highly prized (and highly priced) in the region. In the past they were

often sold dried, since transport was difficult for fresh mushrooms, and at one time they were also preserved in salt.

Today you can freeze ceps. Use firm, small specimens, slice them, sprinkle with salt, and fry in goose fat or butter before freezing. Then serve them cooked in a tomato sauce with parsley and garlic. You can still buy them preserved in jars or cans; to revive these, first rinse and drain them, then fry them in duck fat until they are crisp, and serve them with coarse salt, chopped garlic, and parsley. Dried ceps, on the other hand, spring back to life when soaked, and give a wonderful flavor to chicken dishes, or any dish with a good sauce. Fresh ceps, though, are supreme, whether eaten raw in salads or fried or broiled, sometimes with walnut oil or goose fat, often with parsley, and always with garlic.

Of course, the best cep is the one you have found yourself, but it is important to know that in the Midi these fungi are closely guarded and the pickers have their own secret *nids* (places) that they visit regularly through the season. If you start helping yourself you may enrage someone; better to buy them in the market.

Chard, Swiss Chard, Seakale Beet (*Blette, Bette*)
This handsome vegetable stands in the garden throughout the winter, even withstanding quite hard frosts. It has a crisp and juicy, flattish, broad middle rib, usually white, sometimes ruby, pink, or golden, topped with a curly, bright green leaf. The rib and leaf are usually cooked separately. A particularly strange Niçoise dish, *tourte* or *torta de bette*, is a covered pie whose crust contains a sweet mixture of chard leaves, pine nuts, raisins, and sugar. The green leaves are also used for making *trouchia*, a sturdy omelette (see p. 72).

A comforting winter dish made in the Dordogne, Quercy, and Provence, is *Côtes de Blettes au Gratin*; stalks of chard, cut diagonally into pieces, are boiled and then baked in the oven with cream or béchamel sauce mixed with egg yolks and grated cheese, and seasoned with nutmeg, garlic, and parsley.

Chestnuts (*Chataignes et Marrons*)
The glorious chestnut forests of the Midi at one time provided, in winter and in times of scarcity, a floury substitute for cereals. The trees are called bread trees, and in winter months a large bowl of steaming, boiled chestnuts was once the daily breakfast in many peasant households.

There are two main species of sweet chestnuts; the trees are grafted, and, accordingly, become *marroniers* or *châtaigniers*. The marroniers produce large, single nuts, rounded on both sides, which are called *marrons*, while the châtaigniers contain two *châtaignes*, each with a flat side where they lie side by side in their prickly husks.

The largest marrons are preserved, the smaller ones grilled in the streets of northern towns when the hard weather sets in. They appear as *marrons glacé*, marrons in syrup, *marrons au naturel*, *purée de marrons*, and *marrons sous vide* (vacuum packed), the last a good cheat for using in stuffings and other cooking, as they save a lot of time—peeling chestnuts is no fun. The French marrons are known to be sweeter and more tender than those from elsewhere.

For roasting or cooking with chestnuts at home, look for the large marrons if possible. Use them quickly as they soon dry out and tend to go moldy. Special roasting pans, like black frying pans with holes in them, allow the chestnuts to be roasted in the embers without burning.

Châtaignes, which are smaller, are also used for eating, either fresh or dried, or even as chestnut flour. Dried chestnuts were once a staple—hard little dark brown lumps dried over smoke in special drying cupboards with a fireplace in the wall. They were soaked for twenty-four hours and the liquid used to make a soup with goat's milk and, quite surprisingly, sugar and lumps of cooking chocolate.

The chestnuts are also crushed, seasoned with salt and pepper, and eaten as *fricot*, sprinkled with olive oil, or ground into flour, with which a puree is made to serve with roast kid or lamb.

Globe Artichokes *(Artichauts)*

Globe artichokes are members of the thistle family; thistles of every exotic kind abound in Provence, and in the Languedoc, of course, artichokes do well too. Along the Rhône Valley, beautiful rows of gray-green leaves shoot up in early spring, and in sheltered, frost-free spots, giant clumps of them flourish all year. Tender little purple artichokes, *le violet hâtif* or *le violet de Provence*, are sold in bunches of four or five. Artichokes are good for your digestive system, and are supposed to be an aphrodisiac if cooked in wine, but the French eat them for pure gustatory pleasure. Some people eat them raw with coarse salt, but a favorite way in the South is to stuff them *à la barigoule* with savory, thyme, and garlic, and braise them with thyme, onions, and carrots, while the little hearts, fried up, are a classic accompaniment to milk-fed lamb. In Bordeaux, they have an early variety called *Macau*, which is stuffed with sausage meat, Bayonne ham, and bread crumbs. And in the Pays Catalan, a pale green variety called *blanc Hyérois* is braised with onions and sometimes potatoes, and served sprinkled with garlic and parsley.

Onions, Shallots, and Garlic *(Les Oignons, L'Ail, Les Echalotes)*

Often the warm, appetizing smell of chopped onions and garlic frying in olive oil is the beginning of the enjoyment of the forthcoming meal for everyone in the house. When that comforting aroma starts up, who would not want to sit down to eat the resulting dish together with friends?

A fifth of all the onions eaten in France are grown in the Languedoc and the Pays Catalan. Specialties include sweet onions from the Cévennes, and large, sweet, white onions called *cèbes de Lézignan*, which are usually eaten baked, perhaps with some roasted chestnuts. In the Pays Catalan there is a fête where the specialty is *la calcotada*, young shoots of sweet onions that are grilled and then wrapped in newspaper. The charred outer layers of the onions are peeled off and the soft inner hearts dipped in hot sauce and eaten like asparagus. The green shoots of onions are also eaten raw, dipped in salt, with wine.

When cooking with onions, it is much better to soften them slowly, stirring occasionally, so that they give up their moisture before they brown. Burned onions impart a bitter taste. Cooked extremely gently in oil for up to thirty minutes, they acquire a sweet flavor and lose their acrid or bitter notes. Cook a little longer and they almost caramelize.

Shallots are almost as useful as onions, but cook in a fraction of the time. There are gray, yellow, and pink shallots and pink banana shallots (*échalotes bananes*), this last really a type of mild onion, which is easy to peel and chop. Probably the best-flavored shallots are the *échalotes grises*, which have hard, gray skins. They are excellent raw in salad dressing and in a particularly good, sharp, refreshing sauce for grilled poultry or game (see p. 152).

Garlic, that familiar friend, appears in early spring, all tender and juicy, with each clove wrapped in several silky shifts. The new garlic is firm and crisp and less resonant than mature garlic, which comes in rustling its papery teguments, in bunches, in skeins, in huge market-barrow-loads, later in the year—the rubric is that you plant it on the shortest day and harvest it on the longest.

There is *l'ail blanc*, white garlic, *l'ail rose*, garlic veined with rose-pink, and *l'ail rouge*, which is, in fact, purple or violet-veined. Vast amounts are grown in the Gard, and Gascons, in particular, if they don't grow it themselves, buy it in quantity, not least for their garlic soup, *le tourain*. Their favorite, the rose-colored garlic of Lautrec, is particularly sought-after. Everybody tries to be clever and buy the cheapest possible supply, bargaining like mad, while at the same time seeing that it is completely dry and free of mold, and will keep through the winter.

In Arles, garlic is also sold smoked, which is supposed to keep even longer, but in my experience this spoils the clean, stinging, garlic taste. Some people think that the green shoots that appear in the center of the cloves after they have passed their best (around New Year) should be removed, as they have a bitter taste, but I find this is not true. However, eaten in large quantities, the green shoots might upset a delicate stomach. The garlic of the Périgord is supposed to have a wonderful, mellow flavor; here, except with green salads, it is

usually eaten cooked rather than raw. I was particularly happy to find a bold sauce from farther south, in the Hérault, called *la Cavilhada*, made of whole cloves of garlic, fried in huge amounts of olive oil, which is equally good with any roast meat, and with rabbit.

Hot Red Chili Pepper *(Piment d'Espelette)*

It is rather cheery to find red pepper on your table instead of black when you eat in the little town of Espelette—but you will have had plenty of warnings that this is hot pepper country before you place your elbows on the red-striped table-cloth. This pepper is made in Espelette each autumn, and at that time, garlands of red peppers hang on house walls, drying in the sun and the dry mountain air. They are also found in the windows of shops, on the ceilings of kitchens, and on all the market stalls.

The market in the town of Espelette is an amiably peppery experience, with its red-peppered charcuterie and jars and bottles of different dried and pickled peppers, olive oil with peppers, sausages and hams preserved and flavored with peppers, pepper sauces, and cans of whole peppers. Ground pimento is used in cooking to add flavor as well as heat. The nearest equivalent outside France is hot Spanish *pimenton*. Harvested between the beginning of August and the first frosts, the peppers are marketed under the following names: *la poudre*—ground pimento used instead of black pepper; *la purée*—pimentos pounded to a paste and mixed with spices; *le xipister*—spicy vinegar flavored with garlic and spices; *le olibizia*—olive oil flavored with pimento and garlic, used in frying and grilling fish.

Espelette pepper mania is not just *touristique* (a tourist attraction), but a genuine, long-established, farm-based industry, with a specialized product and knowledge. And there is one note of relief in all the pepperiness: The town is also famous for its little chocolate factory.

Red, Yellow, or Green Bell Peppers *(Pimentos, Piments, Poivrons)*

These usually small, sweet, thin-skinned green or red peppers are a crucial part of Basque cooking. There are many varieties —one revelation is the *piment doux* or *piment du pays*, a long, narrow, tender green pepper that looks like a large chili but tastes sweet, not hot. Peppers can be deep-fried, sautéed, broiled, or perhaps roasted, and then torn into pieces or strips, or stuffed. They are best freshly prepared, but in ordinary restaurants they often come out of cans. You can buy cans of whole pimentos for stuffing or, much cheaper but not as good, cans of ready-cut strips. I usually prepare my own (see p. 64). They are useful for *oeufs sur le plat* (see p. 70), *pipérade* (see p. 221), salads, omelettes, rice dishes, and so on. Once prepared, they keep in the refrigerator, covered, for a week.

Walnuts *(Noix)*

The walnut is my favorite tree, and the Lot and Dordogne, particularly around Sarlat, are full of them. The nuts are chiefly used for making the heavenly tasting, sweetish walnut oil for salads, but they are also for eating on their own and in salads, for *pâtisserie* (cakes), and for drinks such as *La Vieille Noix*, a blackish, sticky, sweet liqueur. *Brou*, a sweet cordial, is made from the green husks. Walnuts are also pickled in vinegar and made into jam.

The main varieties are the soft-shelled *corne* and the *marbot*. They are at their best as wet walnuts, recently picked, while the inside skin covering the nut is still moist. As they dry they become lighter and feel more hollow, and the nuts taste harsher.

The business of cracking the nuts is extraordinary; they are all cracked by hand, even those going to the oil-mills. People get together in the winter, drink wine and tell stories as they hammer away at the nuts. The shells are sometimes used to light fires.

Wild Leeks *(Pouraganes)*

Little wild leeks, quite recognizable as such by their smell when you step on them or pull them up, although they are in fact a type of onion. Grown among the vines in late winter, with the other wild herbs, they are well-liked in the Médoc, where they are eaten boiled, with vinaigrette, and halved hard-boiled eggs.

Black-Skinned Turnips from Pardhailan
(Navets du Pardhailan)

Turnips may not seem much to get excited about, but these are long-rooted and black-skinned, and particularly crisp and white inside. Grown in the mountains, they are ancient, and famous from Béziers to Saint-Pons to Narbonne as a vegetable to be eaten in its own right, not just thrown into the soup. According to food writer Albin Marty, who was brought up in Béziers, the way to deal with them, after peeling, is to whittle them into chips and fry them in goose fat, then caramelize them with a tablespoon of superfine sugar.

Salads and

Small Dishes

Most meals in the South of France seem to have a salad in them somewhere; salads need olive oil, and there is no shortage of that in the region, at least not until recently, when exporters started to realize how good French olive oil is. The light golden oil from Nice is ideal for summer salads, and the nutty, amber oils from Nyons, Bize-Minervois, Beaucaire, and the Vallée des Baux are good for salads with bell pepper, tomato, basil, onion, capers, or anchovies and the tougher salads such as *frisée*, *escarole*, *batavia*, *endive*, and *pissenlit*.

Each region has its favorite salad. In the Médoc they love looking for wild leeks, which grow among the vines (or at least those vines that are cultivated without herbicides). These are boiled and served cool with hard-boiled eggs and a strong vinaigrette. In the Dordogne and the Lot, they like to dress the salad—a cushion of yellow, inner leaves of lettuce—with walnut oil, and they may put a piece of sautéed duck confit, or some preserved duck giblets and a few fresh walnuts on top, or a thick slice of *terrine de foie gras*. The Basques like charcuterie in their salads, a few lardons, and some slices of sausage with batavia, tomatoes, and hard-boiled eggs, while the Catalans love anchovies, and serve them with hard-boiled eggs and grilled red bell peppers. Along the Mediterranean coast and into the Languedoc you will find, out in the country, especially during Lent, a salad of hot chickpeas (garbanzo beans), and in town, grilled or marinated goat's cheese salad. Provençals like a simple mix of hard-boiled eggs, anchovies, tomatoes, onions, and garlic, with plenty of Italian parsley, while farther along the coast *salade Niçoise*, now a universal cliché, is the summer staple, with its green beans, tuna, eggs, anchovies, tomatoes, black olives, and, if you are lucky, basil.

The Southwest, as well as its many salads, has a great repertoire of light, quick dishes, many of them based on eggs and bacon—this is an area whose tradition of poultry-keeping has always been central to the rural economy, and whose charcuterie is second to none. I like these *casse-croûtes* (snacks) because they depend on everyday ingredients, are easily made, and, if the best ingredients are used, are far from humble.

L'Heure de l'Apéritif

Late in the afternoon, on a hot summer's day in the South, delicious, herb-scented air wafts down from the hills, and the light changes from white to gold to pearl. The habit in the Midi, a habit that translates well anywhere, is to have a gentle stroll in the early evening before returning home to sit outside as it gets dark, to talk, and to drink apéritifs—a cloudy *pastis*, nicknamed *la jaune*, perhaps, or a glass of cool *vin rosé*—accompanied by a few simple *amuse-gueules* (appetizers). (A *gueule* is literally a fish's huge maw, but more colloquially means "kisser.") In the Pays Catalan they go further and have tapas, like the Spanish, things to eat with the fingers, stimulating to the appetite and to conviviality.

There is a huge selection of appetizers to choose from in the South. First of all there are, always and ever, simple olives, salted almonds, and sliced saucisson, a form of cured sausage similar to salami. Or the following:

Radis aux beurre—French breakfast radishes, white, pink, and crisp, served with ice cubes, butter, and sea salt.

Féves nouvelles—raw baby broad (fava) beans are eaten straight from their furry pods, and dipped into sea salt. In early spring, raw baby artichokes, *artichauts violets*, are eaten in the same way.

Crevettes grises—tiny brown shrimps, which are eaten shells and all (but not the heads), perhaps with a squeeze of lemon, some *pain integral* (whole-wheat bread), and unsalted butter.

Camarons (gambas)—Mediterranean shrimp, grilled or fried with parsley, garlic, and chili.

Pain à la tomate—grilled or oven-toasted *pain de campagne* (country bread), rubbed or stroked with garlic, then rubbed with half a cut tomato. The squashy, tomato-soaked upper surface is drizzled with olive oil and sprinkled with crystals of sea salt and coarse black pepper. It should be eaten at once while it is still warm. Press a few leaves of fresh basil on top if you like.

Croûtons à l'ail—the same as pain à la tomate but without the tomato.

Anchoïade—drained anchovies served with fresh olive oil, black pepper, and a mashed clove or two of garlic. To serve, put a plate of cubes of bread on the table. Toast some pieces of a baguette cut lengthwise. Place a few of the anchovies on each piece of toast. Let everyone dip the cubes of bread into the oil and garlic mixture and use them to mash the anchovies into the toast. The cubes of bread can be eaten, too.

Brandade de morue—salt cod pounded to a purée with olive oil, garlic, and milk and, sometimes, mashed potato. Add nutmeg, chopped lemon peel, and pepper, if desired, and serve with mounds of toasted baguettes.

Rillettes de canard, rillettes d'oie, rillettes de porc—duck, goose, or pork, slow-cooked for a long time in fat, shredded and seasoned, then allowed to cool. It is sold in charcuteries. Serve it spread on fresh baguettes and accompanied by pickled cornichons.

Grenier médoquin—a tasty saucisson from the Bas-Médoc made with pig's stomach rolled with plenty of pepper; serve it sliced.

Saucisson d'Arles—this famous Arles sausage is made mainly with pork and bull meat from the Camargue.

Figatelli—a Corsican slicing sausage, dark in color, containing dried liver, and eaten with radishes.

Jambon de Bayonne—raw, cured Bayonne ham, cut into shavings and placed next to black olives.

Chorizo—fiery or sweet orange-red, pimento-flavored *saucisson sec*, which comes in various sizes and textures, and which can either be hot-and-spicy or plain.

Tortilla—this omelette-like dish has crossed the border from Spain and is popular in the Pays Catalan. It usually contains onion and potato, and is served cut into small cubes with toothpicks stuck into them. You could also serve the zucchini omelette (see p. 74), cooled to room temperature and cut in cubes—but don't refrigerate it. A traditional *trouchia*—a type of spinach omelette (see p. 72)—sprinkled with fresh lemon juice or vinegar is good, too.

The impact of this dish from Languedoc–Roussillon depends on the person making it; present it on a giant platter decorated with your choice of vegetables.

Anchoïade Salad
LA GRANDE ANCHOÏADE

Serves 6

For the garlic mayonnaise:

1 egg yolk, 1 large clove garlic and ¾ cup oil

For the salad:

9 oz. slender asparagus

2 tbsp. olive oil

7 oz. cherry tomatoes

9 oz. green beans

7 oz. baby carrots

4 eggs, hard-boiled

1 fennel bulb

2 red bell peppers, roasted

9 oz. small cooked new potatoes (optional)

2 baby lettuce heads, washed, leaves separated

7 oz. radishes, trimmed

7 oz. anchovies in oil, drained (reserve 6 for the dressing)

½ cup black olives

2 tbsp. baby capers or berries

salt and freshly ground black pepper

For the anchovy dressing:

6 reserved anchovies, chopped

6 scallions, sliced

4 tbsp. Italian parsley, chopped

juice of half a lemon

2–3 tsp. sherry vinegar

⅔ cup olive oil

First of all, make the garlic mayonnaise by putting the egg yolk in a small bowl. Mince the garlic clove with a pinch of salt into a paste and mix in with the egg yolk. Gradually add the oil, literally drop by drop. When the mayonnaise begins to look thick, stir in a teaspoon of water, then continue adding the oil until it is all incorporated into the mayonnaise. Season, cover the bowl, and keep in the refrigerator until required.

Next, prepare the salad ingredients. Cook the asparagus spears in the olive oil and allow them to cool. Cut the tomatoes in half. Briefly cook the beans in well-salted water, drain and cool. The carrots can also be cooked, or they can be left raw. Cut the eggs lengthwise into halves or quarters, and chop the fennel into narrow strips. Cut the bell peppers into fairly large strips.

In a small bowl, mix together all the ingredients for the anchovy dressing, season, and put to one side.

Start assembling the salad by placing the drained, cooled beans in a mound in the middle of the dish (or the small new potatoes if you are using them). Arrange all the other vegetables around the edge, dividing each vegetable into four bunches. Place the eggs, anchovies, olives, and capers on top. Spoon the anchovy dressing over the top. Serve the garlic mayonnaise separately and let everyone help themselves to salad and mayonnaise.

This is a beautiful-looking salad, and if you can find a blue or blue-black dish to put it on, it will look even more striking. These quantities are for a starter. If you want to eat it as a lunch dish, bulk it up with tomatoes, but be careful when increasing the amount of bell peppers and anchovies, as it may become too rich.

Catalan Salad
SALADE CATALANE

Serves 4 as a starter

2 fennel bulbs, each cut into 6 pieces

4 tbsp. olive oil

7 oz. anchovies in salt (if these are not available, you can use anchovies packed in oil)

2 red and 2 yellow bell peppers, roasted and torn into broad strips (see p. 64)

2 large cloves garlic, coarsely chopped

3 tbsp. Italian parsley, coarsely chopped

3–4 tbsp. olive oil, for serving

4 hard-boiled eggs, halved or quartered lengthwise

sea salt and freshly ground black pepper

Preheat the oven to 375°F.

If the fennel pieces seem tough, blanch them first in boiling water; otherwise put them into a roasting pan, pour over the olive oil, and season. Roast until tender, about 30 minutes. It is good if they start to blacken on the edges.

Wash the anchovies to remove all the salt and carefully run your fingers along the back to separate the two fillets, then peel off the backbones. Rinse again, and dry on paper towels.

Arrange the bell peppers in a circle on a large, round dish, alternating two yellow and two red strips. Place the fennel in between, and the anchovies on top of the pepper strips. Sprinkle with garlic and parsley, and drizzle with olive oil. Arrange the eggs on top and serve with plenty of fresh bread.

Good additions to this Basque and Catalan salad are anchovy fillets and hard-boiled eggs. If possible, use small, thin-skinned, long bell peppers, called piments doux *or* piments du pays, *for this dish.*

Sautéed Green Bell Pepper and Tomato Salad
SALADE DE TOMATES AUX PIMENTS VERTS Ⓥ

Serves 4

4 green bell peppers

½ tsp. salt

½ cup olive oil

5 tomatoes, peeled and sliced

4–5 tbsp. olive oil, for serving

2 tbsp. white wine vinegar

**1 large clove garlic,
finely chopped**

¼ cup black olives

**sea salt and freshly ground
black pepper**

Cut the green bell peppers in half lengthwise, remove the seeds, cores, and any whitish parts with a small knife. Sprinkle the interiors with the salt and leave the peppers, cut-side up, for an hour or more. Rinse, drain, and cut or tear into wide strips.

Heat the olive oil in a skillet and cook the pepper strips on both sides until cooked through and beginning to brown. Remove, drain, and allow to cool slightly, then remove the skin from the strips.

Arrange the peppers and the sliced tomatoes in alternating lines on a large plate. Season with salt and pepper, drizzle with the olive oil and white wine vinegar, and sprinkle with the chopped garlic and black olives.

This is a great autumn and winter salad from the Toulouse area of Midi-Pyrénées, best made when the walnuts are fresh, creamy in texture, and have a sweet and slightly tannic flavor.

Walnut and Garlic Salad

AILLADE Ⓥ

Serves 4

1¼ cups shelled walnuts—they should be fresh and good quality

1–2 tbsp. cold water

¼ cup cloves garlic, peeled

½ cup olive oil

juice of half a lemon

inner leaves of 2 baby lettuce heads, washed

sea salt and freshly ground black pepper

Pound the walnuts in a mortar or blend in a food processor, together with the cold water. Pound or blend in the garlic, then gradually add the olive oil. Season with salt and pepper, and stir in the lemon juice.

Heap onto the inner leaves of the lettuce and serve with other starters, or with drinks. Eat with your fingers.

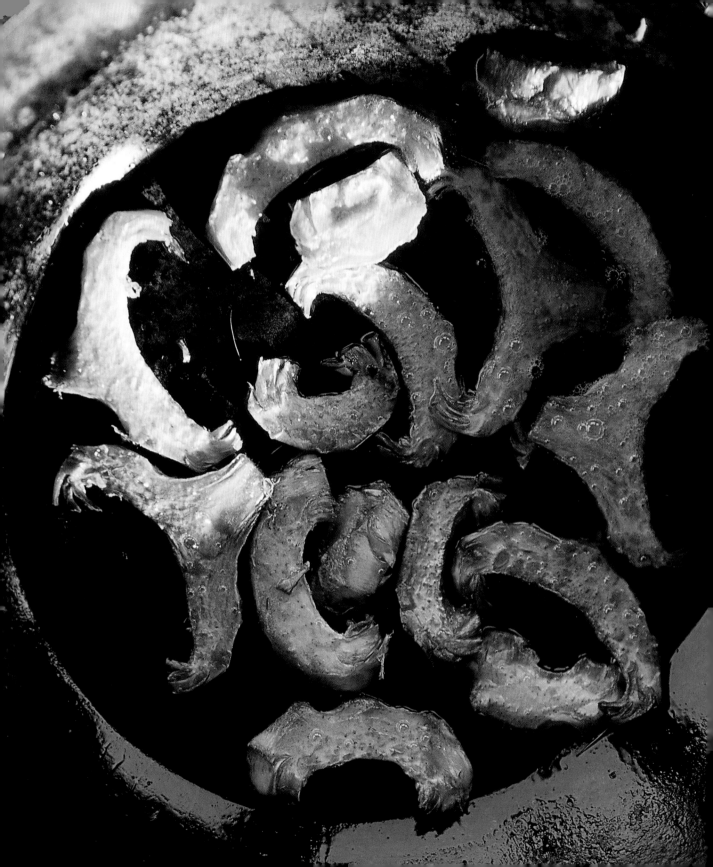

Small, violet artichokes, sold in bunches of four or five, are a specialty of the Languedoc-Roussillon, coming early in the spring. They can be used for this dish, or in the autumn you can use the large, green variety vert de laon, *which are less fiddly to prepare and more easily found.*

Salad of Artichokes Sautéed in Walnut Oil
SALADE D'ARTICHAUTS AUX NOIX ⓥ

Serves 6

For the salad:

12 fresh, wet walnuts or a handful of shelled walnut halves (about 2 oz.)

6 very fresh large globe artichokes, or 12 small violet globe artichokes

1 lemon, cut in half

¼ cup walnut oil (or more if needed)

4–6 cups mixed greens, use 2 types (oak leaf lettuce and curly endive would be a good combination, as would baby spinach and baby lettuce)

2 tbsp. Italian parsley, coarsely chopped

For the dressing:

2 tbsp. walnut oil

2 tbsp. olive oil

1–1½ tbsp. white wine vinegar

2 shallots, finely chopped

1 clove garlic, finely chopped

sea salt and freshly ground black pepper

Crack the walnuts and extract the kernels, pulling off some of the inner skin to expose the white nuts. The kernels can be left in halves or quartered. Remove the artichoke hearts using a sharp knife (see p. 216), and rub them with the cut lemon as you expose the pale inner heart.

Heat the walnut oil in a skillet and, while it is heating, slice the artichoke hearts and throw the slices straight into the pan. Do this a few at a time to avoid overcrowding. Cook until tender and golden on both sides, adding more oil if it is needed. Remove the artichokes, drain, and keep them warm.

Make a dressing with the walnut oil, olive oil, vinegar, shallots, and garlic. Season well.

Put the salad in a bowl, throw on the artichoke hearts, walnuts, and parsley, toss in the dressing, and serve as a first course or a classy salad.

A crucial part of Basque cooking, these are usually small red bell peppers (piquillos), broiled or roasted and skinned, and then torn or cut into pieces or strips, or stuffed. They are best freshly prepared, but in less impressive restaurants they often come out of cans; you can buy cans of whole pimentos for stuffing or, much cheaper but not as good, cans of ready-cut strips. It is certainly easy to make your own when there is time, and to keep the cans for when you need them unexpectedly. They are useful for oeufs sur le plat (see p. 70), pipérade (see p. 221), salads, omelettes, rice dishes, and so on. Once prepared, they can be kept in the refrigerator, covered with plastic wrap, for a week.

Red Bell Peppers
LES PIMENTS ROUGES Ⓥ

Serves 6

3 red bell peppers

3 yellow bell peppers

Preheat the oven to 375°F.

Place the bell peppers in an ovenproof dish and roast them for 25–30 minutes, turning them over once or twice, so that they blacken and blister evenly all over.

Transfer them to a plastic bag or a covered saucepan, or wrap them in a clean dish towel and leave to cool.

With a small knife, cut the peppers around the stalk end. Remove the cores, open the peppers out, scrape off any loose seeds, and remove the skin. Either pull apart into sections or trim and cut into strips. Keep in a covered container in the refrigerator, or in a jar of olive oil.

This omelette from Provence has an unusual and satisfying earthy taste. Make it in April, when dandelions (pissenlits) are young and tender. Choose young dandelions with long lush leaves—not the flat rosette type that grow in dry places or where grass is cut.

Bacon, Dandelion, and Sorrel Omelette
OMELETTE AUX LARDONS ET AUX PISSENLITS

Serves 2–4

9 oz. mixed curly endive, young dandelions, sorrel, and Italian parsley

2 tbsp. butter or goose fat

5½ oz. dry-cured bacon, or *lard maigre* or pancetta, coarsely chopped

1–2 large cloves garlic, finely chopped

3 free-range eggs

sea salt and freshly ground black pepper

Wash all the greens thoroughly and trim off the dandelion roots, but retain the small, tight buds. Spin all the greenery so that it is dry. Remove any coarse or wilted bits, then chop the rest fairly coarsely, using a large, heavy knife.

Heat half the butter or fat in a large skillet or sauté pan and put in the bacon. When it has started to give up its fat, but is not too brown, add the garlic, and then the greenery. Season with plenty of black pepper and let everything wilt down for 10 minutes, stirring. Remove from the heat and allow to cool. Break the eggs in a bowl and season with salt. Whisk lightly and stir in the bacon mixture.

Heat the remaining butter in a trustworthy skillet and, when it smokes, pour in the omelette mixture and let it frizzle. Shake the pan until you can see bubbles on the surface, then give it an abrupt shake to make sure that the omelette is loose and set enough to turn. Slide it onto a plate and turn it over onto a second plate—this is easier and lighter to do than attempting to turn the whole skillet. Slide the omelette back into the skillet, cooked side up, and cook for a minute or two longer until just set. Serve warm or cool.

In the Bouches-du-Rhône, there are strong Algerian and Moroccan influences, and Arles market now has many North African traders. There are spice stalls worthy of any souk, and herb stalls selling huge basins and buckets of mint, fresh cilantro, dill—and many other tender herbs. I use them to make herb salads to eat with wood-grilled lamb, poussins or partridge, or with lobster.

Fines Herbes and How to Make a Herb Salad
SALADES D'HERBES Ⓥ

Handfuls of fresh herbs, such as mint, chervil, Italian parsley, dill, chives, tarragon, and basil

Take a generous handful of as many fresh herbs as you can pick or buy. You can add lamb's lettuce, and a few sprigs of cilantro, although the flavor can be overpowering.

If necessary, increase the quantity with a few salad leaves, but only use the smallest, tenderest leaves you can find. Season with olive oil, lemon juice, salt, and pepper, and serve.

Pale and nacreous white asparagus, grown underground, is more subtle in flavor than the green and pleasant variety, picked when it has emerged above the ground, which is grown particularly in the Lauris, the Rhône valley where the Languedoc and Provence touch shoulders, and the plain of Beaucaire. The white variety, blanched and very thick, with luminous pink, violet, or creamy tips, has a slightly astringent, bitter, earthy taste reminiscent of blanched Belgian endive, although many French growers think that their less cosseted green is superior.

Asparagus Omelette
OMELETTE AUX ASPERGES Ⓥ

Serves 2–3

12 oz. green or white asparagus

4 tbsp. butter

1 tbsp. olive oil

6 free-range eggs, as fresh as possible

sea salt and freshly ground black pepper

Wash the asparagus several times. If it seems sandy, you can scrape the stems, removing the papery scales that lie flat against the stalk. Place a few stalks at a time on a chopping board and cut into thin little round slices, using only the parts that feel tender, and discarding the tough bits.

Melt the butter with the oil in a heavy-bottomed skillet and throw in the asparagus. Let it cook gently until it is tender and lightly browned; this takes a surprisingly long time.

Break the eggs into a bowl, whisk lightly with a fork, season, then pour into the asparagus pan and make one large omelette. Alternatively, allow the asparagus to cool a little, then stir it into the eggs and make two or three smaller omelettes. Serve hot or warm, and make sure the omelette is still soft in the middle; if sloppy and running with juice, just serve with lots of bread to mop up with.

Sometimes it is easy to forget the pleasure of using hands in cooking. A friend who had taken a winter job picking olives in the Languedoc told me that he learned this recipe from watching his companion making an onion omelette for his lunch every day in the olive groves. For this method, I describe his technique.

Olive Picker's Omelette
OMELETTE D'OLIVEUR Ⓥ

Serves 1

1–2 tbsp. olive oil

1 small-to-medium onion

2–3 eggs

salt and pepper

First the picker heated some olive oil in a small black pan over a fire. Holding a peeled onion in his hand, he shredded it into the pan with his pocket knife. Hands and knife were then wiped on an outsized handkerchief. The shredded onion quickly browned, then two or three eggs were broken in and stirred around. A little salt and pepper was added and he had the most appetizing lunch.

This is a minimalist, everyday dish from the Landes and the Pays Basque. It is simple and spiced, and quick to make. The trick is to have the strips of grilled or sautéed red and yellow bell peppers ready in the refrigerator (see p. 64), or you can use canned peppers.

Eggs "On a Dish"
OEUFS SUR LE PLAT

Serves 1

1–2 tbsp. olive oil

$1/3$ cup lardons
(either buy them ready-cut or cut some dry-cured bacon, *lard maigre*, or pancetta into batons)

2 oz. red and yellow bell peppers, broiled or sautéed and cut in strips (see p. 64)

$1/4$–$1/2$ tsp. hot or sweet paprika

2 free-range eggs

1 small clove garlic, finely chopped

1 tbsp. fresh cilantro or parsley, coarsely chopped

Heat most of the oil in a small, heavy, nonstick pan or, better still, a small dish with handles on each side that you can bring to the table. Fry the lardons and bell peppers with a pinch of the paprika, until they start to sizzle and brown.

Break the eggs on top, cover the pan, and continue to cook over low heat until the eggs are just set. Transfer to a plate.

In the remaining oil, cook the garlic, cilantro or parsley, and the rest of the paprika for a moment. Pour this over the eggs and serve. If you are serving the eggs in the cooking dish, either make the spiced oil in another pan, or leave it out.

In the Pays Basque this dish is more or less the equivalent of eggs and bacon. It is made in little flameproof, earthenware dishes, which can be heated on an open fire or a gas flame; unfortunately they do not work on the top of an electric or solid-fuel stove. However, I have discovered that if you cook the dish in a reliable nonstick pan with a metal handle, it can be transferred whole, first to the oven, and then to a hot plate, like a flat omelette. Otherwise, use small, flameproof gratin dishes.

Fried Eggs with Black Pudding
OEUFS AU PLAT AU BOUDIN NOIR

Serves 1 (repeat the process for each person)

1 tbsp. olive oil

2 medium-size tomatoes, thickly sliced

1 clove garlic, roughly chopped

1 tbsp. Italian parsley, coarsely chopped

3 oz. black pudding, thinly sliced

2 free-range eggs

1 tbsp. sheep's milk or other hard cheese, finely grated

sea salt and freshly ground black pepper or cayenne pepper

Preheat the oven to 475°F.

Heat the oil in a flameproof, earthenware dish or an 8½-inch nonstick skillet. Put in the sliced tomatoes, season them with salt and black pepper (or cayenne pepper), then sprinkle with the garlic and parsley. Let the tomatoes cook for a few minutes, then turn them over, season again, and let them cook until they start to disintegrate.

Add the slices of black pudding and cook until the pudding looks crumbly, then remove from the heat. Break the eggs on top, add the cheese, and cook in the oven for 3–4 minutes or until the egg whites are just set.

Alternative

Another way of cooking this dish, without cheese this time, is to cook the tomatoes and black pudding on their own, without the garlic and parsley, then break in the eggs and cover with a lid. Continue to cook on top of the stove until the tops of the eggs are white and opaque. Meanwhile, fry the garlic, parsley, and ¼ teaspoon of cayenne pepper in a tablespoon or two of olive oil and pour it sizzling over the eggs just before serving. If you like, you can replace the cayenne with ¼ teaspoon of hot paprika, and the parsley with chopped cilantro.

Trouchia, similar to a tortilla, was once sold in Nice, in all grocers' shops and traiteurs, and you may still be lucky enough to find it. Originally made with chard, it could contain wild herbs, which, I suppose, must have been such things as dandelion and orache (wild spinach), as well as parsley, chervil, or mint. I use arugula and parsley. Long-cooked, trouchia tastes quite different to a normal omelette and is perfect for a simple lunch, and for picnics.

Open Spinach Omelette
TROUCHIA ⓥ

Serves 2–4

4 free-range eggs

a pinch of freshly ground nutmeg

¾ cup Parmesan cheese, finely grated

8 oz. spinach, stalks removed and leaves coarsely chopped, or 8 oz. chard leaves, coarsely chopped

1 bunch arugula, weighing approximately 1 oz., coarsely chopped

1 bunch Italian parsley, weighing approximately 1 oz., coarsely chopped

3 tbsp. olive oil

sea salt and coarsely ground black pepper

1 lemon, quartered, to serve

Preheat the oven to 350°F.

Break the eggs into a large bowl and season lightly with nutmeg, salt, and black pepper. Whisk in the Parmesan, spinach, arugula, and parsley, and mix thoroughly.

Heat 2 tablespoons of olive oil in a 10-inch pan that has a lid and can go into the oven. Spoon in the spinach mixture and cook gently until you see the egg beginning to come up from underneath, approximately 4–5 minutes.

Cover the pan, transfer it to the preheated oven, and cook for 15 minutes. Remove from the oven, bang the pan down, and then shake it to loosen the trouchia. Slip it out onto a plate, put another plate on top, and reverse it quickly.

Heat the remaining oil in the same pan, remembering that it is already hot. Slide the trouchia back into the pan, cooked-side up. Cover the pan again and return it to the oven for 10–15 minutes.

Transfer the trouchia to a plate and serve hot or cold with quarters of lemon. Originally, this would have been eaten, sliced like a cake, sprinkled with a good dash of wine vinegar.

L'araignée de mer, spider crab, is a beautiful creature with succulent meat that is particularly liked in the Basque country, where it is eaten stuffed with tomatoes, bread crumbs, and hot paprika, or dressed with mayonnaise and mint, which makes it particularly refreshing. Ordinary crab is also excellent prepared this way.

Spider Crab Dressed with Mint and Lemon
ARAIGNÉE DE MER À LA MENTHE

Serves 4

1 free-range egg

5 oz. brown crabmeat

½–1 tsp. Dijon mustard

⅓ cup olive oil

¼ cup fresh mint or wild mint, finely chopped

juice of 1 lemon

5 oz. white crab meat

inner leaves of a romaine lettuce, or 2 baby lettuces, washed

sea salt and coarsely ground black pepper or cayenne pepper

Boil the egg for 6 minutes if very fresh, otherwise 5 minutes. Cool quickly under running water and remove the top as if you were eating a soft-boiled egg. Spoon out some of the white, and then transfer the yolk to a bowl.

Mix the coral, the brownish, creamy parts of the crab, with the mustard and the egg yolk, and whisk in the olive oil, drop by drop at first as if you were making mayonnaise. Stir in the salt and pepper, finely chopped mint, and the lemon juice. Add the white crabmeat and place on the crisp lettuce leaves.

This luscious, open-faced Provençal omelette, based on the Trouchia recipe on p. 72, is cooked flat, like a tortilla, but instead of being turned is glazed to a beautiful buttercup-yellow under the broiler, or baked in the oven.

Open Yellow Courgette (Golden Zucchini) Omelette
TROUCHIA AUX COURGETTES JAUNES Ⓥ

Serves 4

3–4 golden zucchini, coarsely grated

1 tsp. salt

¼ cup olive oil

1–2 cloves garlic, thinly sliced

5 fresh farm eggs

1½ cups Raclette, Gruyère, or other good melting cheese, finely grated

sea salt and freshly ground black pepper

Put the zucchini shreds into a bowl and sprinkle them with the teaspoon of salt, mixing it in with your hands to make sure it is evenly distributed. Tip the zucchini into a colander and leave to drain for about an hour. Squeeze them for a minute with both hands to release as much liquid as possible. Preheat the broiler to its highest setting, or the oven to 400°F.

Heat half the oil in a large, heavy-bottomed skillet, cook the garlic to a pale toast color, add the zucchini, and cook gently, stirring, for 10 minutes. Drain them of most of their oil and let them cool.

Break the eggs into a bowl and whisk lightly with a fork, season with black pepper and a little salt, and stir in the zucchini.

Clean out the skillet and reheat it with the remaining olive oil. When it starts to smoke, pour in the egg and zucchini mixture and let it cook until the omelette starts to set, drawing in the sides gently with a spatula, to keep them thick and chunky, so that they do not burn.

Sprinkle the top thickly with grated cheese and broil or place in the hot oven until the cheese melts and perhaps starts to brown. Don't overcook or the omelette will become tough.

Serve hot, with the melted cheese still runny, cutting the omelette into quarters.

The glory of Nîmes—creamy pureed brandade—is a lunchtime dish, according to Austin de Croze, author of Les Plats Regionaux de France *(it is too rich and heavy for the evening, he suggests). True, it is saturated in olive oil, and also true, it is easy to go on eating more and more. This version is less rich, as it contains potatoes. In Marseille, grated truffles are sometimes added to the brandade.*

Puree of Salt Cod
BRANDADE DE MORUE

Serves 4–6

1 lb. 2 oz. salt cod, cut from the thick part, soaked in cold water for 24–36 hours, water changed occasionally (see p. 32)

6 oz. baking potatoes, peeled and cut into small chunks

$^2/_3$ cup olive oil

$^1/_2$ cup milk

3 large cloves garlic, or more to taste, peeled and minced

squeeze of lemon juice

a pinch of freshly grated nutmeg

white pepper

12 croutons of fried bread or toast, to serve

Put the salt cod in a large pan and cover with cold, fresh water. Bring to simmering point, then turn down the heat so that the water just moves; a very slow simmer is required. Simmer for 5 minutes, then remove the salt cod and let it drain.

Place the potatoes in a pan of cold water, cover with a lid, and bring to a boil. Simmer until tender, then drain thoroughly and force through a ricer or sieve (there should be no lumps).

Skin the salt cod and flake the flesh, removing any bones as you do so. Heat 2 tablespoons of the olive oil in a saucepan, and gently reheat the fish. Keep it warm.

Warm the milk and mix it with the remainder of the olive oil. Warm a large bowl.

To make the brandade in a food processor, put the salt cod in the bowl of the processor and process it for approximately 10 seconds. Then, with the motor running, gradually pour in the warm milk and olive oil. Transfer to the warmed bowl and stir in the sieved potatoes and the garlic; you should have a beautiful, white, creamy puree.

If you are using a mortar and pestle, crush the garlic to a paste, add the flaked fish, and pound it well until it has turned into a creamy mass. Mix in the sieved potatoes, then gradually add the warm milk and olive oil, a tablespoon at a time, working them into the succulent mixture.

Check the taste, adding lemon juice, nutmeg, white pepper, or more garlic to taste. Serve with croutons of fried bread or toast.

It seems that everyone prefers red, yellow, orange, or even black bell peppers to the green ones, which are really just unripe, without the sweetness of ripe capsicums. However, in the Basque country, where the pepper is the favorite vegetable, green ones are considered good eating. But they must be cooked; raw, they are indigestible and taste dull. The Basques often use the green piments du pays, described on p. 49. If you are cooking with ordinary bell peppers, it is better, but not essential, to skin them before eating (see p. 64). Cook them in this way, and serve hot with chorizo, or serve cool with anchovies and olive oil.

Green Bell Peppers with Chorizo
CHORIZO AUX PIMENTS VERTS

Serves 4

4 green bell peppers

¹/₂ tsp. sea salt

¹/₂ cup olive oil, plus extra for serving

8 oz. chorizo, thinly sliced

Cut the green bell peppers in half lengthwise, remove the seeds, cores, and any whitish parts with a small knife. Sprinkle the interiors with the salt and leave the peppers, cut-side up, for an hour or more. Rinse, drain, and cut into fairly wide strips.

Heat the olive oil in a skillet and cook the strips on both sides until cooked through and beginning to brown. Remove, drain, and allow to cool slightly, then remove the skin from the strips.

Eat them sprinkled with olive oil, together with the chorizo and olive bread.

In several French pasta recipes, the dish is an excuse to eat a huge amount of cheese—often equal quantities of pasta and cheese—and the result is a lesson in the excellence of simple food. While macaroni is traditionally the main pasta in the Languedoc, tagliatelle, ravioli, and gnocchi are common in Provence.

Tagliatelle with Sheep's Milk Cheese
NOUILLES AU FROMAGE DE BREBIS ⓥ

Serves 4

12 oz. tagliatelle

¹/₂ cup (1 stick) butter, cut into small pieces

2¹/₂ cups hard sheep's milk cheese or Pecorino (Romano), finely grated

sea salt and freshly ground black pepper

Cook the pasta in a generous amount of boiling, salted water until it is tender, approximately 6–7 minutes. Drain and return to the hot pan, together with 1–2 tablespoons of the cooking liquid.

Add the pieces of butter and mix them in by gently lifting the pasta with a large wooden fork. Once the butter has melted and the pasta is well coated, add the grated cheese and continue to lift the pasta with the fork until the cheese is dispersed evenly.

Season with freshly ground black pepper and serve with a good salad.

French ravioli is often poached in stock and served with a little butter and grated cheese. Originally stuffed with a mixture of cow's and goat's cheese, this recipe from Maussane les Alpilles in Provence uses a green olive stuffing. For a very extravagant version, replace the green olive filling below with slices of foie gras, drain thoroughly, and serve sprinkled with black truffle oil and salt crystals.

Green Olive Ravioli
RAVIOLES D'OLIVES VERTS Ⓥ

Serves 4

For the pasta:

1³/₄ cups all-purpose flour

3 medium free-range eggs, lightly beaten

1 tbsp. olive oil

For the green olive filling:

1¹/₄ cups pitted green olives, drained

¹/₂ cup Ricotta or soft fresh goat's cheese, mashed with a fork and drained in a sieve if at all wet

1¹/₂ cups Parmesan cheese, finely grated

2 free-range eggs

a little finely grated lemon zest (optional)

freshly ground black pepper

¹/₂ cup (1 stick) butter, cut into small pieces, and Parmesan cheese, finely grated, to serve

To make the pasta by hand, sift the flour onto a clean work surface and make a large well in the center. Pour the eggs and the olive oil into the well and, using your fingers, mix them together, gradually incorporating the flour until you have a firm dough. Knead for 10–15 minutes until smooth and silky, then cover with plastic wrap and allow to rest in a cool place for one hour.

If you would rather use a food processor to make the pasta, sift the flour into the bowl of the processor and add one egg and the olive oil. Process for about 5 seconds to incorporate the egg and the oil, then, with the motor running, add the remaining egg and process until the mixture begins to come together. Gather up the dough with your hands and knead as above.

Prepare the filling. Dry the drained olives on a piece of paper towel, chop them finely, and place in a bowl. Add the Ricotta, Parmesan, eggs, and lemon zest (if you want a sharper taste). Season with black pepper and mix thoroughly.

Divide the pasta dough into four pieces. Working on a well-floured surface, take one piece of dough (keeping the others under a damp cloth) and roll it out into four thin strips measuring approximately 27¹/₂ x 4³/₄ inches. (You can, if you prefer, use a pasta machine, following the manufacturer's instructions.)

At one end of the strip, place two rounded teaspoons of the green olive filling in one heap, leaving a ³/₄-inch margin all around. Repeat this twice more so that you have three heaps of filling, leaving a 1¹/₂-inch gap between each lot. Next, lightly brush the pasta around the filling with water, then carefully fold the other half of the pasta strip on top, thus covering the filling (try to remove any air pockets as you do so). Press all around the filling to seal, then cut out three square parcels, measuring approximately 4 x 4 inches. Repeat with the remaining pieces of dough, so that you have twelve large ravioli in total. Leave to dry on a tray for 30 minutes to one hour, turning the ravioli over halfway through.

When you are ready to cook the ravioli, bring a large pan of salted water to a boil. Add the ravioli and simmer for 6–7 minutes. Drain and return to the hot pan, together with 1 tablespoon of the cooking liquid. Add the pieces of butter, allow them to melt, shaking the pan gently to distribute the butter and emulsify it, then sprinkle in plenty of finely grated Parmesan cheese.

This wobbly and almost fluffy polenta, crisp outside and succulent inside, was made, above all, when country households killed their pig in winter, and was a staple food in Gascony. In the twelfth century, when it was made with millet, it was offered to pilgrims on their way to St.-Jacques-de-Compostelle; they liked it because it was satisfying, and it could be kept for days. From the sixteenth century, a new import from South America, corn, became the staple ingredient. The ground corn was cooked, like polenta, into a thick gruel and then spread out on a plate and allowed to cool. It was then cut up and could be cooked crisp and golden on the outside and served covered with tomato sauce, or layered with grated cheese and cooked in a gratin dish. Some people dipped the pieces of millas in beaten egg before frying. One of the favorite ways of cooking millas was to make it with the water in which blood puddings from the pig were boiled. Now it is frequently made with milk and eaten as a dessert, often with eggs, sugar, and perhaps some almond or orange and lemon flavoring. Or it is cooked quite plainly, sautéed and eaten sprinkled with superfine sugar and fig jam, or quince jelly. I like the savory version best; it has a splendid texture and flavor.

Millas

MILLAS DES LANDES ⓥ

Serves 4

$^2/_3$ **cup cornstarch**

3 tbsp. duck fat or butter

$^2/_3$ **cup instant polenta (cornmeal)**

1 tsp. olive oil, plus extra for oiling the dish

1 tsp. sea salt

Lightly brush a rectangular dish (10 x 8 inches) with olive oil.

Mix the cornstarch to a smooth, creamy consistency with $^1/_3$ cup of water.

Bring 4$^1/_4$ cups of water to a boil in a reliable pan, together with 1 tablespoon of the butter or duck fat, and the salt.

Slowly pour the polenta into the boiling water in a steady stream, whisking all the time with a balloon whisk. Next, pour in the cornstarch mixture, still whisking continuously. Swap your balloon whisk for a wooden spoon and stir the millas for 5 minutes over medium heat. It should bubble slowly with big, bursting blops; wear an apron. Check the seasoning, adding more salt if necessary, then pour the mixture into the greased dish, spread it out evenly, and drizzle a teaspoon of olive oil over the top, distributing it quickly with the palm of your hand. Allow to cool.

Cut the solid, slightly jellified millas into pieces about 3$^1/_2$ x 1$^1/_4$ inches.

Heat the remaining butter or duck fat in a large skillet and cook the pieces, in batches, to a light golden color on both sides. This takes some time, about 10 minutes on each side. Drain for a moment on paper towels and serve with tomato sauce (see p. 278) and cheese, or eat with a rich poultry stew such as Alicot (see p. 165) or Guinea Fowl with Ceps (see p. 163).

Soups

There may no longer be the obligatory pale orange soup with pasta in it at the start of every restaurant meal in the South, but soup is still a major part of home cooking. Provence would not be Provence without *soupe au pistou* and bouillabaisse, while the great signature soups of the Southwest are the Gascon *garbures*, substantial and rich with cabbage, meat, and beans, and a variety of onion and garlic soups.

One of the blessings given by the Côte d'Azur, the Golfe du Lion, and the Golfe de Gascogne is the vast repertoire of fish soups. On the market fish-stalls, the crates of blue, yellow, red, and brown barred, banded, striped, speckled, stippled, and spotted rock fish are labeled *soupe de poisson*, *soupe de chaluts*, or even just *soupe* when they are small, and *bouillabaisse* when they are larger fish. The smaller ones are sieved after cooking to remove the bones and spines, but usually left ungutted; when large, they are served whole or in chunks, sometimes in their broth, sometimes separately. The rich smell that rises from the pot, the warm colors of saffron, the pungent aïoli, and the ritual of serving the soup, all make bouillabaisse a special dish.

Vegetable soup, although a more everyday affair, has equal importance. In the Lot, when the farmer's wife calls across the meadow "Have you made your soup?" it is like saying good morning, but she also means it as a phrase of approval if you have, and disapproval if not, since soup is lunch, and a household without soup at lunchtime would be considered wanting.

In fact, making vegetable soup, which lies at the heart of family cooking, is simple and a good way of using up all the vegetables in the garden; in the Médoc, a vegetable soup is *la soupe du jardin*, in Provence, *soupe à la paysanne*.

This big, southern potage from the Pays Basque completely transforms the notion of brown soup; it is brown with black flecks and has a deep, earthy flavor that comes from combining dried fava beans and olives. To make it even more rustic, add dried thyme.

Olive Soup from St.-Jean-de-Luz
POTAGE LUZIENNE Ⓥ

Serves 6

1 cup dried fava beans, soaked for 2 hours until tender

6 oz. potatoes, peeled and diced

4½ oz. leeks, cleaned and sliced thinly

1 cup pitted black olives

2 shallots, finely chopped

2 cloves garlic, finely chopped

sea salt and freshly ground black pepper

6 slices of *pain de campagne* (country bread), cut in half and toasted and 1 quantity of aïoli (see p. 279), to serve

Put the beans, potatoes, leeks, olives, shallots, and garlic into a large pan with 4¼ cups water. Bring to a boil, cover, and simmer for 1½ hours, adding more water if necessary.

Taste for seasoning and blend briefly with a handheld mixer.

When you have made the soup, reheat it and serve it in one of two ways: either float the toast on each soup bowl with spoonfuls of aïoli on top of each piece, or stir the aïoli into the soup and serve the toast separately. Either way, it adds the essential bite to a very simple country soup.

Alternative
Another traditional local specialty, *Purée de Ciboure*, is the same soup, pureed. Remove the skins from the fava beans before making the puree, or sieve before serving.

*Staying in a friend's French retreat, I watched him making this soup for lunch.
Early in the morning he got up and turned on the oven full blast. He put the
tomatoes into a roasting pan and sloshed on some olive oil and a bit of salt. He
put them in the oven and went away to do other things. Later he got them out,
pulled off the blackened and burning skins, put the burst tomatoes and their
juices into the food processor and whizzed them with some crème fraîche until he
had a thickish soup. Then he let it cool. It was delicious, but of course there was
no recipe. I have tried to reproduce it here.*

Provençal Tomato Soup
SOUPE PROVENÇALE AUX POMMES D'AMOUR Ⓥ

Serves 4

3 lb. 5 oz. large, ripe tomatoes

¼ cup olive oil

pinch of sugar

¾ cup crème fraîche

**sea salt and freshly ground
black pepper**

Preheat the oven to 375°F. Put the tomatoes into a roasting pan and sprinkle
them with the olive oil. Season with salt, black pepper, and a pinch of sugar,
then roast for an hour. When you come back, the tomatoes should have burst and
have black tops. Take them out of the oven and leave them to cool. Pick off all the
skins and put the tomatoes and all their juices into a food processor. Puree until
you have a thickish soup, add the crème fraîche, check seasoning, and continue
to puree until smooth. Eat lukewarm, or iced with ice cubes.

Alternative
You could add fresh basil or chopped scallions and coarsely chopped Italian parsley.

Eggplants are often pureed, but it is rare to find them in soup. I like the rustic nature of this summer mixture from Provence, and the warm color of eggplants, tomatoes, and olive oil with green basil leaves.

Eggplant Soup with Basil
PURÉE D'AUBERGINES AU BASILIC

Serves 6

1 lb. 8 oz. eggplants, peeled and sliced

1 tbsp. salt

¼ cup olive oil

1 lb. tomatoes, skinned and coarsely chopped

4 cloves garlic, finely chopped

½ tsp. dried thyme (if using fresh thyme, remove stalks)

2 bay leaves

⅔ cup long-grain rice

6¼ cups good chicken stock or consommé

sea salt and freshly ground black pepper

few sprigs basil, shredded, and olive oil, to serve

Sprinkle the eggplant with the tablespoon of salt. Leave to drain in a colander for about 30 minutes, then rinse and pat dry.

Heat the olive oil in a saucepan and soften the eggplant until it looks translucent and is tender all the way through, then add the tomatoes, garlic, thyme, and bay leaves. Cook until the tomatoes have given up their liquid and are reduced to a puree.

Add the rice, stir it around, and then add the stock or consommé. Season lightly and bring to a boil. Cover and simmer for 35 minutes.

Remove the bay leaves, then stir briefly; the soup should not be too fine a consistency. Taste for seasoning and serve with the shredded basil and a trickle of olive oil in each soup bowl.

If you are successful in your cep hunting, or if you see them at a reasonable price in the market, you can freeze them, either as they are, or preserved in melted butter. It is best not to keep them for too long. Use older, larger specimens for making this Bordelaise soup. They give it a velvety smooth quality.

Cep and Potato Soup
SOUPE AUX CÈPES

Serves 4

12 oz. large ceps (frozen are perfect for this), or 2 cups dried ceps

¼ cup butter or goose fat

2 tbsp. butter or goose fat

1 onion, finely chopped

1 large shallot, finely chopped

3–4 cloves garlic, finely chopped

9 oz. potatoes, peeled and cut into small cubes

3 cups good chicken stock

3 tbsp. parsley, finely chopped

sea salt and freshly ground black pepper

Wipe the fresh ceps with a damp dish towel (avoid washing them if possible) and carefully pare the lower ends of the stalks, to remove gritty parts. Cut them into chunks. If using dried ceps, soak them in a bowl of lukewarm water for 20 minutes. Drain and rinse thoroughly to remove any grit.

Heat ¼ cup butter (or goose fat if you are using it) in a large saucepan and throw in the onion and shallot. Let them soften over a low heat for about 10 minutes. Add two-thirds of the ceps, 2 cloves of garlic, and all the potatoes, and let them sweat for a further 10 minutes, stirring from time to time. Add the stock, season, and simmer over a low heat until the potatoes are tender.

Test the potatoes, and when they are done, prepare the following *persillade* or *fricassée*: heat the rest of the butter or goose fat in a small skillet and add the remaining ceps and garlic, together with the parsley. When the ceps are a beautiful golden color, ladle the soup into hot bowls and put a spoonful or two of the fricassée into each bowl.

This is real rustic Gascon food, perfect in the winter if you are planning a serious walk, either before or after lunch. Garbure is always a thick soup; in the eighteenth century it would have been served in a tureen lined with several layers of bread. It is commonly made with salt pork, or a piece of pork confit, but is particularly good made in the Landaise way with confit de canard; thigh or wings of duck. It is said that in the eighteenth century, Marie Antoinette inhaled the scent of this soup as the performer Montaniser, from Bayonne (who arranged entertainments at Versailles), secretly cooked her garbure behind the closed doors of her quarters. As the appetizing steam percolated through the gratings and corridors of the palace, Marie Antoinette, who was never served anything so common, was heard to sigh enviously: "Ah, que ça sent bon!" This version is from the Landes. Make sure the soup cooks for 1 1/2 hours altogether.

Cabbage Soup
LA GARBURE LANDAISE

Serves 6–8

1 1/3 cups dried *rose coco* or cranberry beans, soaked overnight and drained

1 leg or 2 wings of duck confit (see p. 168)

10 oz. potatoes, peeled and cut into small pieces

1 bunch herbs containing parsley, thyme, and a bay leaf

1/2–1 tsp. pimenton or hot red pepper flakes

1 tbsp. duck or pork fat (see p. 283)

1 onion, coarsely chopped

2 leeks, thinly sliced

6 oz. turnip, peeled and cut into small chunks

7 oz. squash, peeled and cut into small chunks

6 Savoy cabbage leaves, cut into thin strips

salt and freshly ground black pepper

slices of pain de campagne (country bread) and 1 cup Cantal or Gruyère cheese, grated, to serve

Put the beans in a large pan of fresh, cold water. Bring to a boil, simmer for 5 minutes, then drain (discarding the cooking water). Add fresh water to the pan, bring to a boil again, and simmer the beans for 45 minutes. Drain the beans, discarding the cooking water once more.

Put the confit, potatoes, drained beans, and herbs in a large casserole and add 6 1/4 cups of water. Bring to a simmer, skim the surface, then add the pimenton or red pepper flakes. Simmer gently for 30 minutes.

Meanwhile, heat the fat and soften the onion, leeks, turnip, and squash until the onion is tender and just turning golden. Add them to the soup and cook for another 30 minutes.

Remove the confit, cut it into pieces, and discard the bones. Continue simmering the soup for 20 minutes more, then add the strips of cabbage and the pieces of confit, and cook for 5–10 minutes more.

While the soup is still simmering, preheat the broiler to its highest setting. Lightly toast the slices of pain de campagne (country bread), sprinkle them with the grated cheese, and broil until the cheese has just melted.

Check the soup for seasoning, remove the herbs, and serve with the toasted bread topped with cheese.

In nature, watercress is a seasonal vegetable; it starts to grow in March and soon small streams and rivers are full of it. In the northern part of Quercy, the Lot, whose valleys and rivers are fed by clear underground streams, I sometimes found farmers gathering wild watercress for this soup and the result is a most bewitching dark green. When making the soup, I use as much of the wild watercress as possible while it is tender. If left uncut, it is soon covered in small, white flowers, and becomes both hot and bitter.

Madame Tresse's Watercress Soup
POTAGE AU CRESSON ET À LA CRÈME Ⓥ

Serves 4–6

3 medium potatoes, peeled and cut in half

1 lb. watercress

2 tbsp. butter

3 tbsp. crème fraîche

sea salt and freshly ground black pepper

garlic croutons, to serve

Boil the potatoes in salted water until they are tender, then add the watercress and cook, uncovered, until soft.

Pour off some of the cooking liquid if there is too much, but reserve it. Puree the soup, add the butter and crème fraîche, and season with salt and black pepper. If necessary, add more of the cooking liquid to get the texture you like.

Serve with garlic croutons (small slices of toasted baguette rubbed with raw cloves of garlic).

Double Watercress Soup
CRESSONIÈRE

Serves 6

1 bunch scallions, coarsely chopped

¼ cup butter

3 medium potatoes, peeled and cut in chunks

6¼ cups duck or chicken stock

1 lb. watercress, washed and coarsely chopped

2 tbsp. all-purpose flour

sea salt and freshly ground black pepper

heavy cream (optional), to serve

In a large pan, soften the scallions in half the butter, without letting them brown. Add the potatoes and the stock and cook, uncovered, until the potatoes are done. Add the watercress and cook until soft.

Melt the remaining butter in a separate pan, stir in the flour, and cook for 1 minute. Gradually add two or three ladlefuls of the liquid from the soup, stirring to make a velvety sauce.

Puree the rest of the soup, and stir this pureed soup into the sauce. Heat, add more stock if the soup is too thick, season, and serve with or without cream.

Pain rassis—stale bread—was, until recently (when bread cooked by modern methods became too soft when steeped in a liquid), used in soups throughout the South, either baked in the oven in the soup, or crammed into the soup tureen with the soup poured over the top and then served, thick, melting, and homely, at the table. It tasted good, it was filling, and bread was never wasted. Sometimes it was layered with cheese, sometimes not. This recipe gives each person a slice of toasted bread and an egg, which mellows the strong, salty flavors of onion, ham, and cheese. It is ideal for lunch on a cold day and it is easy to make, using everyday ingredients—except that the ham should preferably be jambon cru and the cheese, traditionally a Pyrenean mountain cheese, should be made from ewe's milk.

Catalan Onion Soup with Ham, Eggs, and Cheese
SOUPE À L'OIGNON À LA CATALANE

Serves 4

¼ cup olive oil

2 medium sweet onions, finely sliced

1½ cups lardons (dry-cured bacon cut into small batons), blanched and drained

4¼ cups good chicken stock

8 sprigs fresh thyme

8 sprigs fresh rosemary

4 slices of day-old *bâtard*, *Parisien*, or pain de campagne (country bread)

4 fresh eggs

4 slices Bayonne ham or other *jambon cru*

4 oz. Ossau Irraty or a similar sheep's milk cheese suitable for melting, cut into 4 slices

sea salt and freshly ground black pepper

Preheat the oven to 400°F.

Heat the olive oil and soften the onions and lardons gently, until the onions are translucent and beginning to color, approximately 20–25 minutes.

Add the stock, thyme, and rosemary, bring to a boil and simmer for 10 minutes. Remove the sprigs of thyme and rosemary, taste for seasoning, and keep at simmering point.

Meanwhile, toast the bread in the oven until pale golden, about 10–12 minutes. In the same oven, heat up four ovenproof, earthenware soup bowls or one large ovenproof dish.

Place a piece of toasted bread in each of the soup bowls, then carefully break an egg on top of each slice of bread. Cover with a slice of Bayonne ham (use the ham to hold the egg in place) and top with a slice of cheese. Ladle the hot soup into each bowl and place in the oven for 10 minutes, until the egg has set and the cheese has melted. Serve straight from the oven.

In autumn, the leaves of the pumpkins die down and you can see the huge orange globes decorating the fields and potagers (kitchen gardens), and piled up in the markets of the Gers, where they are sold, as they are throughout the Southwest, by the kilo, in huge slices. If you can find haricots grains (fresh white beans), they are perfect for this dish.

Pumpkin, Leek, and White Bean Soup
POTAGE À LA CITROUILLE AUX HARICOTS BLANCS

Serves 6

1¼ cups large fresh white beans (*haricots grains*), or dried navy or cannelini beans, soaked overnight

2 onions, finely chopped

2–3 sprigs fresh thyme

1 bay leaf

1 tbsp. butter or goose fat

1 lb. pumpkin, peeled and cut into 1-in. pieces

4¼ cups good goose, duck, or chicken stock

1 leek, finely sliced

sea salt and freshly ground black pepper

6 slices of bread, toasted, and 1 cup Cantal or Gruyère cheese, grated, to serve

Drain the soaked beans, put them in a large pan of fresh water, and bring to a boil. Simmer for 5 minutes, then drain and throw away the cooking water. Return the beans to the pan with fresh water, 1 chopped onion, the thyme, and the bay leaf. Cook until tender, approximately 1½ hours, drain, and reserve the cooking liquid. Discard the thyme and bay leaf.

Soften the remaining chopped onion in the butter or goose fat for 10 minutes in a large pan. Add half of the pumpkin pieces and cook them for 3–4 minutes, stirring once or twice. Add the stock, remaining pumpkin pieces, cooked beans, and enough of the bean cooking liquid to make soup for six people (about 2½ cups should be enough). Season well and cook, covered, for 40 minutes.

Remove the lid, add the leek, and cook, uncovered, for 30 minutes. Stir vigorously—this will thicken the soup. Serve with toast and grated Cantal or Gruyère cheese.

Alternatives
Use chickpeas (garbanzo beans) for a darker, "meatier" soup. Butternut squash also works well in place of pumpkin.

Eating soupe au pistou, *with its stinging slap of raw garlic and basil, is one of the rites of passage when you sit down to your first meal of the summer season in the Var. This springtime version from Hyères is made with Gorgonzola.*

Pumpkin, Bean, and Fava Bean Soup with Pistou
SOUPE AU PISTOU DE GORGONZOLA Ⓥ

Serves 6

For the soup:

1 cup dried *coco de Prague* (cranberry beans) or navy beans, soaked overnight

8⅓ cups water or chicken stock

1 large onion, finely chopped

1 tbsp. olive oil

9 oz. pumpkin, peeled

7 oz. potatoes, peeled

7 oz. golden zucchini, diced

2 carrots, peeled and diced

9 oz. tomatoes, skinned

7 oz. spinach, coarse stalks removed and leaves chopped

1½ cups shelled fava beans, blanched

sea salt and freshly ground black pepper

For the pistou:

6–8 cloves garlic

3 heaping tbsp. chopped basil

1 small tomato, skinned, deseeded, and chopped (optional)

2 oz. Gorgonzola, crumbled, and/or ⅓ cup Parmesan, finely grated

2–3 tbsp. olive oil

olive oil and grated Parmesan or Gruyère cheese, to serve

a pinch of sea salt

Put the soaked beans in a large pan of fresh water and bring to a boil. Simmer for 5 minutes, then drain the beans (discarding the water) and return them to the pan. Pour in the chicken stock, bring to a boil again, and simmer for 45 minutes.

Stir in the onion and olive oil, and cook for 15 minutes. Dice the pumpkin and potato, then add to the onions with the zucchini and carrots. Deseed the tomatoes, chop coarsely, and also add to the pan. Season with salt and pepper, bring back to a boil, and simmer, covered, for 30 minutes. Finally, add the spinach and fava beans (you can skin them if you prefer) and cook, uncovered, for 15 minutes more.

While the soup is simmering, make the pistou. You can either use a mortar and pestle or a food processor, but take care not to overprocess the pistou; it should be slightly coarse rather than a smooth puree. First, pound together the garlic and salt, then mix in the basil, tomato, and cheese. Next, add the olive oil, slowly, as you would for mayonnaise.

Serve the soup with the pistou on the side, which is stirred in by the *convives* (diners), helping themselves straight from the mortar in which it was made. Pass a bottle of olive oil with a drizzler and a bowl of grated cheese, to add to the soup.

I am not suggesting a fully authentic mixture of fish for this bouillabaisse from Valras in the Languedoc, because it is so hard to find them outside Provence and southwest France. But when you are there, you find that every fish stall has at least two piles of different striped, banded, transparent, highly colored rockfish. In Paris, they gut the fish, in Marseille they don't. I do not gut the small fish for fish soup, but I like to fillet the larger ones and use the bones for a stock.

Bouillabaisse from Valras
BOUILLABAISSE DE VALRAS

Serves 4

For the bouillabaisse:

1 lb. monkfish, on the bone

1 lb. gurnard or large *rouget* (red mullet)

2 small John Dory

1 leek, white part roughly chopped and green part reserved

¼ cup Italian parsley, roughly chopped, stalks reserved

3 tbsp. olive oil

1 onion, chopped

2 cloves garlic, finely chopped

half bulb of fennel, coarsely chopped

1 piece dried orange peel

1 bay leaf

½ cup lardons, cut from *poitrine fumée*, or pancetta (optional)

½ tsp. saffron, soaked in ⅓ cup dry white wine

3 tomatoes, skinned and chopped

sea salt and coarsely ground black pepper or cayenne pepper

1 small baguette, sliced and toasted, and 1 quantity of *rouille* (see p. 279), to serve

Either ask the butcher to take the fillets off the fish and to give you the bones and heads, or do it yourself at home with a filleting knife. Chop up the bones a bit and put them in a pan with the green part of the leek, the parsley stalks, and some seasoning. Cover with 6¼ cups cold water, bring to a boil, and simmer for 25–30 minutes to obtain a good fish stock. Skim off any foam, but the stock need not be clear for this soup. Strain and set aside.

Heat the oil and soften the onion, garlic, leek, fennel, and parsley, together with the orange peel, bay leaf, and lardons. When the onions are turning golden, add the saffron and white wine, and let the mixture come to a boil. Next, add the tomatoes, 4¼ cups of the fish stock, salt, and pepper. Cook, uncovered, for 20 minutes, letting it boil.

Meanwhile, cut the fish into pieces about 1½ inches across, small enough to go on a spoon and large enough to retain some succulence. Add the fish to the soup, cook for 3–4 minutes, and then remove from the heat. Discard the bay leaf and orange peel.

To serve, place the toast in the soup bowls on top of the soup, and spoon some rouille on top.

Langouste (crawfish or spiny lobster) is eaten all along the Mediterranean coast; in the Pays Catalan it is eaten as a civet or stew, or cooked with snails, and in Provence it may be broiled or boiled and served with mayonnaise, eaten with tomato sauce and tapenade, or made into this bouillabaisse. It is worth sacrificing the most infant new green peas for the sake of this sublime dish.

Bouillabaisse of Crawfish with Peas
BOUILLABAISSE DE LANGOUSTE AUX PETITS POIS

Serves 4

For the bouillabaisse:

2 live or freshly cooked crawfish or lobsters, weighing about 1 lb. each

¼ cup olive oil

½ tsp. saffron threads dissolved in 1 cup dry white wine

2 cups light fish or chicken stock, fresh or made with a bouillon cube

2 bay leaves

a few sprigs parsley

1 medium onion, finely chopped

2 cloves garlic, sliced

half bulb of fennel, finely chopped, or ½ tsp. fennel seeds

3 tomatoes, peeled, deseeded, and finely chopped

1 lb. 9 oz. fresh peas in pods, shelled (or use 8 oz. frozen peas)

sea salt and freshly ground black pepper

1 quantity of aïoli (see p. 279), slightly softened with a few drops of hot water, and slices of pain de campagne (country bread), toasted, to serve

If using live crawfish, bring a large pot of well-salted water to a boil. Drop them into the fast-boiling water and cover the pan. Turn down the heat and simmer for 10 minutes. Remove them and let them cool.

With a large knife, cut the crawfish in half lengthwise so that you have four halves. Remove the tails from the shells and set them aside. Chop heads and shells into large pieces.

Heat 2 tablespoons of the olive oil in a saucepan and sauté the shells for 5 minutes, crushing them with the back of a spoon. Add the saffron-flavored white wine and the stock, put in the bay leaves and parsley, and season lightly. Simmer for 20 minutes and strain.

Meanwhile, in a separate saucepan, heat the remaining olive oil and add the chopped onion, garlic, and fennel. Season with salt and soften over a low heat until tender and transparent (or add fennel seeds to the chopped onion). Add the crawfish tails and turn in the oil for 2–3 minutes, then remove them and keep them hot. Add the tomatoes to the pan and cook for 5 minutes, then add the strained crawfish-flavored stock. Bring to a boil, throw in the peas, and boil for 5–6 minutes until the peas are tender. Taste for seasoning.

Ladle this soup into four heated soup plates. Place half a crawfish tail in each and serve with rounds of toasted bread with spoonfuls of aïoli on top.

The favorite place to eat bouillabaisse is the old port in Marseille, where there are still some good restaurants. The origin of this recipe is La Cuisinière Provençale *by J. B. Reboul, published in Marseille in 1895 but usefully reprinted in paperback in 1970. Reboul is a great one for soups. He starts every dinner throughout the year with a plate of it, but bouillabaisse is his favorite and he suggests serving it for lunch on New Year's Day. This version, made with salt cod, is a Friday soup, and he suggests it should be followed by cardoons with a cream sauce.*

Bouillabaisse of Salt Cod
MORUE EN BOUILLABAISSE

Serves 4

For the bouillabaisse:

1 lb. salt cod, soaked in cold water for 24 hours, water changed occasionally (see p. 32)

3 tbsp. olive oil

1 medium to large onion, finely chopped

12 oz. tomatoes, peeled and coarsely chopped

3 cloves garlic, minced

bunch of herbs containing fennel, bay leaf, and thyme

9 oz. small, waxy red potatoes, peeled and thinly sliced (about $\frac{1}{8}$ in.)

$\frac{1}{2}$ tsp. saffron

sea salt and freshly ground black pepper

For the aïoli:

1 large clove garlic

1 egg yolk

$\frac{2}{3}$ cup olive oil

sea salt

8 slices of baguette, toasted, and $\frac{1}{2}$–1 tsp. fennel seeds, to serve

After soaking the salt cod, remove the skin and bones, and cut it into 1½-inch squares.

Heat the olive oil in a heavy saucepan. Sweat the onion for approximately 15 minutes, without letting it color. Add the tomatoes and cook for 5 minutes, then add the garlic, herbs, and potatoes.

Pour in 4¼ cups of water, add the saffron, and season with pepper, but do not add salt at this stage, as the fish will be salty. Bring to a boil, and boil vigorously for 5 minutes. Add the salt cod, reduce the heat, and simmer for 5 minutes more. Turn off the heat, remove the herbs, and taste for seasoning.

Meanwhile, make the aïoli; mince the garlic to a fine pulp with a little salt, then put it in a small bowl and mix in the egg yolk. Gradually add the oil, a few drops at a time, working it in with a pestle or whisk. When the aïoli becomes thick, add a teaspoon of hot water, then continue adding the oil until it is all used up.

Ladle the soup into very hot soup plates. Put a slice of toast on each soup plate and top with a spoonful of aïoli. Sprinkle with the fennel seeds and serve.

You can use either palourdes (rough-shelled carpet clams), which are quite muscular and may be large; clovisses (the smoother Venus clams), which are smaller and flatter with less dense flesh; or chopped razor clams (couteaux or rasoirs). This combination of clams with beans comes from the sandy Bassin d'Arcachon on the Atlantic coast. If you can make the soup with fresh beans (haricots grains), so much the better.

Bean Soup with Clams
SOUPE DE HARICOTS BLANCS AUX PALOURDES

Serves 6

1½ cups dried white navy beans, soaked overnight

1 red onion, finely chopped

1 rib celery, finely chopped

3 tbsp. olive oil

3 medium potatoes, peeled and cut into small cubes

2 cloves garlic, finely chopped

6¼ cups chicken stock

3 tomatoes, peeled and coarsely chopped

1–2 bay leaves

1 lb. clams, washed well

1 tbsp. parsley, coarsely chopped

sea salt and freshly ground black pepper

Put the soaked beans in a large pan of fresh water and bring to a boil. Simmer for 5 minutes, then drain the beans, add fresh water, and return to the heat. Bring to a boil again, simmer for 30 minutes, and drain.

Soften the onion and celery in the olive oil over a low heat for 15 minutes, add the potatoes, beans, and garlic, and cook for an additional 5 minutes.

Add the chicken stock and simmer for 40 minutes, uncovered, then add the chopped tomatoes and bay leaves. Mash the vegetables a bit, season lightly, and cook for an additional 30 minutes. You can prepare the soup to this point and keep it on one side until you are ready to eat.

Add the clams to the hot soup, cook for 3 minutes, then stir in the parsley and cook for 2 minutes more. Remove the bay leaves and serve hot or lukewarm.

Mouclade, *mussel soup with saffron, is well liked in the quayside restaurants of the Mediterranean coast. When you cook it at home, try to find a supplier who sells clean* moules de bouchot, *mussels grown on wooden piles, with shiny, satiny shells. Once you have removed the beards and the odd barnacle, tap each one with the back of a knife, immerse them in a bowl of salted water, and swish them around for a minute. Throw out any that float or will not close when tapped. Any that are dubious can be put into a separate pan with a little water and steamed. If they open and are not stuck to the shell (except by the small muscle at the base), they are good. Strain the grit out of the cooking liquid and keep this broth, so important to the final flavor, as it embodies the taste of the sea.*

Saffron Mussel Soup
MOUCLADE

Serves 4

2¼ lb. small, thin-shelled mussels, cleaned

3 tbsp. olive oil

1 onion, finely chopped

1 large tomato, skinned and chopped

3 cloves garlic, finely chopped

2 bay leaves

pinch of fennel seeds

1 dried red chili

¼ tsp. saffron, soaked in ½ cup dry white wine

3 tbsp. long-grain rice (optional)

sea salt and freshly ground black pepper

1 tbsp. Italian parsley, roughly chopped; 1 tbsp. coriander (cilantro), roughly chopped; and 2 tsp. lemon rind (zest), finely chopped, to serve

Put the cleaned mussels into a saucepan with ½ cup of water. Cover the pan and bring to a boil, shaking over a fairly high heat until the mussels are all open.

Take the pan off the heat and let the mussels cool until you can pick them up. Remove two-thirds of them from their shells. Reserve the liquid, straining it through cheesecloth or paper towels in a sieve, if it is at all sandy.

Heat the olive oil in a saucepan, soften the onion thoroughly, and, when it is tender and just beginning to change color, add the tomato, garlic, bay leaves, fennel seeds, and chili. Let it simmer until the tomato becomes a light puree.

Next add 2 cups of water, the mussel cooking liquid, and the saffron in wine. Bring to a boil, throw in the rice (if desired) and season with pepper and, if needed, salt. Cover with a lid and cook for about 10–12 minutes.

Fish out the chili and the bay leaves, throw in the shelled mussels, and heat through. Ladle into soup bowls, put the remaining mussels in their shells on top, and serve sprinkled with the parsley, cilantro, and lemon zest.

Fish and

The Atlantic, with its huge sand beaches and energetic surf, and the calmer Mediterranean, whose rocky coasts shelter fascinating marine life, form the western and southern boundaries of the Midi. The center of this vast region did not see fresh sea fish until the invention of refrigeration; today, in contrast, it is one of the best places for cooking and eating fish and shellfish, all available in the most pristine state. In the seaside towns of the Midi, people jostle to get into such restaurants as Nice's Bar Turin on the corner of the Place Garibaldi, with its impeccable credentials for serving the best fresh fish and shellfish. Outside this impressive but unpretentious restaurant, the pavements are full of counters encrusted with oysters and shellfish, which are opened at speed for the customers crowding the old-time banquettes. They serve nothing but oysters, *plâteaux de fruits de mer*—a mound of raw oysters, clams, cooked *langoustines*, halved boiled crabs, winkles, and whelks piled on a dish of crushed ice and seaweed and placed on a stand in the middle of the table—whole crabs, bowls of mussels, and french fries and, of course, a quantity of chilled, white Entre-Deux-Mers.

At Chez Hortense, another dizzily crowded restaurant, this time in Cap Ferret on the west coast, the succinct menu offers roasted or raw oysters, mussels cooked with crumbs of sausage meat, and little else apart from the most enormous pieces of skate or turbot, or whole sole or sea bass, partnered with burning salty *pommes frites* (french fries).

Shellfish

In the Pays Basque, at St.-Jean-de-Luz, every visitor eats golden-red fish stews, hot with chilies, and in Collioure the favorite dish is *grillade de poissons*, a mixture of fish such as daurade, squid, and shellfish cooked over vine-prunings or charcoal, or grilled blue sardines straight out of the Mediterranean.

Inland Meridians have, of necessity, developed their tastes in a different direction; landlocked, they were obliged to rely on salt cod, which was not just allowed, but almost forced upon them by the church for Lent, Fridays, and fast days, of which there were many. This was supplemented with local freshwater fish, *écrevisses* (freshwater crayfish), fried or baked trout, carp stuffed with ham, a rustling *friture* (platter of fried fish) including tiny river fish such as *goujons* (gudgeons) dipped in milk and flour and fried, pike, eels, and in the Gironde, lampreys. There are still some *étangs*—pools, small or large—in the Aveyron that are emptied once every other year in March, when all the large fish, particularly carp, are caught. The largest are kept and the small thrown back to grow. Some are kept to breed, others are stuffed with bacon, bread, garlic, and parsley and baked, a traditional Lenten feast.

But it is seafood that captures our imagination; the pleasure of sitting for happy hours at a table overlooking the sea, eating fresh fish and enjoying the moment . . . these recipes may bring back some of those feelings of well-being.

Little baby squid (calamari), chipirons, *and octopus are loved both in the Mediterranean and on the Atlantic coast. This particular recipe comes from the Pays Basque. Completely fresh squid are clean little things that can usually be emptied without much washing (see p. 34), and their ink sacs can be removed without breaking for use in the cooking. However, once they are frozen or kept chilled for some time, the ink sacs become fragile and must be removed gingerly, or they may break and spoil the color of the squid. The thin speckled skin rubs off quite easily.*

Squid Braised with Green Bell Peppers
CHIPIRONS AUX PIMENTS DOUX

Serves 4

1 red onion, finely chopped

3 tbsp. olive oil

2 large or 4 small green bell peppers, deseeded and cut into thin strips

1 lb. 2 oz. squid, cleaned, skinned and cut into thin strips (see p. 34); use tiny squid, *chipirons*, or baby octopus, if possible

4½ oz. ripe tomatoes, peeled and coarsely chopped

juice of half a lemon

⅓ cup dry white wine

ink sacs from the squid (see p. 34), or a small packet of squid ink (optional)

sea salt and freshly ground black pepper

Soften the onion in the olive oil, over a moderate heat, for 5 minutes. Add the green bell peppers, season, and cook for an additional 10 minutes, stirring occasionally, until they are just beginning to brown.

Add the squid and the tomatoes, then pour in the lemon juice and the white wine. Season with salt and black pepper, cover the pan, and braise for 20–30 minutes or until the squid is tender. If, halfway through cooking, the squid seems too dry, add a little water. Lastly, if you have it, stir in the squid ink (see p. 130).

Serve with boiled potatoes, or triangles of fried bread rubbed with garlic. If you intend it as an appetizer, serve with a pile of small, young arugula leaves.

This Basque soup could be described as a stew. Rich and beautiful to look at, it is found from Biarritz to the Spanish border and is traditionally made with hake, gurnard, monkfish, or, as here, with cod. The vegetables and the mussels can be cooked up to 2–3 hours beforehand, leaving you simply to reheat them, and to add the fish, just before serving.

Basque Fish Soup
TTORO BASQUE

Serves 6

6 slices cod, each weighing
7 oz., skinned, or 6 thick pieces
cod fillet, weighing 5 1/2 oz., skinned

6 tbsp. olive oil

1 large onion (preferably Spanish),
finely chopped

2 ribs celery, finely chopped

1 large red or yellow bell pepper,
finely chopped (optional)

2 cloves garlic, sliced

1/2 tsp. pimenton or crushed red
pepper flakes

6 tomatoes, skinned and
coarsely chopped

1 bay leaf

1/4 tsp. fennel seeds

1 cup dry white wine

3 lb. 5 oz. mussels, carefully
cleaned and bearded

24 raw Mediterranean shrimp or
24 small raw spotted shrimp,
shelled and deveined

3 tbsp. parsley, coarsely chopped

sea salt and freshly ground
black pepper

Sprinkle the cod with 1/2 teaspoon of salt and set aside.

Heat the olive oil over a moderate heat in a large pan, and soften the onion, celery, pepper, and garlic, together with the pimenton or red pepper flakes. Let them cook gently, stirring occasionally, for at least 20 minutes. Add the tomatoes, bay leaf, and fennel seeds, and simmer until the liquid has reduced to a sauce, approximately 15 minutes.

Meanwhile, pour the wine into another large pan and bring to a boil. Throw in the mussels and let them cook, covered, for approximately 5 minutes. Take a look to check if they have all opened and remove from the heat as soon as they are really wide open. (Discard any that remain closed.)

All these steps can be prepared in advance.

When you are ready to cook the fish, reheat the rich vegetable stew and the mussels in their juice. Add the cod and the shrimp to the vegetables and cook gently for 3 minutes. If the mixture begins to stick to the pan, add a little of the mussel juice. Taste for seasoning. Turn the cod over carefully, and cook for an additional 3 minutes. The shrimp should turn pink and the cod should be flaking.

Add the mussels and their juice, season with salt and pepper if necessary, and stir carefully with a large metal spoon, without breaking up the fish too much. (You can, if you prefer, transfer the cod to soup bowls beforehand, so that the pieces remain whole.) Remove the bay leaf and sprinkle over the parsley. Ladle into hot, flat soup bowls and put large bowls on the table for the shells. You can eat this soup with pain de campagne (country bread) and unsalted (sweet) butter.

Note

Mussels can be salty so it is best not to season until the end. If the liquid is too salty, dilute it with white wine or water, or a mixture of both. If you are using gurnard, a good and underrated fish, ask the fish merchant to fillet it for you.

In Provence this would originally have been made with langoustines or gambas, but it can be made with shrimp; the point is to keep the shells. It isn't essential to have the heads, but they add color and flavor. Use Spanish or Camargue rice if possible, or substitute with a risotto rice such as arborio, although this will give a thicker result because it has been specially milled. Or you can try red Camargue rice, which takes a long time to cook, as it is unrefined. It behaves like wild rice and has an extraordinary nuttiness of flavor.

Shrimp Pilaf
PILAU DE GAMBAS

Serves 4

16 large raw gambas or deveined shrimp, or *langoustines* in their shells

2 tbsp. dry white wine

3 tbsp. unsalted butter

1 small onion, finely chopped

1 young small leek, finely sliced

1¼ cups Camargue rice, or risotto rice, such as arborio

1 tbsp. dill or Italian parsley, coarsely chopped

sea salt and freshly ground black pepper

Remove (but do not discard) the shells and, if you have them, the heads from the shrimp. To devein the shrimp, cut down the back of each shrimp with a small, sharp knife. The cut should be deep enough to enable you to remove the black vein that runs down the body. Keep the shrimp to one side.

Put the shells and heads into a pan with 2½ cups of water, the white wine, and just a small pat of the butter. Bring to a boil, season, and simmer gently for 20 minutes, then strain through a sieve, mashing the shells to extract all their flavor.

In a pan with a heavy base, melt the remaining butter. Cook the shrimp gently, without browning, for about 2 minutes on each side, then transfer to a dish. Add the onion and leek to the pan, and soften them for about 10 minutes, or until tender and transparent.

Add the rice, stir it around, and cook for a few minutes more. Pour in the strained liquid from the shrimp shells and bring to a boil. Reduce the heat, cover the pan, and simmer for 20–45 minutes, according to the type of rice, checking it from time to time. If you are using risotto rice, you may need to add a little water.

When the rice has swelled and almost all the liquid has been absorbed, add the shrimp and cook for an additional 3–4 minutes. Remove from the heat and allow to stand for 10 minutes, still covered. Sprinkle with the coarsely chopped dill or parsley, and serve.

I have not been able to find out exactly who Mère Figon was; sometimes she is described as Mère Pigeon. But she was evidently a celebrated Provençal cook, as she appears in Austin de Croze's famous Plats Régionaux, *and her recipe for cooking monkfish, with all its strong, salty flavors, keeps her name alive.*

Monkfish with Anchovies, Capers, and Black Olives
LA BAUDROIE DE LA MÈRE FIGON

Serves 4

4 pieces of monkfish fillet, weighing approximately 6 oz. each

all-purpose flour, for dusting

¼ cup olive oil

1 large onion, finely chopped

2¼ lb. plum tomatoes, peeled, seeded, and finely chopped

8 anchovy fillets, pounded

⅓ cup dry white wine

2 tbsp. basil, finely chopped

2 tbsp. Italian parsley, finely chopped

½ cup black olives

2 tbsp. capers, drained

sea salt and freshly ground black pepper

Season the pieces of monkfish with salt and black pepper, then dust them in flour. Heat 3 tablespoons of the olive oil in a skillet and cook the monkfish on all sides, approximately 7 minutes altogether. Transfer the fish to a warmed dish.

Add the remaining oil to the pan and sauté the onion for 5–10 minutes, until soft. Stir in the tomatoes, anchovies, white wine, basil, and parsley and bring to a boil. Reduce the sauce down until it is soft and jammy. Slide in the monkfish, add the black olives and capers, and cook for an additional 3 minutes.

One version of this dish, a lively Basque fish stew, from the useful Manuel de Cuisine Basque *by Maïté Escurignan, uses cooked mussels, made into a puree, to thicken the sauce. You can also use red bell peppers instead of green.*

Marmitako of Squid
MARMITAKO AUX CHIPIRONS

Serves 4

1 Spanish onion

¹⁄₂ cup olive oil

1 lb. squid, cleaned thoroughly and cut into rings (see p. 34)

1 lb. potatoes, peeled and chopped into rough cubes

1 red chili, seeded and finely chopped

2 green bell peppers, roasted, skinned, and cut into thin strips (see p. 64)

2 large cloves garlic, finely sliced

3 tbsp. Italian parsley, coarsely chopped

sea salt and freshly ground black pepper

Cut the onion in half, then into crescents, and finally cut the crescents across the middle.

Heat 3 tablespoons of the olive oil in a sauté pan and soften the onion for approximately 15 minutes, without browning it. When it is limp and translucent, add the squid rings and cook for 5 minutes. Next, add the potatoes, the chili, and enough water to almost cover the contents of the pan. Season with salt and black pepper, cover the pan, and simmer for 45 minutes.

Heat another tablespoon of oil in a pan and cook the strips of green bell pepper with 1 clove of the garlic for a few minutes, then add them to the squid. Continue to cook, uncovered, for an additional 10 minutes, until everything is tender and mellow. If the cooking liquid needs thickening, strain it and reduce over a high heat.

Finally, using the remaining oil, cook the second clove of garlic (or more if you like) together with the chopped parsley. Throw this *persillade* (see p. 28) over the stew just before serving.

A grand specialty of Sète, where it is made with monkfish, Bourride is popular in Marseille made with mullet. One version uses white fish with a creamy aïoli; the other uses cuttlefish, or squid, potatoes, and allspice. This combines both versions.

Bourride
LA BOURRIDE

Serves 4

For the fish stock:

1 cod's head or other white fish bones

1 rib celery, cut into chunks

1 carrot, peeled and cut into chunks

1 onion, cut into large chunks

1 leek, cut into chunks, washed

1 bay leaf

a few parsley and thyme sprigs

1 tsp. olive oil

For the bourride:

3 tbsp. olive oil

14 oz. squid, cleaned and cut into 2-in. squares (optional)

4 cloves garlic, finely chopped

2 tbsp. Italian parsley, finely chopped

2 large pinches crushed allspice

1 lb. 2 oz. waxy potatoes, peeled and diced

4 fillets white fish (monkfish, bream, or John Dory), weighing 7 oz. each, or 4 boneless pieces of hake, mullet, or brill, weighing 7 oz. each

salt and freshly ground black pepper

For the aïoli:

6–8 cloves garlic

1 egg yolk

²/₃ cup olive oil

Make the fish stock by placing all the ingredients in a large pan. Cover with 6¼ cups of cold water, bring slowly to a boil, and simmer gently for 25–30 minutes. Skim off any foam, strain, and set aside. Alternatively, you can use half a bouillon cube to make a stock.

For the bourride, heat the olive oil in a heavy casserole. When it is very hot, put in the pieces of squid; take care because they may spit. Cook for 1 minute, stirring once or twice. Turn down the heat, throw in the garlic and parsley, and stir them around briefly. Pour in 4¼ cups of strained fish stock, add the crushed allspice berries, and season with salt and pepper. Bring to a boil and simmer gently, covered, for 40 minutes.

While the squid is simmering, make the aïoli using all 6–8 cloves of garlic (see p. 279).

Add the potatoes to the squid, cover the pan, and simmer for 10 minutes. Place the pieces of fish on top and simmer, covered, until they are just cooked through, about 10 minutes. Carefully transfer the pieces of fish to a plate, without breaking them.

Ladle the bourride into four warmed bowls, stir a spoonful of aïoli into each, and top with a piece of fish.

This well-known Basque recipe is also known as Merlu Koskera. *It is a light broth containing fish and clams, and embellished with peas and hard-boiled eggs, rather than a fish stew. The broth can be spiced with more chili and mopped up with bread or eaten with a spoon. Occasionally, mussels are added.*

Hake in Green Sauce
MERLUZA SALZA VERDE

Serves 6

1 lb. 2 oz. peas in pods, shelled, or 2 cups fresh peas

1 lb. 2 oz. asparagus, cut into 1¼-in. lengths (optional)

6 hake cutlets, weighing approximately 4 oz. each

3 tbsp. all-purpose flour

¼ cup olive oil

2 cloves garlic, coarsely chopped

1 red chili, seeded and coarsely chopped

2 tbsp. parsley, coarsely chopped

2 bay leaves

¾ cup dry white wine

¾ cup fish stock or water

14 oz. clams

2 eggs, hard-boiled and cut into quarters lengthwise

sea salt and freshly ground black pepper

First, simmer the peas and asparagus (if using) separately in boiling salted water for 4–5 minutes. Drain them well and set aside.

Lightly dust the pieces of hake in the flour. Heat the olive oil in a sauté pan and soften the garlic, chili, and parsley. Add the bay leaves and the hake, and cook the cutlets briefly on both sides, without letting them brown.

Pour the white wine and stock (or water) over the fish, and stir in the clams, peas, and asparagus. Season with salt and black pepper, cover, and simmer for 5 minutes. Add the quarters of egg and simmer for an additional 5 minutes or until the clams open. Taste for seasoning and serve in hot soup plates.

In spring, Basque cooks often combine fresh fish with new peas and young fava beans, a marriage that is both fresh and symbiotic. They might choose hake or, as in this version, monkfish.

Monkfish Tails with Peas and Fava Beans
BAUDROIE À LA SAUCE VERTE

Serves 4

For the monkfish:

5½ oz. monkfish tail fillets, gray membrane removed

2 tbsp. olive oil

1 lb. 10 oz. fava beans in pods, shelled

1 lb. 2 oz. peas in pods, shelled, or 2 cups fresh peas (or use frozen)

¼ cup unsalted butter

1 tbsp. Italian parsley, coarsely chopped

sea salt and freshly ground black pepper

For the dressing:

½ cup olive oil

¼ cup lemon juice

1 clove garlic, finely chopped

1 tbsp. parsley, coarsely chopped

Season the monkfish fillets with salt and pepper and coat them with the olive oil. Leave them to marinate in the oil for 30 minutes.

Bring a pan of salted water to a boil and blanch the shelled beans for 4–5 minutes, or until they are just cooked, then rinse them under cold water and drain well. If they are larger than a thumbnail, skin them carefully. Prepare the peas, blanching them for 3–4 minutes.

For the dressing, whisk together all the ingredients and season with salt.

When you are almost ready to serve, melt the butter in a sauté pan over a low heat and warm the peas and beans through gently. Meanwhile, heat a heavy griddle or large skillet and cook the fish over a medium heat for 4 minutes on each side; it should be hot enough to sear the fish and prevent the liquid from escaping, but not so hot that the fish burns.

When the fillets are just cooked, place them on hot plates. Give the dressing a last whisk, then pour it over the fish, scatter the peas and beans over the top, and sprinkle with the parsley.

Wild trout from the mountain streams of the Southwest are well worth eating if you can find them, but farmed trout are more easily available and can be eaten very fresh. One such farm, outside Souillac in the Lot, has a restaurant serving the trout straight from their large, cold, source-fed pools. This dish, with the greens reduced to sorrel on its own, has become a classic. It can be made with salmon, John Dory, turbot, or brill, but in the Languedoc, where it originated, it was always made with wild river trout or, a great favorite in the Médoc, alose (shad).

Pink Trout with Greens
TRUITES À LA VERDURE

Serves 4

For the sauce:

¼ **cup butter**

2 shallots, finely chopped

4 ½ **oz. baby spinach leaves and** 5 ½ **oz. spinach beet (leaves only), coarsely chopped, or 10 oz. baby spinach leaves, coarsely chopped**

1 ½ **oz. sorrel leaves, coarse stalks removed and coarsely chopped**

1 oz. mint leaves, coarsely chopped

²⁄₃ **cup white vermouth**

²⁄₃ **cup heavy cream**

sea salt and freshly ground black pepper

For the trout:

4 pink trout, weighing about 9 oz. each

juice of half a lemon

sea salt and freshly ground black pepper

Preheat the oven to 400°F.

Start by making the sauce. Melt the butter in a large pan and soften the shallots over a medium heat for 5 minutes, then add the chopped greens and let it wilt down. When it is wilted, add the vermouth and reduce for 5 minutes. Add the cream and cook for 5 more minutes. Season well and pour into a large gratin dish.

Season the trout inside and out with salt and pepper, then squeeze the lemon juice into the insides. Place the trout on top of the green sauce and bake in the preheated oven for 10 minutes. Turn the trout over carefully and cook for an additional 5–10 minutes.

If you like them brown, you can brush each trout with 1 tablespoon of cream and brown them quickly under a preheated broiler. Serve them in their dish.

The fishing for tuna starts in mid-June in the Golfe de Gascogne, and from Agde to Sète on the Mediterranean, and ends in autumn. The boats, some loaded with amateurs, may go as far as Africa after the thon rouge, *red tuna, which looks almost like beef when cooked. Traditionally, much of the catch was salted for canning, but fresh tuna has always been so popular that it got the name of* saumon du pauvre; *ironically, it is now more expensive than salmon.*

Use fresh red tuna if possible for this dish, but you can also use white tuna or swordfish. Serve with grilled slices of baguettes spread with tapenade (p. 282).

Tuna Steaks with Roasted Tomato and Onion
THON AUX TOMATES ET AUX OIGNONS RÔTIS

Serves 4

four 8-oz. fresh tuna steaks

½ cup olive oil

1 tsp. black peppercorns, crushed

1 lb. onions, finely sliced

1 lb. 10 oz. fresh ripe plum tomatoes, peeled, seeded, and coarsely chopped

6 sprigs fresh thyme

2 bay leaves

2 large cloves garlic, finely chopped

1 tbsp. Italian parsley, coarsely chopped

sea salt and freshly ground black pepper

Coat the tuna steaks with 2 tablespoons of the olive oil and the crushed black peppercorns, and allow them to soak up these flavors in a cool place for an hour or so.

Preheat the oven to 300°F.

Cook the onions gently in 4 tablespoons of the olive oil for 20–25 minutes, until golden and beginning to caramelize. Season lightly, then spread them over the bottom of an oval gratin dish large enough to take all the tuna steaks side by side. Sprinkle the tomatoes over the top and cover with the thyme, bay leaves, and garlic. Season, sprinkle with a little olive oil, and bake, uncovered, for 20 minutes.

Meanwhile, heat a cast-iron griddle until it is very hot and sear the tuna steaks on both sides. Place them on top of the roasted tomatoes and onions, and bake for 10 minutes. Sprinkle with the parsley and a little more olive oil, and serve with pureed potatoes.

Alternative
A version of this dish in *Gastronomic Tour de France* by Jean Conil suggests pouring a glass of Calvados over the fish at the last moment.

This recipe from Provence has some interesting variations. One combines chard with the sorrel, another suggests shredded lettuce hearts instead, and another studs the tuna with pieces of anchovy before cooking.

Fresh Tuna Braised with Sorrel
THON À L'OSEILLE

Serves 4

¼ cup olive oil

4 young carrots, peeled and thinly sliced into rounds

2 small red onions, thinly sliced

1 large clove garlic, thinly sliced

3 sprigs fresh thyme

a few sticks dried fennel or ¼ tsp. fennel seeds

four 1½-in.-thick steaks fresh tuna, well trimmed

3 oz. sorrel, coarse stalks removed

¼ cup dry white wine

sea salt and coarsely ground black pepper

Heat 3 tablespoons of the olive oil gently in a sauté pan and add the carrots, onions, garlic, thyme, and fennel. Cover and let them sweat for 5 minutes.

Meanwhile, season the tuna steaks with a liberal amount of salt and pepper. Sprinkle with the remaining olive oil and rub it into the steaks. Place the tuna on top of the vegetables and cook, covered, for 2–3 minutes. Turn the fish over and cook for an additional 2–3 minutes. Transfer the tuna to a warm dish.

Throw the sorrel into the pan with the braising vegetables and sweat for 1–2 minutes, then add the white wine, season, and cover the pan. Cook for 15–20 minutes, or until the cooking juices begin to thicken and turn syrupy. Remove the thyme and fennel sticks.

Meanwhile, either prepare a wood or charcoal fire, or heat a cast-iron griddle. When it is very hot, sear the tuna steaks on each side; do this as rapidly as possible. Place them on top of the vegetables and serve, giving each person a wonderful, rare steak.

Alternative

If you want to try the alternative recipe using small lettuce hearts with the sorrel, baby lettuce heads, cut in half lengthwise, work well.

I first ate cod cooked in this way at a Sunday lunch with friends. We had foraged to and fro in the market all Saturday morning, immersed in making purchases such as mammoth artichokes and fresh walnuts. But the queen of all finds was the giant cod, the staple fish of the Pays Basque, once so common, now so sought after and almost an endangered species. With the cod perfectly roasted, we had its black skin cut in squares and fried to a crisp texture, hollandaise sauce, and plain boiled potatoes rolled in finely chopped parsley, followed by a fresh endive salad and a large piece of Vacherin.

Roast Cod with Hollandaise Sauce
CABILLAUD RÔTI, SAUCE HOLLANDAISE

Serves 4

For the cod:

2 pieces from the thick part of a large, whole cod, weighing about 1 lb. 4 oz. each

1 tbsp. olive oil

sea salt

For the hollandaise sauce:

1 tbsp. white wine vinegar or lemon juice

2 free-range egg yolks

½ cup unsalted butter, cut into small cubes and softened to room temperature

sea salt and freshly ground black pepper

Preheat the oven to 400°F.

Rub a roasting pan with a little olive oil, then put in the pieces of cod and sprinkle them with the oil and some sea salt. Roast in the preheated oven for 20–25 minutes.

If you want to serve the cod skin with the fish, preheat the broiler to its highest setting. Once the cod is ready, carefully remove the skin and sprinkle it with a little oil and salt. Broil it until it is crisp.

For the hollandaise sauce, use a double boiler or place a small saucepan or a bowl in a larger pan. Partly fill the lower part with hot water and place over a gentle heat. In order to avoid curdling the sauce, keep the water well below the boiling point, and make sure it does not touch the base of the upper container.

In the upper bowl or pan, beat the vinegar or lemon juice together with the egg yolks. Set this mixture over the water and stir continuously with a wooden spoon. Add the cubes of butter, one at a time, making sure that each one melts before adding another. Keep scraping the sides of the pan or bowl with your wooden spoon to incorporate everything into the sauce. If the sauce shows any sign of thickening too fast or of curdling, immediately remove the pan from over the hot water and set it in a bowl of cold water, stirring all the time. In contrast, if the sauce refuses to thicken, turn up the heat a little.

Taste the sauce and season with a little salt and pepper, and perhaps a little more vinegar or lemon juice. Hollandaise should be smooth and creamy in texture. If it is too thick, add a teaspoon of cream or a few drops of water and stir gently.

To serve, put the cod on a dish, without removing the bone, and let each person take one side of the luscious, shimmering white fish and plenty of hollandaise sauce and potatoes. The black, crisp skin makes a good foil for the succulent fish.

A quayside restaurant in St.-Jean-de-Luz on the Côte Basque produced this glorious dish. The colors on the plate—black, white, and red—remind one of nearby Spain. The original dish uses piquillos, *the small, pointed bell peppers.*

Salt Cod–Stuffed Bell Peppers with Squid Ink Sauce
PIQUILLOS FARCIS DE MORUE AU FUMET NOIR

Serves 4

For the stuffed bell peppers:

8 small red bell peppers

9 oz. salt cod, soaked in cold water for 24 hours (see p. 32)

10½ oz. potatoes, suitable for mashing, peeled and cut into small chunks

¼ cup milk, at room temperature

3 tbsp. olive oil, at room temperature

2 strips lemon peel, finely chopped

1 clove garlic, minced

pinch of grated nutmeg

sea salt and freshly ground black pepper

For the squid ink *fumet* (sauce):

1 large squid, weighing approximately 1 lb., or 2 small packets of squid ink

¾ cup red wine

1 red onion, finely chopped

2 cloves garlic, finely chopped

2 tbsp. olive oil

1 large tomato, peeled and coarsely chopped

2 tsp. all-purpose flour

⅔ cup fish stock from cooking the salt cod

1 tsp. lemon juice

Preheat the oven to 400°F.

To obtain the squid ink, take hold of the squid's body in one hand and the tentacles in the other; pull gently but firmly to separate them. You will find the ink sac of the squid, a small, long, silvery pouch, lying underneath the tentacles. Put this ink sac into a cup and mash it up, then dissolve it in the red wine, stirring it around to extract all the ink. You can clean and freeze the squid's body and tentacles for another time. You can also freeze the ink.

Place the bell peppers in an ovenproof dish and bake them for 20 minutes. Cook the salt cod using the method described on page 76. Drain the fish, reserving the cooking liquid, and allow to cool. Boil the potatoes in salted water until they are very soft, then mash thoroughly.

Make the sauce by softening the onion and garlic in the olive oil over low heat. When they are tender, stir in the tomato and let it soften and reduce for 10 minutes. Stir in the flour and cook for 1–2 minutes. Next, using a sieve, pour in the wine and squid ink, and simmer gently for 10–15 minutes. Measure ⅔ cup of the salt cod cooking liquid and add it to the sauce, together with the lemon juice. Taste for seasoning, then set aside, ready for reheating later.

Flake the salt cod flesh and remove all the skin and bones. Puree it by mashing it with a fork, with your fingers, or in the food processor, together with the milk and 1 tablespoon of the olive oil. Combine it with the mashed potatoes, adding more milk or oil if necessary. The mixture should not be too wet, as it is to be used as a stuffing and must hold its shape. Add the lemon peel, garlic, and nutmeg and season with black pepper and possibly some salt.

Carefully cut the tops off the peppers and stuff them with the salt cod mixture. Replace the tops and, if necessary, secure with toothpicks. Lightly oil an ovenproof dish and place the stuffed peppers in it. Sprinkle with the remaining olive oil and cover with foil. Bake for 30 minutes, pushing any escaped stuffing back inside the peppers.

To serve, reheat the black sauce, pour it onto four plates, and place two red bell peppers on each—the colors of Goya.

This daube, as you might expect, comes from Provence, where octopus is not feared but regarded as a splendid seafood; long and slowly cooked, it turns a delicate brown-pink and develops a rich meatiness. Nonetheless, octopus can be daunting to tackle for the first time and is very tough. One method of dealing with octopus is as follows: Choose an octopus of not more than 3 pounds 5 ounces, ask the butcher to clean it if this has not already been done, and, at home, wash it thoroughly under cold water. Cut off the tentacles as close to the head as possible. There are two ways of tenderizing the flesh, a process that makes the essential difference to the end result and considerably shortens the cooking time. Either place the trimmed tentacles, one at a time, on a worktop and thump them hard with a heavy wooden pestle until they lose their resilience, or pick each one up and swing it hard, hitting the worktop (or a rock). Do this with both ends, until the whole tentacle feels slightly limp. You can now cut the suckers off and, with the help of a knife, remove the dark skin. Slit the head, empty it out, and remove the beak if this has not been done. Cut the head to lay it flat and beat with a pestle. Cut the tentacles into short pieces and the head into squares.

Daube of Octopus
DAUBE DE POULPE

Serves 4

1 medium octopus, or a few smaller octopuses weighing 3 lb. 5 oz., prepared as above and cut into 1¼-in. pieces

⅓ cup dry white wine

2 small organic lemons, sliced

2–3 bay leaves

3 cloves garlic, minced

2 tbsp. Italian parsley, coarsely chopped

3 tbsp. olive oil

1 large onion, finely chopped

1 lb. plum tomatoes, peeled, squeezed, and coarsely chopped

1 lb. small new potatoes, cut in half

sea salt and crushed black pepper

Put the pieces of octopus in a bowl with the white wine, sliced lemons, bay leaves, garlic, and parsley. Sprinkle with some crushed black pepper and leave to marinate for an hour in the refrigerator.

Heat the olive oil in a skillet and soften the onion gently to a golden color, approximately 15 minutes. Strain the octopus (reserving the marinade), add it to the onion, and let it cook for a minute or two. Stir in the tomatoes and continue cooking for 5 minutes, then add the marinade, together with the bay leaves, garlic, and parsley (discard the slices of lemon).

Cover the pan and cook very gently, at the slowest of simmers, for 2 hours. Next, add the potatoes and a little salt and black pepper, and continue to cook until the octopus and potatoes are tender. This will take another 30–40 minutes. If, at the end of that time, the cooking juices need thickening, strain the octopus and potatoes, and reduce the liquid down. Remove the bay leaves and serve.

Alternative

In some versions the octopus is marinated in brandy, and it may be sprinkled with cinnamon before serving.

Skate is best eaten when not too fresh—the texture firms up and the fish comes off the bone in characteristic long strands. Like most skate recipes, this one from the Pays Basque uses a fair amount of vinegar; the strong smell of hot vinegar, garlic, and paprika is tantalizing. You can increase the quantities of vinegar and pimenton for a stronger flavor.

Skate with Red Sauce
RAIE GASTAÏKA

Serves 4

For the skate:

1 leek, cut into large chunks

1 onion, cut into large chunks

1 carrot, cut into large chunks

bunch of Italian parsley

3 lb. 5 oz. skate, cut into 4 pieces

sea salt and freshly ground black pepper

For the red sauce:

5 tbsp. white wine vinegar

¼ cup olive oil

5 cloves garlic, minced

1 tsp. pimenton or hot paprika

Bring 8 cups of water to a boil in a large pan and put in the leek, onion, carrot, and parsley. Season and simmer for 20 minutes or until the vegetables have given up their flavors. Remove the vegetables and the parsley from the water and discard them.

Slide the pieces of skate into the simmering water and cook very gently for 10 minutes. Lift the skate carefully onto a dish and keep hot.

Meanwhile, in a saucepan over a high heat, reduce the vinegar by half. In a separate pan, heat the oil and gently cook the garlic until it turns a pale golden color. Add the pimenton or paprika, cook briefly, then turn off the heat.

Arrange the skate on four plates and sprinkle the fish first with the vinegar, then with the red sauce. Serve hot.

Small pearly squid, delicately stippled with deep claret spots, cleaned, dried, and simply sautéed in olive oil for 5–10 minutes, are delicious on their own, served with aïoli or cooked in this Basquaise way, in a little garlic sauce with green peas.

Squid with Green Peas
CALAMARS AUX PETITS POIS

Serves 4

2¼ lb. squid

¼ cup olive oil

2 medium onions, finely sliced

4 large cloves garlic, halved lengthwise

1 cup shelled fresh green peas

½ cup dry white wine

sea salt and freshly ground black pepper

Carefully skin the body of each squid. Remove their heads and the contents of their bodies, including the transparent backbone. Cut the tentacles from the heads, reserving the tentacles. Wash the tentacles and the body pockets thoroughly and drain them well.

Heat the oil and cook the onions and garlic gently for approximately 20 minutes, until they are cooked through and beginning to turn a golden color. Add the squid and the peas, and season well. Continue cooking, over a medium heat, for about 5 minutes, until the squid has turned opaque.

Add the white wine and bring to a boil. Simmer for a minute or two, then remove the squid and keep them hot. Reduce the sauce until it is fairly thick, pour it over the squid, and serve hot, with fried squares of millas (see p. 82).

Any clams can be used for this dish—larger clams can be steamed open in advance and the top shells removed, although the pleasures of this dish are the beauty of the shells—and eating with your fingers! It can be served as a main course, an appetizer, or as an accompaniment to, for example, a squid dish. The rice can be prepared ahead of time, and the last stage, from the cooking of the shrimp and chili, done just when you need it.

Clam Pilaf

PILAU DE RIZ AUX PALOURDES

Serves 2 as a main course or 4 as a starter or an accompaniment

¼ **cup olive oil**

4 **cloves garlic, thinly sliced**

¾ **cup long-grain rice**

1 **lb. small clams**

a strip of lemon peel

1 **green chili, seeded and thinly sliced**

8 *langoustines* **or whole jumbo shrimp, or 9 oz. shelled jumbo shrimp**

1 **tbsp. lemon juice**

2 **tbsp. Italian parsley, coarsely chopped**

sea salt and coarsely ground black pepper

Heat half of the olive oil in a heavy saucepan and gently cook 2 cloves of garlic until they are a pale golden color. Throw in the rice and stir it around until it has absorbed the oil, then add the clams and the strip of lemon peel. Stir for a moment or two, then pour in 2 cups of water and bring to a gentle boil.

Season with salt and black pepper, cover the pan, and simmer over a gentle heat for 20 minutes, stirring occasionally. The rice should be tender and the liquid more or less absorbed. Once ready, remove from the heat and discard the lemon peel.

Just before serving, heat the remaining oil in a large skillet. Cook the chili, the rest of the garlic, and the shrimp, turning them over once or twice, until they are lightly browned and cooked through. Pour over the lemon juice, then add the rice and the clams, and stir everything together. Check the seasoning, sprinkle with chopped parsley, and serve.

Rice has been popular in southern France since the Middle Ages, when it was imported from the Middle East and from Spain. The French subsequently used rice from the French colonies of Indochina and, to a small extent, riz de Camargue grown in the marshes of the Camargue and around Arles. There is a road shaded by plane trees outside Arles, where Vincent van Gogh painted himself walking along with his paints and easel, wearing a sun hat. On the side of this road, rather exotically, are vivid green paddy fields, where the round rice called cigalon, used for paella and rice salads, is cultivated. This Provençal pilaf, however, can be made with long-grain rice such as ariete, which is also grown locally, or with imported long-grain rice.

Mussel Pilaf
MOULES AU RIZ

Serves 4

3 tbsp. olive oil

1 leek, finely chopped

1 red onion, finely chopped

2 cloves garlic, finely chopped

1 tomato, peeled and coarsely chopped

2 sprigs fresh thyme

1 bay leaf

1 tbsp. green fennel leaves and seeds, chopped, or ½ tsp. fennel seeds

1¼ cups long-grain rice

large pinch of saffron, soaked in 3 tbsp. dry white wine

juice and finely chopped zest of half a lemon

3 lb. 5 oz. mussels, cleaned and bearded

sea salt and freshly ground black pepper

Heat the olive oil in a large pan, and soften the leek and onion over a low heat until tender, approximately 10 minutes. Add the garlic and let it cook for a few minutes, then add the tomato, thyme, bay leaf, and fennel and stir them briefly until they have wilted into the oil.

Stir in the rice, thoroughly coating it with the oil, then pour in the saffron and wine, the lemon juice, and 2 cups of water. Season with salt and pepper. Bring to a boil, then reduce the heat, cover the pan, and simmer gently for 10 minutes, without stirring.

Add the mussels, letting them sit on top of the rice, cover the pan again, and cook for 5 minutes. Sprinkle over the lemon zest, then cook for an additional 5 minutes or until the mussels are open and just cooked.

Remove the thyme and bay leaf, then serve in soup bowls, with finger bowls for each person and a large bowl in the middle of the table for the empty mussel shells. This is a soupy pilaf, and can be eaten with spoons and forks, as well as with fingers.

Note

If you want to be neater, you can remove the mussels from their shells after steaming them for 5 minutes in a closed pan, with a few spoonfuls of water, until they open. Stir them, with their liquid, into the rice with the lemon peel, and perhaps keep a few back in their shells to decorate the top; the black shells and saffron-colored rice dotted with pink onion make this a handsome dish.

Poultry

and Game

Geese, ducks, chickens, and guinea fowl are a common sight around the roadside farms of the Southwest and in particular the Landes, the Gers, Périgord, and the Lot, indulging themselves in dust-baths under the apple or walnut trees, or strutting through the grass.

The following recipes are from an area where keeping birds is an art, although the introduction of intensive farming has meant fewer *artisanes* (small, independent farmers) rearing geese and ducks for foie gras, and fewer *marchés au gras* to sell it. These markets still thrive, though, in the Gers, where they proudly hang on to the tradition of hand-rearing poultry, and large quantities are still sold at the February markets in Gimon and Samatan.

Often it is the farmers' wives who tend to the fowl, making sure that healthy birds are turned into good food. While hens are kept for eggs and for long-cooked dishes, and chickens for quick-fried or sautéed meals, the ducks and geese are reared for foie gras that is not eaten by the family, but sold in the markets. As a result, there is plenty of duck and goose meat, and their fat available, which accounts for the local tradition of cooking in duck or goose fat.

In the past, the art of making confit, which preserves the meat in salt and its own fat was hugely important in the region, as it dealt with this excess. Today, plump *magrets* or *suprêmes de canard* (duck breasts), grilled fresh or cured and eaten sliced like ham, are fashionable.

This is a springtime dish, to be eaten when the artichokes are small and tender, and the new season's garlic is at its most succulent and delicate. The artichokes should be the smaller southern varieties, such as the violet artichoke. If using a large variety, such as vert de Laon, *cut the hearts in slices rather than quartering them. Note that the artichoke and lemon combination affects the flavor of wine, so do not waste your best Bordeaux with this. Better to drink a simple red or white wine, or even water, which acquires a sweet taste in contrast to the astringency of the dish.*

Chicken with Artichokes
POULET AUX ARTICHAUTS

Serves 4

1 yellow, corn-fed chicken, cut into 8 pieces (plus heart and gizzard if you like these)

¼ cup olive oil, or 2 tbsp. olive oil and 2 tbsp. goose fat

8 small young artichokes, prepared and quartered (see p. 216)

1 red onion, finely chopped

4 large, juicy cloves garlic, finely chopped

¼ cup lemon juice

¼ cup Italian parsley, chopped

sea salt and freshly ground black pepper

Season the chicken pieces with salt and black pepper. Heat the oil, or oil and goose fat, in a huge sauté pan or paella pan or, failing that, in two pans. Put in the quartered artichokes and the chicken drumsticks, thighs, and giblets, and let them brown for 10 minutes. Next, add the wings, cook for a few minutes, and lastly add the breasts, the onion, and the garlic. Keep turning the chicken pieces and cook them to a golden color on all sides.

Once the chicken has browned, turn the heat down, cover the pan with a lid, and cook gently for about 30 minutes altogether, until everything is tender, turning the pieces so they cook evenly. Remove the lid and skim off the fat from the juices. Lastly, add the lemon juice and parsley and cook a few minutes more, stirring and scraping the pan. Allow to sit in a warm place for 10 minutes before serving.

This is essentially Provençal food, but there are popular versions all over the Midi; the dish uses everyday ingredients but has a simple balance and harmony that many more complex recipes lack. The secret is not to allow it to become watery. After the chicken is cooked, do not keep the pan covered or it will start to steam, which spoils the texture. For added interest, you can add an herb or a spice with the garlic. In the Basque country it might be pimenton—either hot or sweet. In the Languedoc, they like to add a large handful of dried ceps, soaked and squeezed dry, then sautéed in butter and olive oil.

Chicken Sautéed with Tomatoes and Garlic
POULET À LA PROVENÇAL

Serves 4

1 yellow, corn-fed chicken, cut into 8 pieces

3 tbsp. goose fat or a mixture of olive oil and butter

3 large shallots, coarsely chopped

2–4 cloves garlic, sliced lengthwise

3 ripe tomatoes, peeled and cut in half

sea salt and freshly ground black pepper

2 tbsp. butter or olive oil; 4 ripe tomatoes, cut in half; 4 sprigs fresh thyme, coarsely chopped; and ¼ cup black olives, to serve

Season the pieces of chicken with salt and black pepper. Heat the goose fat, or olive oil and butter, in a sauté pan, add the pieces of chicken, and cook them on all sides to a beautiful, rich amber color. Add the shallots and garlic and lightly brown them, but do not let them burn.

Take the peeled tomato halves, squeeze out their seeds and some of their liquid, then cut into coarse pieces and add to the pan. Cover the pan and cook, turning the chicken frequently, for 15–20 minutes or until the meat is cooked through. Remove the lid.

For the garnish, heat the butter or oil in a small skillet and add the tomato halves. Sprinkle with the thyme, season with salt and black pepper, then slowly cook the tomatoes for approximately 5–10 minutes, or until they lose their moisture, but still retain their shape. Add the olives and heat them through in the butter or oil, then serve with the sautéed chicken.

This Provençal rice dish is closely related to risotto. If there is too much oil and goose fat for your taste, you can cut them down, but they do give a sumptuous texture to the rice and help prevent it from sticking to the pan.

Chicken with Saffron Rice
POULET AU RIZ AU SAFRAN

Serves 4

For the chicken:

one 4-lb. free-range chicken

3–4 cloves garlic, peeled

1 tbsp. goose fat or butter

1 tbsp. olive oil

6 shallots, peeled

5–6 medium tomatoes, peeled, cut in half, and stalks removed

a few sprigs thyme and marjoram

small piece celery

1 bay leaf

$^2/_3$ cup white wine and $^2/_3$ cup stock

$^1/_2$ tsp. saffron threads

salt and freshly ground black pepper

For the rice:

1 tbsp. onion, finely chopped

1 tbsp. goose fat or butter

$^1/_2$ tbsp. olive oil

$^3/_4$ cup Spanish, Italian, or Camargue rice

For the spiced oil:

6 tbsp. olive oil

4 cloves garlic, coarsely chopped

4 tbsp. Italian parsley or cilantro, coarsely chopped

$^1/_2$–1 tsp. mild pimenton or paprika

Preheat the oven to 225°F.

Season the inside of the chicken with some salt and pepper, and slip in one of the cloves of garlic.

Heat the goose fat, or butter and oil, in a casserole that will hold the chicken and brown the bird on all sides over a moderate heat. Add the shallots and let them brown at the same time. Throw the tomatoes into the pan, together with the remainder of the garlic, the thyme, marjoram, celery, and bay leaf. Season well, add the wine and stock, and simmer, covered, for 40–45 minutes.

To cook the rice, sweat the chopped onion in the goose fat, or butter and oil, in a large skillet until it is tender and transparent. Stir in the rice, keeping it moving for about a minute, then add the chicken cooking liquid, still containing the shallots, tomatoes, etc. Season well, cover, and cook gently for 20–25 minutes, until just tender. It should absorb all the liquid and still be juicy. Remove the thyme, marjoram, and bay leaf.

For the spiced oil, heat the olive oil in a small saucepan and throw in the garlic and parsley or cilantro. When the garlic starts to turn a pale golden color, add the pimenton or paprika.

Remove the chicken and keep it hot in the preheated oven. Stir the saffron threads into the chicken juices.

To serve, carve the chicken into four pieces, put one on each of four plates with some of the yellow rice and throw hot, red, spiced oil and herbs over each piece of chicken.

Alternative

Another way to cook this dish is to put the rice in with the chicken halfway through the cooking. Place the casserole on a heat diffuser over a very low heat and cook until the rice is tender, about 20 minutes.

This good-natured rice dish from the Hautes-Pyrénées (a simplified form of paella) is undoubtedly "comfort food." Easily made, its sweet and nutty aromas fill the air with those glorious southern smells—hot olive oil and sizzling garlic.

Basque Chicken with Rice
RIZ À LA GACHUCHA

Serves 4

3 tbsp. olive oil

1 small, corn-fed chicken, cut into 8 pieces

1 red onion, coarsely chopped

2 large cloves garlic, sliced

¾ cup lardons, cut from *poitrine fumée*, or pancetta

1 red bell pepper, roasted, skinned, and cut into thin strips (see p. 64)

4 oz. chorizo, sliced

¼ tsp. hot red pepper flakes

1 cup Spanish, arborio, or Camargue rice

2 cups chicken stock

12 black olives

sea salt and freshly ground black pepper

Heat the olive oil in a large skillet, sauté, or paella pan. Put in the pieces of chicken and brown them until they are a good, golden color, then lift them out onto a plate.

Lower the heat a little, add the onion, garlic, and lardons, and cook them gently in the same oil. When they are tender and translucent, add the pepper and chorizo, together with the chicken pieces. Sprinkle over the hot red pepper flakes and

season well. Sauté for 5 minutes, then add the rice, stirring it in between the pieces of chicken, until it is well coated with oil.

Lastly, pour in the stock, cover the pan, and simmer for 20–30 minutes, or until the liquid has been more or less absorbed and the rice is tender. Place the black olives on top and allow to stand for a few minutes before serving.

Cornish game hens can be bland, but in this Gascon recipe, which can be used for chicken, poussins, duck breasts, pigeons, or even pheasant, their flavor is heightened by a strong vinaigrette with warm shallots. Best grilled over the fire, the birds can also be cooked on a charcoal grill or a ridged cast-iron griddle.

Hot Wood-Grilled Cornish Game Hens with Vinegar and Shallot Dressing

POUSSINS À LA CRAPAUDINE

Serves 2

2 Cornish game hens, backbones removed (if the butcher has not done this, it is easy to do with scissors)

juice of half a lemon

¼ cup olive oil

3 tbsp. red wine vinegar

1–2 cloves garlic, finely chopped

3 shallots, finely chopped

sea salt and freshly ground black pepper

Flatten the game hens slightly with the palm of your hand. Sprinkle them inside and out with the lemon juice, 1 tablespoon of the olive oil, and some salt and pepper. Rub this into the game hens, then leave them for 1 hour in a cool place to absorb the lemon.

Make a vinaigrette with the remaining oil and the vinegar, and season it well.

Over a wood or charcoal grill, cook the game hens for 5 minutes on the inner side, and then 10–15 minutes on the skin side, basting with the lemon marinade once or twice. The grill should be far enough from the heat to cause slight spitting sounds as the birds cook, but not so close as to cause flare-ups and burning fat.

Test by pricking the thickest part of the leg with the point of a knife; when the juices run clear, place the birds in a warmed dish and sprinkle at once with the garlic and shallots. Cover and keep hot for 5 minutes, then pour on the vinaigrette dressing, and cover again. Keep hot for an additional 10 minutes, turning the game hens over in the dressing from time to time.

Serve with a vegetable gratin and a green leaf salad.

Alternative

The game hens can be cooked on a ridged cast-iron griddle, over the stove. Cook them for 10 minutes on the inner side, and approximately 20 minutes on the skin side, or until the juices run clear. Sprinkle with garlic and shallots, cover, and transfer to a 300°F oven for 5 minutes. Next, pour over the vinaigrette and return the game hens, still covered, to the oven for an additional 10 minutes. If you are wood grilling (*le grillade*), remember that the wood should be seasoned before it is burned on the fire. One-year-old wood is good but two-year-old wood is better.

A simple Mediterranean dish, I used to make it in Provence with local yellow chickens, and wonderfully fresh lemons, whose juicy skins perfumed the air when cut. If you can grill the chicken over a wood fire, it gives a most extraordinary depth of flavor. If not, grill it over charcoal or cook on a ridged cast-iron griddle over the stove. The caramelized, lemony onion sauce and the smoky taste of the chicken make this a satisfying, full-flavored dish.

Grilled Chicken with Lemon and Onions
POULET GRILLÉ

Serves 4

1 corn-fed chicken, cut into 8 pieces and trimmed

juice of 2 large lemons

3 tbsp. olive oil, or 2 tbsp. olive oil and 1 tbsp. goose fat

5 medium onions, thinly sliced into crescents

1 tsp. fresh thyme leaves

2 bay leaves

sea salt and freshly ground black pepper

Two hours before cooking the dish (or less if you are in a hurry), put the chicken pieces into a bowl and pour the lemon juice over them. With your hands, rub the lemon juice over the chicken, then add 1 tablespoon of the oil, some salt and pepper, and rub that into the chicken as well. Leave to marinate while you prepare a wood or charcoal fire.

You can also prepare the onions at this time. Heat the remaining oil in a large sauté pan and add the onions, thyme, and bay leaves. Soften the onions slowly until they are transparent, limp and golden brown, about 40–50 minutes.

When you are ready to cook the chicken, drain the pieces well by leaving them in a colander on top of the bowl containing the marinade, so that none of the juices are lost.

Grill the chicken pieces over the fire until the skin is crisp and turns golden, and is striped with the bars of the grill. It is better not to have too fierce a heat or the skin will blacken and become bitter; aim for a mellow fire that sizzles but does not flame or burn. Alternatively, preheat a ridged cast-iron griddle and brown the chicken on that.

When the chicken pieces are brown on both sides, arrange them in one layer on top of the golden onions, skin-side up. Pour the lemon marinade over the top, season well, and cover the pan. Simmer gently for 15–20 minutes, then test the chicken by prodding the thickest part of the leg pieces with a knife. If the juices run clear, remove the pieces of chicken and keep them hot while you finish the sauce.

Skim any oil from the top of the sauce and, if necessary, reduce until slightly thickened and velvety. Serve by spooning the sauce onto plates and putting the pieces of chicken on top.

This recipe originally came from a book of French Catalan cooking by Eliane Thibaut-Comelade—Ma Cuisine Catalane. I have included it because it is one of those simple dishes where the results far outshine the amount of effort put in. Also, it does not mind being kept waiting; the sauce keeps it from drying out too much, although it will eventually do so. The dish can be reheated, but make the sauce a bit more liquid in this case. Although green olives are mentioned, I have also made it with black olives and it is just as good. You could use sliced, fresh artichoke hearts instead of olives, or even large whole cloves of garlic cooked in with the chicken.

Chicken Breasts Wrapped in Ham
FRÉGINAT

Serves 4

4 chicken breasts, skin left on

¼ cup olive oil

4 sprigs fresh thyme

4 slices serrano ham or unsmoked bacon

2 tbsp. all-purpose flour

1 large onion, finely chopped

8 cloves garlic, finely chopped

¼ cup Italian parsley, finely chopped

1 ripe tomato, peeled and chopped

½ cup dry white wine

1¾ cups pitted green olives

sea salt and freshly ground black pepper

Rub the chicken breasts with 1 tablespoon of the olive oil and season them with a little salt and black pepper. Place a sprig of thyme on each, wrap around with a piece of ham or bacon, and secure it in place with string or a toothpick.

Heat 2 tablespoons of the olive oil in a sauté pan. Roll the chicken breasts in the flour, put them in the pan, and brown them on both sides. Transfer them to a plate and keep to one side.

Add the chopped onion to the pan, and the remainder of the oil if needed, and let it soften and start to brown a little. Next, add the garlic and parsley, cook for a minute or two, then add the tomato and cook for 5 minutes or until it has deepened in color to a dark red. Return the chicken breasts to the pan and add the white wine and the olives. Cover and simmer for 20 minutes, or until the chicken is cooked through.

Check the sauce, which should be fairly dry, adding more wine or water, if necessary. Remove the string or toothpicks from the chicken, together with the sprigs of thyme, and serve.

This dish, a chicken with a whole head of garlic nestling inside it, sitting in a reddish gold sauce, was the signature dish of a restaurant in Juan-les-Pins in the Alpes-Maritimes. Although it is described in Secrets of the Great French Restaurants *by Louisette Bertholle as "a typically Provençal chicken* fricassée," *it has a Spanish touch,* pepitoria, *meaning with seeds and nuts. Note that if the bread is not stale enough, it will become soggy when soaked in the vinegar. You will still be able to fry it, although it may take longer to brown and will need plenty of stirring.*

Chicken with Almonds and Garlic
POULET À LA PEPITORIA

Serves 4

For the chicken and stuffing:

4 oz. stale white bread, crusts removed, cut into cubes

3 tbsp. white wine vinegar

¼ cup olive oil

1 free-range chicken, weighing approximately 4 lb.

1 whole bulb garlic, cloves separated and peeled

⅓ cup flaked or blanched almonds, coarsely chopped

For the sauce:

2 tbsp. olive oil

1 small onion, finely chopped

1 large carrot, peeled and cut into batons

1 lb. tomatoes, peeled, seeded, and finely chopped

6 tbsp. dry white wine

¼ cup chicken stock

2 tbsp. Italian parsley, finely chopped

a few sprigs of fresh thyme

sea salt and freshly ground pepper

Preheat the oven to 350°F.

Soak the cubes of bread in the vinegar for 5–10 minutes, squeeze, and then crumble into coarse crumbs.

Heat the olive oil in a casserole large enough to take the chicken. Brown the chicken lightly all over, then transfer to a plate. Next, in the same oil, brown the crumbled bread and the whole cloves of garlic over low heat for 10 minutes. Stir in the almonds and continue browning for an additional 5 minutes, or until the almonds are golden.

Remove these ingredients with a slotted spoon and transfer them to a mortar, or food processor, pounding them to the consistency of a stuffing. Stuff into the cavity of the chicken and secure with a toothpick.

Using the same casserole, add the 2 tablespoons of olive oil and soften the onion and carrot for 5–10 minutes, or until the onion is tender and translucent. Add the tomatoes, white wine, chicken stock, parsley, thyme, and any leftover stuffing. Season with salt and black pepper, put in the chicken, and cover.

Place in the oven, covered, and cook for 15 minutes, then turn the bird onto its breast, turn down the oven to 300°F, and cook for another 15 minutes, adding more stock if necessary. Finish by stirring the sauce and cooking the chicken for an additional 30–45 minutes, breast-side up.

Transfer the chicken to a dish and cover with foil. Skim the fat from the top of the sauce and remove the sprigs of thyme. If the sauce needs thickening, reduce it down over a high heat, then serve with the chicken and steamed potatoes or tagliatelle.

Alternative

Leave out the tomatoes and, when the chicken is cooked, combine the cooking juices with ⅔ cup of lemony mayonnaise for a fresh delicate sauce. To do this, after skimming the sauce, whisk it into the mayonnaise, a little at a time, away from the heat.

This stuffed chicken has strong southern flavors. The recipe comes from Les Belles Recettes des Provinces Françaises, *a collection of winning recipes from a competition run by Radio Paris in the 1930s. The idea was to archive all the old provincial recipes before they disappeared and were lost to new generations. It gives a unique insight into the sort of food that people were eating at home in those days.*

Chicken Stuffed with Sausage and Black Olives
POULARDE À LA TOULOUSAINE

Serves 4–6

For the stuffing:

1–2 tbsp. olive oil

1 tbsp. butter

9 oz. Toulouse or other coarse-cut sausage, skinned and coarsely chopped

2 chicken livers, coarsely chopped

1 clove garlic, finely chopped

1 cup pitted black olives

For the chicken:

2 tbsp. butter

1 plump chicken, weighing approximately 4 lb.

2 small onions, finely chopped

1 bunch parsley

3 bay leaves

2–3 sprigs fresh thyme

$\frac{1}{2}$ cup dry white wine

1 tomato, peeled, coarsely chopped, and squeezed

sea salt and coarsely ground black pepper

To make the stuffing, heat the olive oil and butter in a casserole large enough to hold the chicken. Sauté the pieces of sausage and chicken liver together with the garlic. When they are lightly browned, add the olives and cook for a minute or two. Allow to cool, then use this loose mixture to stuff the cavity of the chicken, fastening the opening with toothpicks or a skewer.

In the same pot, heat the butter and brown the chicken all over. Add the onions, cook for a few minutes more, then add the parsley, bay leaves, thyme, white wine, and seasonings. Cover the pot and simmer gently over low heat, basting the chicken occasionally. After an hour, add the chopped tomato and simmer for an additional 40 minutes or until the chicken and stuffing is cooked through.

Remove the chicken and let it rest in a warm place. Skim the fat off the juices and, if necessary, reduce them by boiling for a few minutes. Taste for seasoning and remove the parsley, bay leaves, and thyme.

Carve the chicken and spoon out the stuffing. Add some of the tomato- and onion-enriched juices to each plate.

Truffled poultry are a specialty of the Périgord. You may prefer to use an organic, free-range capon, or a turkey, weighing about 10 pounds, as it makes a good alternative with its juicy texture and flavor, and is ideal for Christmastime.

Truffled Chicken or Turkey "in Half-Mourning"
POULET EN DEMI-DEUIL

Serves 8–10

For the court-bouillon:

6 leeks, washed thoroughly and cut into large pieces

6 small carrots, peeled and cut into large pieces

4 ribs celery, cut into large pieces

2 bay leaves

12 black peppercorns

sea salt

For the chicken:

1 large or 2 medium black truffles, fresh or preserved (1 oz.)

4 lb. top-quality free-range chicken, skin intact

For the leek sauce:

2½ cups clean, strong chicken or turkey giblet stock

¼ cup butter

¼ cup flour

1 cup heavy cream

sea salt and freshly ground black pepper

You will also need 1 large piece of cheesecloth

Make a well-flavored court-bouillon by placing the ingredients in a large pan, together with 16 cups of cold water. Bring slowly to a boil and then simmer gently for 40 minutes. Allow to cool, then strain, reserving the leeks for the sauce. If you have bought a fresh truffle, scrub it clean with a wet brush, then peel it thinly, and reserve the peel. Slice the truffle into thin rounds. Using your hands, carefully loosen the skin around the chicken breast from both neck and cavity ends and insert the slices of truffle between the skin and the flesh, spacing them out evenly. Any broken bits of truffle can go in the sauce with the truffle peelings.

When the breast of the chicken is patched all over with truffle slices, wrap the whole bird in a large piece of cheesecloth or other thin cloth (I use a muslin ham bag, made to hang ham in an airy place to keep it from deteriorating). Tie the cloth with string underneath the chicken, securing it firmly so that it is tightly wrapped over the breast.

Put the chicken into the pan with the cooled court-bouillon. Bring it slowly to a boil, skimming it well. Cover the pan and lower the heat so that it cooks at a slow simmer for 1¼ hours.

While the chicken cooks, start making the leek sauce by reducing 2½ cups of the chicken stock by about half. Melt the butter in a pan and stir in the flour, letting it cook gently for a minute or two. Gradually add the stock, stirring until smooth after each addition. Take the leeks that were used for the court-bouillon and finely chop the white parts (discard the green), or puree them with a handheld mixer, then add them to the sauce together with the cream. Simmer until the sauce starts to get thick and creamy, then finely chop the truffle peelings, add them to the sauce, and season well.

When the chicken is cooked, remove it from the court-bouillon and drain it well over the pan. Let it rest for 10–15 minutes, then unwrap carefully (the cloth will still be very hot). When you carve the pearly white bird, with its black truffle–studded breast, make sure everybody has some white meat with bits of truffle, and some dark meat.

Serve with the velvety leek-and-cream sauce, Roasted Forgotten Vegetables (see p. 238), and follow with a herb salad.

This recipe from the Languedoc is a way of making really good dried ceps give their best performance. The flavor of this rich, warm, brown sauce is meaty and earthy. If you can add some fresh ceps, then you will have an even finer dish.

Guinea Fowl with Ceps
PINTADE AUX CÈPES

Serves 4

4 cups best-quality dried ceps, in large pieces

1 free-range guinea fowl, weighing approximately 2 lb. 12 oz.

1 stick butter

1 cup dry white wine

1 heaped tbsp. all-purpose flour

½ chicken bouillon cube

2 tbsp. parsley, leaves and stalks, coarsely chopped

2 large cloves garlic, peeled and coarsely chopped

sea salt and freshly ground black pepper

Preheat the oven to 300°F.

Soak the dried ceps in 3 cups warm water for 20 minutes, or for as long as it takes for all the pieces to soften—leave tougher pieces in for longer. Remove the ceps from their liquid, squeeze them gently, and cut any large pieces in half. Strain the liquid through paper towels in a conical sieve to remove any grit.

Season the guinea fowl inside with salt and black pepper and remove any excess fat around the neck area. Melt 3 tablespoons of the butter over a gentle heat, in a pan into which the guinea fowl will just fit snugly. Brown the guinea fowl in the butter, turning frequently until it is the palest straw color all over, then pour in the white wine and 2 cups of the ceps' soaking liquid.

Place the guinea fowl so that it rests on one side of its breast. Cover the pan and simmer gently for 20 minutes, then place the guinea fowl on the other side of its breast and simmer for another 20 minutes. When ready, transfer the guinea fowl to a plate, cover with some dampened waxed paper, and allow it to rest in the preheated oven for 15 minutes. Skim off the fat from the cooking liquid, bring to a boil, and reduce it by about half.

Meanwhile, melt the remaining butter in a sauté pan and put in the sliced ceps. Sauté them until they are a rich chestnut brown; it takes about 20 minutes over a low heat. Sprinkle the flour over the ceps and stir over the heat for 3 minutes or so, then add the reduced cooking liquid, a little at a time, stirring to make a smooth sauce. Simmer for 15 minutes, then season to taste with the parsley, garlic, salt, and pepper.

Serve each person some breast and some brown meat, a few ceps, and a lot of delicious sauce. Sprinkle on the *persillade* of chopped garlic and parsley. *Pommes Sarladaises* (see p. 235) would go well with this, or *pommes purées* (pureed potatoes).

Albigensian Duck with Baby Onions, Lardons, and Fennel
CANETON ALBIGEOIS

Serves 2

1 Barbary duck, weighing about 3 lb.

2 tsp. fennel seeds

2 tbsp. olive oil

16 baby onions, peeled

¾ cup lardons, cut from *poitrine fumée* or pancetta

1 cup chicken stock

1 tsp. thyme

1 tsp. pimenton or paprika

1 tbsp. all-purpose flour

1 tsp. sugar or 2 tsp. honey

sea salt and freshly ground black pepper

Preheat the oven to 350°F.

Open the cavity of the duck and remove the giblets and the excess pieces of fat. Season the inside with salt and black pepper, and some of the fennel seeds. If it is not trussed, tie around the legs with string.

Heat the oil in a casserole large enough to take the duck quite snugly. Put in the duck, breast-side down, add the onions, and begin to brown. After 5 minutes, add the lardons and cook, turning, until everything is a light, golden color.

Pour the stock over the duck and add the rest of the fennel seeds, the thyme, and pimenton. Sprinkle the flour and sugar around the duck, season with salt, and plenty of coarsely ground pepper, and cover. Put into the preheated oven and leave to simmer for 1¼ hours, removing the lid after 45 minutes. Check from time to time to make sure that the liquid does not evaporate entirely.

When the duck is done, transfer it to a dish and skim all the fat from the sauce. Carve the duck and serve with the onions and bacon, the fennel-perfumed sauce, and with *pommes purées* (pureed potatoes) or lentils.

One of the forgotten flavors, and now almost unknown, is that of the giblets of duck, turkey, or chicken, although these have always been eaten with relish by small farmers, particularly the people of the Landes. They are carefully trimmed and cooked in a succulent and velvety alicot *or* alycot *(a little* ragoût *or stew made in autumn when lots of poultry were traditionally slaughtered), or made into* gésiers confits *(preserved giblets) to be fried up later for a* salade de gésiers *(salad of giblets). Some butchers will sell duck or chicken giblets in small containers. They should include the neck, heart, liver, and gizzard of the bird, perhaps with some of its fat. The liver and gizzard need to be inspected, and any bitter yellow or greenish parts cut away. This is a dish for two people as it may be hard to find enough giblets for more.*

Duck Giblet Stew with Ceps
ALICOT

Serves 2

1⅓ cups dried ceps

3 cups warm water or chicken or duck stock

1 large onion

2 cloves garlic

2 slices dry-cured bacon

2 tbsp. *graisse* (pork or goose fat), or a mixture of olive oil and butter

2 sets extremely fresh duck or turkey giblets (containing necks, hearts, livers, and gizzards)

1 large carrot or turnip, chopped into coarse chunks

1 tbsp. all-purpose flour

½ cup dry white wine

3 medium potatoes, peeled and chopped into coarse chunks

sea salt and coarsely ground black pepper

Soak the ceps in the warm water or stock for 20 minutes. Drain and rinse the ceps thoroughly, then gently squeeze out their excess moisture. Strain the soaking liquid through a conical strainer, lined with paper towels, to remove any grit. Set aside.

Chop the onion, garlic, and bacon into a *hachis* (see p. 281).

Heat the fat, or oil and butter, in a small casserole and brown all the giblets, except the livers, lightly. Transfer to a dish and put in the hachis; let it sweat and soften, stirring from time to time until the onions are transparent and tender. Stir in the carrot or turnip, the ceps, and the flour, and when it has frizzled a bit, add first the wine, then 2½ cups of soaking liquid from the ceps, a few tablespoons at a time, stirring until smooth after each addition.

Add all the giblets, except the livers, season with salt and plenty of coarsely ground pepper, cover the pan, and cook for 30 minutes, then add the potatoes and cook for an additional 20 minutes. Drop in the trimmed livers and cook for an additional 10 minutes or until the giblets are tender. Serve with a green salad dressed with walnut oil.

Eat confit de canard cooked in a little of its own fat until crisp and golden, with a fresh green salad, or with sorrel.

Preserved Duck
CONFIT DE CANARD

For 6–8 pieces

1 fresh duck, weighing 5 lb. 8 oz.

³/₄ cup coarse sea salt

6 dried bay leaves, crumbled

1 lb. 2 oz. *graisse* or rendered pork fat (see p. 283), melted

coarsely ground black pepper to taste

Place the duck, breast-side up, on a large board. Remove the fat from the cavity and set aside. Make an incision along the breastbone, cut around the wishbone, and remove the two breast fillets and the wings, cutting through to remove the wings intact but leaving the wishbone in place. Wiggle the wings about to find the point at which you can cut through cleanly.

Grasp hold of a leg, slide a knife between it and the carcass until you reach the top thigh joint, then pull it away from the carcass in order to expose the ball-and-socket thigh joint; cut through this joint where it joins the carcass. Cut off any excess fat from the duck but don't throw it away. You should end up with two wings (keep only the largest, using the rest to add to the soup), two breasts, (whole or cut in half), and two legs each consisting of drumsticks and thigh pieces (separated or left whole).

To make the confit, first preheat the oven to 275°F. Put all the pieces of fat in a roasting pan and cook for 2 hours, until all the fat has run out. Drain the remaining crispy bits on a rack over the pan. These are *grattons* and can be eaten. The fat, known as *graisse*, provides the medium in which the duck is slowly cooked to a consistency so soft that you can cut it with a spoon. But first the flesh has to be salted.

Place the pieces of duck in an earthenware terrine and rub them with the salt, crumbled bay leaves, and pepper. Leave covered in a cool place for 12 hours, turning the pieces once or twice. Then remove the pieces of duck, wash them in cold water, and dry with a clean dish towel or paper towels.

Put the pieces, skin-side down, in a preserving pan over a moderate heat and let them sizzle gently for 15–20 minutes, making sure that they do not stick. Add 2 cups of water, the rendered duck fat, and the melted lard or pork fat. Bring slowly to a boil, then reduce the heat and cook gently for 2–2½ hours over a low heat. If the pieces become uncovered, add a little more fat.

Allow to cool somewhat, then transfer the pieces of duck to earthenware pots or a terrine of glazed earthenware or pottery, or large glass preserving jars, packing the pieces in tightly. Pour the fat over and bang the pot to remove air bubbles.

Push the pieces well under the surface of the fat so they are completely covered, and allow to cool. Cover with a circle of waxed paper, placing it directly in contact with the surface of the fat. Store for a week in a cool, dry pantry before eating, or keep in the refrigerator for several months.

The rustic cavilhada, *a recipe from the high country of the Languedoc, consists of roasted garlic mashed into the cooking juices from the meat.*

Whole Roast Rabbit à la Cavilhada
LAPIN À LA CAVILHADA

Serves 4

1 young, farmed rabbit, weighing approximately 1 lb. 10 oz.

1 tsp. fresh thyme leaves

2 tbsp. sunflower oil

2 tbsp. olive oil

3½ oz. piece of *poitrine fumée* or pancetta

10 cloves garlic, peeled

½ cup rabbit or chicken stock

10 cloves garlic, peeled

sea salt and ground black pepper

Sprinkle the rabbit inside and out with a little salt and pepper, and the thyme.

Heat the oil in a large sauté pan. Put in the rabbit, the poitrine fumée, and the unpeeled garlic. Let the rabbit brown, turning it once or twice, for 10–15 minutes; it should be brown all over.

Cover the pan and cook for an additional 10 minutes, then turn the rabbit over onto its other side and cook, still covered, for another 10 minutes. Add the stock and the peeled garlic and cook on for an additional 10–15 minutes. At the end of this time, the rabbit should be cooked.

Transfer the rabbit to a hot dish and reduce the juices in the sauté pan until they are only a few tablespoons. Squeeze the pulp from the unpeeled cloves of garlic and mash it roughly into the juice with a fork (discard the garlic skins).

Taste for seasoning and serve the rabbit, carved into pieces, with pieces of poitrine fumée, the whole, peeled garlic cloves, and this fragrant, succulent sauce.

The idea for this dish originally came from Jean-Marc Banzo at the Clos de la Violette in Aix-en-Provence.

Partridge Roasted with Forgotten Vegetables
PERDREAUX RÔTIS AUX LÉGUMES OUBLIÉS

Serves 4

For the partridge:

4 partridges, weighing about 13 oz. each

¼ cup all-purpose flour

2 tbsp. butter

2 tbsp. olive oil

sea salt and ground black pepper

For the vegetables:

1 roasting pan of Forgotten Vegetables (see p. 238)

Preheat the oven to 375°F.

Prepare the vegetables acccording to the recipe on p. 238; start to roast them.

Dust the partridges lightly with the flour and season them with a little salt. Heat half of the butter and olive oil in a large skillet and, over a medium heat, cook two of the partridges until they are golden brown all over. Transfer to a plate, add the remaining butter and olive oil to the pan, and brown the other birds.

Season the birds with black pepper, then, 20 minutes before the vegetables are due to come out of the oven, place the partridges on top of them and roast for 20 minutes, basting the birds from time to time with their juices.

Remove the vegetables from the pan with a slotted spoon and let the partridges cool for 5 minutes. Skim the fat from the roasting juices left in the pan and serve the juice with the partridges, which will be perfectly tender (provided they are young birds) and will have imparted some of their flavor to the vegetables.

This Catalan recipe is my own, more homely version of a delicate dish I ate in a restaurant called Miura after a morning's market shopping in Bayonne. It adds a similar sweet-and-sharp flavor to the bird that is the correct result of a well-made caneton à l'orange, *but I think duck marries more harmoniously with carrots than it ever did with orange.*

Spiced Crisp Duck with Honey-Roasted Carrots
CANETON EPICÉE AUX CAROTTES

Serves 4

1 duck, weighing approximately 4 lb. 8 oz.

pinch of sugar

1 lb. carrots, peeled and cut into batons

½ tsp. ground coriander

¼ tsp. ground cinnamon

2 heaping tbsp. honey

2 tbsp. lemon juice or white wine vinegar

sea salt and freshly ground black pepper

Unwrap the duck, remove the giblets, and place it uncovered in the refrigerator until you are ready to cook it; this will dry out the skin and help to make it crisp.

Preheat the oven to 400°F.

Bring a saucepan of water to a boil and season with a little salt and a pinch of sugar. Add the carrots, blanch them for a minute or two, then drain them in a colander.

Take the duck and remove any excess pieces of fat around the cavity, then rub the bird inside and out with salt, coriander, and cinnamon. Put it into a roasting pan, breast-side up, and roast in the preheated oven for 25 minutes. Then turn the duck breast-side down and roast for an additional 35 minutes.

Next, skim off the duck fat, leaving just 1 tablespoon of fat in the roasting pan. Turn the duck breast-up again and surround it with the carrots. Mix together the honey and the lemon juice or vinegar, then spoon them over the duck and the carrots. Season the carrots with salt and black pepper and return to the oven for an additional 15 minutes.

Remove and drain the duck and let it rest for 15 minutes in a warm place, uncovered (if you cover it, the skin may lose its crispness). Meanwhile, if the carrots need more cooking, return them to the oven. Once tender, remove from the oven, skim off any excess fat, but reserve the duck cooking juices.

Carve the duck into four or eight pieces and serve with the roasted carrots and their juices, watercress, and small new potatoes.

Meat and

My favorite traditional butcher's shop is in Martel, in the Lot. The butcher talks at length about everything he sells, and offers old-fashioned items like *couennes* (cooked pork rinds) and *grattons* (frizzled pieces of pork left over from rendering lard from pork fat), which he makes himself. He chooses the meat from the market himself and makes sure it is hung properly so that it is tender and juicy.

This butcher's shop is not typical of the majority in France; in general they are well-equipped, with stainless-steel cabinets as clean as operating theaters. The men and women are fast, skillful, and efficient, their customers are incredibly demanding, and want everything trimmed and tied like a neat parcel—as a result, the meat looks much more enticing. They sell vast quantities of *biftek* and *biftek haché* (steak and ground beef), sausages, and homemade hamburgers, which are just biftek pressed in a little mold.

Tender steak, in fact, is not something associated with most of the Midi, although the Médoc is close to the Charente, where the climate is right for prime beef cattle. So the Médoquins have a fairly recent tradition of eating the best steak, *entrecôte Bordelaise*, cooked over a scented fire of vine prunings. Here they also enjoy their famous *agneau de Pauillac*, milk-fed lamb, a few weeks old, with its delicate liver, sweetbreads, and kidneys, which are eaten grilled on skewers.

Sausages

In the South, the pastures are too scanty—and until recently people were too hard up—to sustain many beef cattle or other animals throughout the year.

But the favorite meat of all was fatty pork. Most rural households kept one huge pig, and killed it in the early winter, working incredibly hard to make all sorts of sausages, preserves, hams, and *graisse* (rendered pork fat for cooking) to tide them over the winter. They loved the pig in all its parts—little pieces, or *lardons*, of cured pork to enrich a simple dish such as *garbure*, whole pork loins studded with garlic, *cassoulet*, pork and beans, black sausage, trotters.

Entrecôte cooked over the fire, tender young lamb, and pork loin all have their place in the Midi's cuisine, but there is something very natural about the slow-cooked dishes, the *daubes*, where the tougher pieces of meat are cut into large pieces that release their flavor slowly in the oven, becoming a tender, melting balsamic emulsion of meat, wine, thyme, and juniper. In Provence, dried orange peel is sold for daubes, and in the Lot, some still add the dried outer casings of walnuts to a marinade. These haunting flavors make it worth the trouble to try and keep some of the older dishes alive, by cooking them from time to time.

Lamb with garlic really is the signature dish of Provençal menus; in the Michelin Guide *every starred Provençal restaurant specifies lamb as a specialty, and yet it is the easiest thing to cook to perfection at home. If you can, cook the cutlets over a wood fire; otherwise use a cast-iron griddle.*

Grilled Lamb Cutlets with Garlic Mash and Roasted Garlic
CÔTELETTES D'AGNEAU À L'AIL

Serves 2

For the roasted garlic and mash:

2 whole heads garlic

3 tbsp. olive oil

1 lb. 2 oz. potatoes, peeled and cut into small chunks

⅓ cup milk

sea salt and freshly ground black pepper

For the peppers:

2 red bell peppers

1 tsp. olive oil

1 tsp. fennel fronds or green fennel seeds

For the lamb:

10 tiny or 8 very small lamb cutlets from the best end (rib chops), carefully trimmed

1 tbsp. olive oil

Preheat the oven to 400°F.

With a sharp knife, cut the top ¼ inch off the heads of garlic. Place them on a sheet of aluminum foil and sprinkle with 1 tablespoon of the olive oil and some salt and pepper. Wrap the foil loosely around the garlic. Put the bell peppers in a small, ovenproof dish and roast them, and the wrapped garlic, in the top of the preheated oven for 25 minutes.

Meanwhile, put the potatoes in a pan of cold, salted water. Bring to a boil and simmer for approximately 20 minutes or until tender, then drain.

Once roasted, put the peppers in a dish towel or a plastic bag to cool, then peel and slice thinly (see p. 64). Mix them with 1 teaspoon of olive oil and the fennel fronds or seeds. Keep them warm.

When the garlic is cool enough to handle, separate the cloves of one head and peel them carefully. Keep warm. Peel the cloves of the second garlic bulb and squash them flat with the blade of a kitchen knife to obtain a thick puree. Mash the potatoes with the milk, 2 tablespoons of the olive oil, and the garlic puree; taste for seasoning and add plenty of salt and pepper.

Heat the grill or cast-iron griddle. At the last minute, rub the cutlets with 1 tablespoon of oil, season, and grill them over a moderate heat for 4 minutes on each side. Turn them once or twice, and lower the heat if they appear to be browning too fast. Let them rest in a warm place for a few moments.

Put some garlic mash, whole cloves of garlic, and some strips of pepper on each plate. Add the cutlets and serve very hot.

The first time I was given this typical Basque dish, I was on a photo shoot at a three-star restaurant. After a long morning fiddling with exquisite plates of lobster medallions and thinly sliced duck breasts spread out into perfect little fans, it was a huge relief when the photographer and I were offered lunch with the workers in the kitchen; nothing much, just lamb with yellow bell peppers. The dish proved that simple, economical food can be unbeatable.

Lamb Fillet with Yellow Bell Peppers
RAGOÛT D'AGNEAU AUX PIMENTS DOUX

Serves 4–6

¼ cup olive oil

2 lb. 4 oz. lamb fillets or boned shoulder, trimmed and cut into large (1½-in.) pieces

3 yellow or orange bell peppers, seeded and cut into large strips

2 red onions, coarsely sliced

2 large cloves garlic, sliced

1 fresh long red chili, seeded and finely sliced, or ½ tsp. hot red pepper flakes

¼ cup red wine

4 sprigs fresh thyme

2 tomatoes, peeled, seeded, and coarsely chopped

sea salt and freshly ground black pepper

Heat 1 tablespoon of the olive oil in a large, heavy pan. Cook the pieces of lamb, a few at a time, until browned all over, adding more oil as necessary. Transfer the lamb to a dish, then add to the pan the remainder of the oil, the bell peppers, onions, garlic, and chili. Cook gently until the onions start to brown, approximately 15 minutes.

Return the meat to the pan, together with any juices that have run out. Add the wine and simmer for 5 minutes, then add the thyme and tomato and season well. Stir everything once, cover the pan, and simmer for 1 hour. Check the meat after 45 minutes and, if there is too much liquid, simmer, uncovered, for the last 15 minutes, or ladle off the juices and reduce by simmering in a shallow pan until syrupy.

Remove the sprigs of thyme and serve with steamed or boiled potatoes.

Note

If you make this ahead of time and let it cool, you can carefully remove the chewy skins from the pieces of pepper to make it more digestible.

If you doubt whether couscous is a Provençal dish, the answer is that thanks to the Algerian community, it has become so over the course of more than a hundred years. There are many variations of this dish but I have used lamb and vegetables.

Lamb Couscous with Seven Vegetables
COUSCOUS AUX SEPT LEGUMES

Serves 10

For the lamb:

half a shoulder of lamb (blade), about 2¼ lb., boned and cut into ¾-in. slices across the grain (ask your butcher)

2 large white onions, chopped

4 large carrots, peeled

3 tbsp. olive oil

2 tbsp. butter

a large pinch of saffron

a pinch of hot red pepper flakes

10 chicken drumsticks

one 15-oz. can chickpeas (garbanzo beans), drained and rinsed, or ½ cup dried, soaked overnight and cooked for 1½ hours

1 medium turnip, peeled

2 golden zucchini, cut into chunks

7 oz. green beans, trimmed

3 tomatoes, peeled and cut into eight sections

1 cabbage heart, cut into eight sections

3 tbsp. cilantro, chopped

3 tbsp. Italian parsley, chopped

2 tsp. harissa paste

salt and ½ tsp. coarse black pepper

For the couscous:

3 cups instant couscous

1½ tbsp. olive oil

2 tbsp. butter

Start by cooking the lamb. Pour 4¼ cups of water into a large, wide pan and add the lamb, onions, carrots (cut into chunks), olive oil, butter, saffron, black pepper, hot red pepper flakes, and 1 teaspoon of salt. Bring to a boil and simmer for 30 minutes. Next, put in the chicken drumsticks and simmer for an additional 30 minutes, by the end of which time the lamb should be tender.

Add the chickpeas (garbanzo beans), turnip (cut into chunks), zucchini, green beans (halved), tomatoes, cabbage, 2 tablespoons of the cilantro, and 2 tablespoons of the parsley. Taste the broth, adding more salt and pepper as necessary, then simmer until the zucchini and beans are just cooked. Stir in the remaining cilantro and parsley.

While the broth is simmering, prepare the couscous; instant couscous is extremely quick and easy to cook. Heat a large, deep bowl for preparing and a large, flattish dish for serving (this is a good chance to use a really beautiful pottery bowl in a good, strong color). Simply pour an amount of boiling water equal to the amount of couscous, in this case 3 cups, into the deep bowl and add some salt. Tip in the couscous, add the olive oil, and stir quickly. Cover with a lid, then let it swell for 5–10 minutes. Rub the grains with your fingers to separate them, or fluff them up with a fork. Add the butter, cut first into small pieces, and stir them through. The couscous should be moist but fluffy and separate.

Tip the fluffed-up couscous grains into the center of the big serving dish, piling it up in the middle. Lift out the lamb, chicken, and vegetables with a slotted spoon and place them in the middle. Mix 2 cups of the broth with the harissa paste and pour into a jug, then pour 2 cups of plain broth into a separate jug. Put the dish in the middle of the table and let everyone help themselves to meat, vegetables, couscous, and spicy or plain broth, or both.

One of southern France's favorite combinations is lamb and beans, but in this recipe the usual haricot blancs *are replaced by brown beans, which give a warm, rich flavor. If you can find fresh beans, so much the better.*

Braised Lamb Shanks with Beans and Black Olives
PISTACHE

Serves 4

1¼ **cups dried** *rose coco* **(cranberry) beans, soaked overnight and drained**

¼ **cup olive oil**

4 lamb shanks

12 shallots, peeled

8 carrots, peeled, halved widthwise and quartered lengthwise

2 cloves garlic, peeled and sliced

2 tomatoes, peeled and chopped

2 bay leaves

¾ **cup dry white wine**

½ **cup black olives**

sea salt and freshly ground black pepper

Put the soaked beans into a pan of cold water, bring to a boil, and simmer for 5 minutes. Throw this water away and start again with fresh water. Simmer the beans until just tender, about 1¾ hours, and drain, reserving the cooking liquid.

Heat the oil in a heavy pan and brown the lamb shanks all over. Add the shallots and carrots, stir them around in the oil, lower the heat, and soften them for 5 minutes. Next, add the garlic, tomatoes, bay leaves, and wine, and season with salt and pepper.

Add the drained beans, together with ⅔ cup of their cooking liquid. Stir everything together and cover the pan. Simmer for 45–60 minutes, turning the lamb shanks over fairly often.

Next, stir in the olives and cook for an additional hour or until the meat and the beans are melting and tender.

You can use small violet artichokes for this spring dish, but if they are very tiny, increase the number to twelve. Buy the smallest, youngest new season's spring lamb you can find.

Ragoût of Artichokes and Lamb
RAGOÛT D'AGNEAU AUX ARTICHAUTS

Serves 4

1 small, young shoulder of lamb, weighing approximately 4½ lbs., boned by the butcher and cut into 2½ x 1¾ x ½-in. pieces; remove excess fat and the skin

3 tbsp. all-purpose flour

3 tbsp. butter, lard, or goose fat

1 tsp. olive oil

12 shallots, peeled

2 fresh or canned plum tomatoes, peeled and coarsely chopped

2 cloves garlic, finely chopped

bunch of herbs (bouquet garni) containing sprigs of parsley, fennel, thyme, and bay leaves

¾ cup dry white wine

8 medium artichokes, prepared and cut into quarters (see p. 216)

sea salt and freshly ground black pepper

Preheat the oven to 375°F.

Lightly coat the pieces of lamb in the flour and season them with salt and pepper. Heat 1 tablespoon of the fat in a large casserole, together with the olive oil, which helps to prevent it from burning. Brown the pieces of lamb, a few at a time, adding more fat as necessary. When they are richly caramelized, transfer them to a dish and brown the shallots.

Add the tomatoes, garlic, and bouquet garni and cook for a few minutes, then add the white wine. Return the meat to the pan, season, and bring to simmering point. Drain the artichoke hearts and add them to the meat, using a large spoon to distribute them evenly. Cover and simmer for 15 minutes, then transfer to the oven and cook until tender, about 45–60 minutes.

Remove the bouquet garni and serve with the best-quality tagliatelle to catch the delicate juices.

In the Lot, this well-flavored enchaud (pork loin) cooked with garlic is often eaten cold, sliced fairly thickly, and accompanied by a green salad. If you can obtain a pig's trotter or two to tuck in with the pork while it cooks, it will give an added richness to the juices, and the gelatin will set when cold. The trotters can be coated with bread crumbs and fried afterward for a separate meal. If you wish to eat it cold, it is best just as it has cooled down; otherwise take it out of the refrigerator an hour before serving.

Garlic Roasted Pork Loin
CARRÉ DE PORC RÔTI À L'AIL

Serves 4

2 lb. pork loin, boned and rolled (rind and bones removed, but keep the bones)

3 large cloves garlic, cut into slivers

$\frac{1}{2}$ tbsp. olive oil

2 tbsp. parsley, coarsely chopped

$\frac{1}{4}$ cup dry white wine

$\frac{1}{4}$ cup water

sea salt and coarsely ground black pepper

Using the point of a knife, make small slits all over the meat and push the slivers of garlic into them. Put the olive oil into a casserole that will just hold the pork and bones. Roll the pork in the oil on all sides, then sprinkle with salt, a generous amount of black pepper, and the parsley. Leave the meat in the refrigerator for an hour or so, or even overnight.

Preheat the oven to 375°F.

Arrange the pork bones in the casserole with the meat on top. Cook, uncovered, in the preheated oven for 30 minutes. Add the white wine and water, then cover the casserole. Reduce the oven temperature to 325°F and cook for an additional 45 minutes.

Place the meat on a serving dish and allow it to rest for 15 minutes in a warm place. If necessary, reduce the cooking juices by pouring them into a small saucepan and simmering them over a high heat.

Serve the pork sliced, with the reduced juices, cornichons (small pickles), and small boiled potatoes. The spinach gratin (see p. 213) goes extremely well with this dish.

Making sausages was an important ritual in winter in country households. When the family pig was killed, there was long cleaning of intestines to be done so that they could be used as sausage casings for saucissons secs *(cured sausages like salami, to be hung up and dried, ready for slicing and eating cold),* boudins noirs *(black puddings), and* saucisses *(fresh sausages). To make sausages at home, you can buy a special machine called a* Porkalt, *which not only minces but also funnels the meat efficiently into the skins or casings. In the Pays Basque, the sausages were turned into chorizo, flavored and colored orange-red with pimento puree, as in this recipe.*

Chorizo

CHORIZO

Makes 6 large or 12 small chorizos

For the filling:

5 cloves garlic

10 dried red pimentos, the dark brown variety called *choriceros*, soaked overnight and drained, or 1½ tsp. hot or sweet pimenton, or hot or mild paprika

2¼ lb. pork shoulder, neck and a bit of fat back or belly, ground

2 tsp. salt

For the casing:

approximately 5 ft. sausage casing, soaked in cold water

In a small bowl, mash the cloves of garlic thoroughly with 2 tablespoons of water. Strain this mixture through a sieve, retaining the water and discarding the pieces of garlic.

Using a sharp knife, split the soaked pimentos in half lengthwise and carefully remove the seeds. Next, scrape the flesh away from the skins and mash it lightly with a fork.

In a large bowl, mix together the garlic water, pimento flesh, meat, and salt. Let the mixture stand in the refrigerator for a couple of hours, or even overnight, giving it a stir from time to time.

Make the chorizos (see p. 187 for method), tying them with string every 6 inches for large ones, or 3 inches for smaller ones. Keep them a day or two before eating, if you can bear to, then sauté or grill them, and serve with lentils or beans. Alternatively, allow the chorizos to dry in a cold, airy place for three to four days, then slice them up and use in Basque dishes such as *Oeufs Sur le Plat* (see p. 70).

In the Pays Basque, sausages are sometimes cooked in white wine, and in Provence, in a little tomato sauce with mushrooms or capers, or with braised Savoy cabbage (chou frisé) or beans. But it is in the Toulouse area that sausage-making and cooking is a real art. This recipe for pure pork sausages with white wine is made to the Toulouse formula; that is, three parts lean to one part fat, as opposed to the usual two parts lean to one fat—it makes a firmer sausage. Fresh sausages were eaten with a puree of haricot beans or split peas—or serve it with lentils.

Fresh Sausages with White Wine
SAUCISSES AU VIN BLANC

Makes approximately fourteen 3-inch sausages (size after cooking)

For the filling:

1 lb. 12 oz. lean pork such as loin, neck, or shoulder, ground or finely chopped

7 oz. pork fat, ground or finely chopped

1 tsp. fennel seeds, crushed, or pinch of five-spice powder (optional)

⅓ cup dry white wine

1½ tsp. salt

1–2 tsp. cracked black pepper

For the sausages:

approximately 5 ft. sausage casing, soaked in cold water

Mix all of the filling ingredients together in a large bowl, then let the mixture mature in the refrigerator for a couple of hours or overnight.

Fit a large piping bag with a plain tip and fill the bag with the sausage mixture. Take approximately one-third of the sausage casing, open up one end, and gently push it onto the tip. Continue doing this until all of this casing is gathered up on the tip.

Tie a knot in the other end of the casing, then squeeze the filling into it to produce one large sausage. Twist at regular intervals to make sausages of the size you prefer, remembering that they will shrink during cooking. Repeat twice more.

Allow the sausages to settle in the refrigerator overnight before cooking or using in any dish that requires 100 percent pure pork sausage.

A bean recipe from Gascony; the ideal sausages are the Toulouse type, with a higher proportion of meat to fat than a normal sausage.

Haricot Bean and Sausage Casserole
HARICOTS BLANCS À LA SAUCISSE

Serves 4

2³/₄ cups fresh white beans (*haricots grains*) or 1 cup dried navy beans soaked overnight and drained

2¹/₂ tbsp. goose fat or butter

1 onion, sliced

3 cloves garlic, cut into slivers

1 *couenne* (piece of pork rind), 3¹/₄-in. square, blanched for 15 minutes (see p. 283); or ³/₄ cup lardons, cut from *poitrine fumée* or pancetta, blanched

3 carrots, peeled and sliced

¹/₄ cup tomato sauce (see p. 278)

1 bunch of herbs to include parsley, sage, rosemary, thyme, and a piece of leek

12 oz. 100% pure pork sausages (preferably *saucisses de toulouse* or similar [see p. 187])

1 tbsp. Armagnac

Cover the beans with cold water, bring them to a boil, and simmer for about 30 minutes. Drain the beans and throw the water away.

Heat 2 tablespoons of the goose fat or butter in a large pan. Put in the onion, garlic, couenne, and carrots and let them soften for 10 minutes. Add the tomato sauce, herbs, and beans. Cover with 5¹/₃ cups water and push the herbs down into the middle. Bring to a boil and simmer for 1¹/₂ hours.

Cook the sausages lightly in the remaining goose fat or butter, until they are just browned. Put them in with the beans, together with the Armagnac. Stir well and simmer for an additional 30 minutes, then remove the bunch of herbs and the couenne.

You *can* eat the couenne; in the Southwest of France, people love this succulent preserved pork rind.

Crépinettes, little parcels of judiciously seasoned ground or chopped pork, wrapped in a piece of lacy caul, are another form of sausage. In Arcachon, you can order small, grilled crépinettes, to arrive spitting hot, with a plate of oysters.

Crépinettes with Armagnac
CRÉPINETTES A L'ARMAGNAC

Serves 6

3 cloves garlic, unpeeled

⅓ cup dry white wine

2–3 tbsp. Armagnac

1 lb. 2 oz. lean pork, such as fillet or loin, ground

3½ oz. pork fat, ground

1 tsp. truffle peelings, chopped (optional)

six 8-in. squares of fresh pig's caul or *crépine*, or 12 slices of dry-cured bacon, rind removed

6 slices of black truffle (optional)

1 tbsp. olive oil

sea salt and freshly ground black pepper

Put the unpeeled cloves of garlic in a small saucepan, together with the white wine. Bring to a boil and simmer gently for 15 minutes or until the garlic is soft. Peel the garlic, mash it into the wine, then strain off the liquid into a measuring cup (discarding the garlic). Add the Armagnac and enough water to bring the amount of liquid back to ⅓ cup.

Put the pork meat and fat into a large bowl and add the white wine and Armagnac mixture. Season with salt and black pepper, add the truffle peelings if you have them, and then allow to mature for an hour or more, stirring occasionally.

Divide the meat mixture into six and form it into oval patties (you can do this easily if you use very lightly floured hands). Spread out the squares of caul (some people find the caul easier to use if it is first soaked in warm water for a few moments, but often allowing it to warm up to room temperature will relax it enough) and place a slice of truffle and a meat patty in the center of each. Wrap the caul around the meat, securing it underneath with a toothpick if necessary, ensuring that the slice of truffle shows through on the uppermost side.

If you are using bacon rather than caul, lay the slices out so that they form six crosses. Place a slice of truffle and a meat patty in the center of each cross and wrap the bacon around them like a parcel.

Allow the crépinettes to rest in the refrigerator for at least an hour, or overnight.

To cook, heat the oil in a large skillet and, in batches, cook the crépinettes gently until they are cooked through and are a golden brown color, approximately 15 minutes.

Alternative

An even more luxurious version of these beautiful crépinettes is to divide the pork mixture into twelve and flatten the pieces into small patties. Place a small slice of foie gras, not more than ¾ ounce, on six of the patties, and top with the remaining patties. Mold the meat around the foie gras so that it is completely encased, and wrap in caul as before.

In the little summer market in Gluges, in the Lot, our favorite foie gras comes from an elegant farmer's wife, who also makes the most beautiful preserves. As well as pâtés, she does her own confit de porc.

Preserved Pork
CONFIT DE PORC

Serves 3

1 lb. 10 oz. free-range pork tenderloin or pork loin, trimmed

10 oz. rendered pork fat (see p. 283), goose fat, or lard

1 cup water

1½ tbsp. coarse sea salt

Cut the pork into large, equal-sized pieces; they should be more or less cubic in shape and measure approximately 2½ inches square. Tie each piece of pork both ways with string, like a package, then sprinkle them with the salt. Place in an earthenware bowl and leave in a cool pantry or in the refrigerator for 12–14 hours, turning the pork from time to time.

Heat the rendered pork fat, goose fat, or lard together with the water in a small saucepan. Brush any remaining salt crystals off the pork and arrange it in the saucepan so that it is completely covered by the melted fat and water. Bring to simmering point and cook gently for 2 hours, topping up with a little water if necessary to keep the pork covered. The pork is ready when it is easily pierced with a fork; it should offer almost no resistance.

Place the pork in a clean, airtight jar and pour in a little fat. Allow to cool, then fill the jar with the remaining fat. Keep for four days in the refrigerator before eating.

To serve, warm the jar a little to soften the fat, then remove the pieces of pork and cook them in the fat that remains on them. Serve with sautéed potatoes and a green salad.

Fabada, a rustic stew with beans from the Pays Basque, uses the large, flattish white beans (soissons) *that we call butter beans. However, this dish could also be made with good-quality dried navy beans.*

Farm-Style Beans

FABADA DE LA FERME

Serves 4

1¼ cups butter beans, soaked overnight and drained

¼ cup olive oil

1 onion, cut into quarters

6 oz. salt pork (*petit salé*), bacon (*lard maigre*), or pancetta, cut into 6 pieces and blanched in boiling water for 5 minutes

2 cloves garlic, crushed

1–2 green chilies, seeded and finely sliced, or 1 dried red chili

1 bay leaf

a large pinch of saffron

1 onion, finely chopped

9 oz. black pudding, thickly sliced

9 oz. chorizo, thickly sliced

sea salt and freshly ground black pepper

Put the beans into a large pan and cover with 4¼ cups of fresh, cold water. Add 2 tablespoons of the olive oil, the quartered onion, the salt pork or bacon, garlic, chilies, and bay leaf.

Bring to a boil, turn down the heat, and simmer, covered, for 1½ hours or until the skins of the beans are lifting off and the beans are just tender, adding more water if necessary. Taste for seasoning toward the end of the cooking time; a fair amount of salt will have come out of the salt pork or bacon. Give the beans a stir to thicken their cooking liquid.

Meanwhile, soak the saffron in 2–3 tablespoons of the bean cooking liquid. Heat the remaining oil in a large skillet. Add the finely chopped onion and let it soften, then stir it into the beans, together with the saffron, and remove the bay leaf and dried chili, if using. Cook the black pudding and chorizo in the skillet, adding a
little more oil if necessary. When they are cooked through and sizzling, spoon the beans and salt pork into hot soup plates and put some slices of black pudding and chorizo on top.

This recipe for beef in a rich, dark sauce, made all the meatier by the addition of dried ceps, should be eaten with macaronade (macaroni) *or with plain or fried* millas, *a type of polenta (see p. 82).*

Beef with Dried Mushrooms
BOEUF À LA LANGUEDOCIENNE

Serves 4

For the beef:

1 lb. 10 oz. shoulder of beef

⅓ cup lardons, cut from *lard maigre*, bacon, or pancetta

2 cloves garlic, cut into slivers

¼ tsp. ground cinnamon

¼ cup olive oil or lard

1 large red onion, finely chopped

2 bay leaves

1⅓ cups dried ceps

¾ cup dry white wine

1 large beefsteak tomato, peeled and coarsely chopped

1½ tsp. tomato paste

2 cloves garlic, finely chopped

2 tsp. fresh rosemary, finely chopped

1 tbsp. Italian parsley, finely chopped

sea salt and freshly ground black pepper

For the pasta:

2¾ cups macaroni

¼ cup butter

a pinch of nutmeg

6 tbsp. Gruyére cheese, grated

Lard the beef by cutting into it all over with the point of a knife and sticking the lardons and garlic slivers into the cuts. Season it with salt and pepper, and the ground cinnamon.

Heat the olive oil or lard in a casserole or heavy-bottomed saucepan. Soften the onion, together with the bay leaves, over a low heat for about 20 minutes until the onion begins to brown. Add the meat and let it cook very gently for about an hour, turning it over from time to time.

Meanwhile, soak the dried ceps in 1¼ cups water for at least 20 minutes. Drain (keeping the soaking liquid) and squeeze them dry. Strain the soaking liquid through a sieve lined with paper towels to remove any grit.

When the beef is thoroughly caramelized all over, add the white wine, chopped tomato, tomato paste, and the soaked ceps, together with the garlic, rosemary, and parsley. Cook gently until the sauce is thick, approximately 30 minutes.

Add the soaking water from the mushrooms and cook, covered, until the beef is completely tender, approximately 2 hours. Add a little water if necessary, in order to keep the beef bathed in a thickish sauce; it should not be too wet, but you want to end up with enough sauce for the pasta. Remove the bay leaves.

When the beef is almost ready, cook the pasta in a large pan of boiling, well-salted water. When the pasta is tender, drain and mix in the butter, nutmeg, 3 tablespoons of the grated cheese, and half the rich, dark sauce from the meat. Serve the pasta with the sliced meat, and the remaining sauce and grated cheese on the side.

In the Southwest, every cook knows this daube. The essential part is the extremely long, slow cooking in red wine. In the past, the daube was cooked all night in the embers of the fire, but, on the whole, meat is just not that tough today and so 3 hours in the oven should be enough. In order to have really succulent, melting beef, cut the meat in very large pieces, about 2 inches square.

Saint André's Daube
DAUBE DE LA SAINT-ANDRÉ

Serves 4

For the hachis:

4 oz. salt pork (*petit salé*) or bacon in a single piece (*lard maigre*), or pancetta

4 large cloves garlic

2 shallots

a large handful of Italian parsley

For the daube:

3 lb. top rump of beef (*gîte à la noix*), cut into 2-in. squares

3–4 *couennes* (see p. 283)

1 onion, studded with a clove

bunch of herbs (bouquet garni)—thyme, bay leaf, dried orange peel—tied in a leek leaf

1½ cups good-quality red wine

a pinch of *quatre-épices* (white pepper, cloves, nutmeg, and ginger)

salt and freshly ground black pepper

dumplings, to serve

Preheat the oven to 300°F.

Finely chop the hachis ingredients together and transfer to a small bowl.

Season the pieces of beef with salt and black pepper. Put the couennes in the bottom of a heavy casserole and place a layer of beef on top, then a layer of hachis (flavoring elements), then another layer of beef, and so on, filling the pot. Push the onion and the herbs into the middle of the dish, then pour in the wine. Sprinkle with the quatre-épices, cover, and cook in the preheated oven for 3–3½ hours, or until the meat is completely tender.

Allow to cool, remove the onion and bouquet garni, and skim the fat from the top. Reheat slowly and serve with *mique* (dumplings) and a green salad.

Dumplings from Sarlat (*Mique Sarladaise*)

This recipe serves four. Break 2 eggs into a large bowl and beat them lightly with a fork. Stir in some bread crumbs (made from 7 ounces of day-old white bread, with crusts removed) and mix thoroughly. Next, add 2 ounces goose or duck fat and 3 ounces all-purpose flour, and season with plenty of salt and black pepper. Using your hands, combine the ingredients thoroughly and roll the mixture into a large ball.

Bring a large pan of salted water to a boil. Add the mique and let it cook in gently boiling water for approximately 30 minutes. As it cooks, it will float toward the surface of the water. When ready, drain and serve with the daube.

The pigtailed boatmen who maneuvered the huge barges that once provided the main form of transportation from the Mediterranean, up the great river Rhône to Lyons, liked their own southern dishes wherever they traveled. They brought this famous grillade up from Beaucaire, where anchovies were used as a seasoning with capers or coriander seeds to give an extra depth of flavor. Sometimes the beef was marinated in vinaigrette for a day or two before cooking.

Mariners' Beef
GRILLADE OR BOEUF MARINIÈRE

Serves 6

3 lb. 5 oz. braising beef

2 tbsp. olive oil

2 tbsp. pork fat, or lard (*graisse*), or olive oil

2 large onions, finely chopped

10 small pearl onions, peeled

2–3 tbsp. dry white wine

a few sprigs of fresh thyme

3 tbsp. capers, chopped, or
1 tbsp. coriander seeds, crushed

1 tbsp. arrowroot

8 anchovies, coarsely chopped

2–3 cloves garlic, minced

1 tbsp. Dijon mustard

1 tbsp. white wine vinegar

sea salt and freshly ground black pepper

Cut the slices of beef into strips measuring 2 x 1¼ inches. Heat the olive oil and half the fat in a large casserole and brown the meat fairly gently, a few pieces at a time. Transfer the pieces to a plate as they brown.

In the same fat, soften the chopped onions and pearl onions slowly for about 15 minutes. Arrange the meat on top of the onions, add the white wine, thyme, and capers or coriander, and season with salt and pepper. Mix the remaining fat with the arrowroot and drop little pieces over the top of the meat.

Cover the casserole with foil and the lid and simmer very gently for 2 hours or until the meat is tender and melting, adding a little water if necessary.

Crush the anchovies with a fork, or pound them in a mortar, then stir in the garlic, mustard, and vinegar. Just before serving, remove the sprigs of thyme from the meat and stir in the anchovy mixture.

Many Moroccans and Algerians shop at the Arles market, where herbs and spices abound, and this is one of their dishes; long-cooked beef with an unusual, silky sauce, slightly thickened with sliced okra. Okra is a member of the mallow family. It has to be picked and eaten young, as it quickly becomes stringy, so look for very small, very green pods.

Braised Beef with Okra
BOEUF BRAISÉ AUX GOMBOS

Serves 6

3 lb. 5 oz. braising beef, cut into 1¼-in. slices

¼ cup olive oil

2 large onions, finely chopped

1½ cups lardons, cut from *lard maigre* (dry-cured bacon), or pancetta

4 large carrots, peeled and cut into thin batons (about the size and shape of a green bean)

3 bay leaves

a few sprigs of fresh thyme

¼ cup parsley, coarsely chopped

4 large cloves garlic, coarsely chopped

1¼ cup red wine

8 oz. okra, ends removed and sliced across into small wagon wheels

4 plum tomatoes, peeled and coarsely chopped

sea salt and freshly ground black pepper

Marinate the beef in a drizzle of olive oil as soon as you get home.

Heat the olive oil in a casserole large enough to hold the beef in one layer, if possible. Cook the beef fairly gently until it is a rich, caramelized brown on both sides. Transfer it to a dish.

In the same pan, sauté the onions and lardons for 10 minutes or more, until they start to turn golden. Add the carrots and toss them in with the onions and bacon, then place the beef on top. Sprinkle the bay leaves, thyme, 2 tablespoons of the parsley, and the garlic on top, pour on the red wine, then add the okra and tomatoes. Season carefully, bearing in mind that the lardons may be salty and that the liquid will reduce toward the end of the cooking.

Bring to a boil and then turn the heat down as low as possible; it should just bubble. Cook for 1 hour, covered, pushing the okra down into the liquid and basting the meat from time to time. Then remove the lid and continue to cook until the meat is very tender when poked with the point of a knife. Depending on the quality of the meat, this could take between 1 and 2 hours, or even longer if you are using shin or another of the more resilient cuts. Turn the meat over from time to time and add a little water if necessary.

The beef should be tender and succulent, and bathed in a satiny juice; if the juice is still too fluid, pour it off and reduce it in a small pan at a fast boil, then return it to the meat. Sprinkle the rest of the parsley over the top at the last minute. Serve with *pommes purées* (pureed potatoes).

In the Médoc, it is fiercely held that entrecôte bordelaise *does not have red wine sauce with it, and that it should be a steak two fingers thick, preferably from the loin end of the* entrecôte, *with a mixture of raw shallots and bone marrow spread over the top halfway through grilling. What is more, the meat should be cooked over a fire of vine prunings. Some butchers sell a ready-prepared mixture of shallots and bone marrow to anoint the steak. I have tried this and it was quite good. But frequently* entrecôte bordelaise *does have shallot and red wine sauce to accompany it, whatever the purists may say; in this recipe both methods are combined and butter is substituted for the bone marrow.*

Entrecôte Bordelaise with Red and White Shallots
ENTRECÔTE BORDELAISE

Serves 2

6 shallots, finely chopped

6 tbsp. butter or bone marrow, softened to room temperature

1³/₄ cups good red wine

²/₃ cup beef or chicken stock

2 thick *entrecôte* steaks (boneless sirloin steak)

olive oil, for brushing

sea salt and freshly ground black pepper

Light the wood fire or charcoal an hour before you want to cook the meat, so that it can heat to the necessary temperature. If you are using a ridged cast-iron pan, preheat it well before you put the steaks on to cook.

Mix together half the shallots and half the butter or bone marrow and keep the mixture on one side. Melt the remaining butter in a medium pan and soften the remaining shallots for 3 minutes. Add the red wine, bring to a boil, and reduce by half. Pour in the stock, then continue reducing until you have 3–4 tablespoons of syrupy sauce.

Brush the steaks lightly with olive oil and season with salt and black pepper. Place them under the broiler and cook on one side for 4 minutes. Turn them over, and spread the butter and shallot mixture over the tops of the steaks, pressing it on with the heated blade of a knife. Continue to cook for about 4 minutes, until the steaks are cooked. Lift them carefully from the grill onto hot plates, taking care that they do not lose their shallots and butter. Serve with the red wine and shallot sauce, and some sautéed potatoes.

Note

If you want to serve this with marrow and can get ahold of marrow bones, ask the butcher to cut them in short lengths. Preheat the oven to 375°F, wrap the bones in foil, and roast them for 20 minutes. Unwrap, and serve beside the steaks, with small spoons to scoop out the marrow.

This sauce is equally good with veal escalopes. It is based on a Bordelaise recipe from Traité de Cuisine Bourgeoise Bordelaise, *written in 1921 by Alcide Bontou. Some of the food in this book is elaborate, clearly meant for people with cooks. For example, there is a recipe that lards the veal chops with ox tongue, ham, and truffles, and another that requires the chops to be dipped in béchamel sauce, chilled, bread crumbed, and baked in pork fat in the oven. This recipe, however, is the one to cook for dinner, as it takes only a moment to put together.*

Veal Chops with Green Sauce
CÔTELETTES DE VEAU, SAUCE VERTE

Serves 4

For the sauce:

1½ tbsp. white wine vinegar

1½ tbsp. Dijon mustard

⅓ cup olive oil

1 large or 4 small dill pickled cucumbers, finely chopped

2 heaping tsp. lemon zest, finely chopped

2 heaping tbsp. small, whole capers

8 anchovies, finely chopped

1 tbsp. Italian parsley, finely chopped

1 tbsp. chervil, finely chopped

sea salt and freshly ground black pepper

For the veal chops:

4 veal loin chops, weighing approximately 10½ oz. each

2 tbsp. olive oil

Make the green sauce by combining the vinegar and mustard together in a small bowl. Stir in the olive oil, a little at a time, to make an emulsion, then add the rest of the sauce ingredients. Season well.

Preheat the oven to 200°F.

Season the veal chops with salt and black pepper, then rub in the olive oil. Heat a cast-iron griddle and cook the chops for about 6 minutes on each side. Let them rest in the warm oven for 5–10 minutes, then serve with the green sauce and some small, boiled new potatoes.

This recipe, remarkably similar to the Venetian way of cooking calves' liver, is in fact Bordelaise. It is important to take the time to cook the onions to perfection to get the best out of this dish.

Calves' Liver with Onions
FOIE DE VEAU À LA BORDELAISE

Serves 2

1 tbsp. butter or goose fat

1 tbsp. olive oil

2 medium-sized red onions (weighing approximately 10 oz.), very thinly sliced

2 large or 4 small, very thin slices of calves' liver, well trimmed

juice of half a lemon

sea salt and coarsely ground black pepper

Heat the butter or goose fat, and olive oil in a skillet large enough to hold the pieces of liver side by side. Add the onions and cook, stirring from time to time, over a very gentle heat, until the onions are completely wilted down and are almost caramelized. It takes about 20 minutes.

Season the slices of liver with coarsely ground black pepper. Push the onions to one side of the pan and sprinkle in a little more olive oil if necessary. Place the slices of liver in the pan and cook for 2 minutes on each side.

Bring the onions back into the middle of the pan again, season with salt, and cook the liver and onions together for 2–3 minutes. Sprinkle with the lemon juice, give the liver a last turn, then serve.

Vegetables

Some of the best vegetable gardens in the world can be found in the southern regions of France, from the small, immaculate *potagers* (kitchen gardens) such as those glimpsed from the train window as you dawdle toward Brive-la-Gaillarde, with their borders of step-over, espaliered apples and pears, to the market gardens of Provence and the Luberon, with their rows of channel-irrigated eggplants, tomatoes, zucchini, and artichokes. Between them lie orchards of peaches, apricots, and nectarines.

Throughout the Midi you can find vegetables in almost any color imaginable; violet artichokes in the Roussillon, splendid purple asparagus in the Gard, coppery-pink flat onions from the Aude, the fantastic long black-skinned turnips of Pardhailan, to mention just a few. How odd, then, that you can have a meal in a cozy restaurant that has no vegetables from start to finish, except for a tiny garnish of cubed tomatoes, crushed pink peppercorns, or two or three artfully arranged wilted baby spinach leaves. Traditionally, it seems vegetables were eaten in soups. However, things are beginning to change, and when you do find local vegetables on your plate, you will be convinced. In the South, cooking such produce, matured slowly out of doors with plenty of sunshine and not too much water, demonstrates that these are infinitely sweeter, denser, and finer in texture and more flavorful than their large, coarse, force-fed, and almost sun-less counterparts from the North. So if thin, pale water oozes out of your *ragoûts* and stews made with hothouse vegetables, pour off that liquid and reduce it fiercely in a small pan until it becomes a velvety juice. This goes some way toward finding the concentration of flavor that sun and soil give to the summer vegetables of the Midi.

I first tasted these tomatoes in stunning Collioure in the Roussillon, where the quayside "museum restaurant" Chez Pous, with its walls full of old paintings, feeds local artists and visitors. These tomatoes make a perfect first course to a simple meal or they can be eaten, like stuffed tomatoes, with roasted or grilled lamb.

Catalan Tomatoes with Black Olives
TOMATES FARCIES À LA CATALANE ⓥ

Serves 4

4 large beefsteak tomatoes

½ tsp. salt

¼ cup olive oil

2 yellow or red bell peppers, seeded and cut into thin strips

3 red onions, thinly sliced

24 black olives

sea salt and freshly ground black pepper

Preheat the oven to 250°F.

Cut the tomatoes in half across the middle and scoop out the insides with a teaspoon. Sprinkle the insides with the salt, turn upside down in a colander, and leave to drain for 30 minutes. Dry the insides with paper towels.

While the tomatoes are being salted, heat 3 tablespoons of olive oil in a skillet and gently cook the strips of bell pepper, seasoned with salt and pepper, until they are soft and starting to brown. Drain well and set aside. In the same pan, season the sliced onions with salt and pepper and sweat them slowly; they should be very well cooked, almost caramelized. Drain them thoroughly.

Turn the tomatoes over and place them in an ovenproof dish. Stuff them with the onions and then put the strips of pepper on top. Arrange three olives on each. Sprinkle with the remaining tablespoon of olive oil and bake for 30 minutes.

The secret of this dish is its concentrated flavors, achieved by sautéing the bell peppers and onions, and finally by baking everything in the oven.

Catalan Tomatoes with Lemon and Capers
TOMATES FARCIES À LA CATALANE 2 ⓥ

Serves 4

4 large beefsteak tomatoes

½ tsp. salt

¼ cup olive oil

2 red bell peppers, seeded and cut into thin strips

3 red onions, thinly sliced

4 strips of peel from an unwaxed lemon, finely chopped

8 caper berries

sea salt and freshly ground black pepper

Preheat the oven to 250°F.

Cut the tomatoes in half across the middle and scoop out the insides with a teaspoon. Sprinkle the insides with the salt, turn upside down in a colander, and leave to drain for 30 minutes. Dry the insides with paper towels.

While the tomatoes are being salted, heat 3 tablespoons of olive oil in a skillet and gently cook the strips of bell pepper, seasoned with salt and pepper, until they are soft and starting to brown. Drain well and set aside. In the same pan, season the sliced onions with salt and pepper, and sweat them slowly; they should be very well cooked, almost caramelized. Drain them thoroughly.

Turn the tomatoes over and place them in an ovenproof dish. Mix together the peppers, onions, and chopped lemon peel and use this mixture to stuff the tomato halves. Sprinkle with the remaining olive oil and bake for 30 minutes. Remove from the oven. Place a caper on top of each tomato. Serve warm or cool.

This gratin is from Provence, with a touch of juniper, a spice that grows wild on the limestone plateaus of the Lot and the Dordogne, and in alkaline areas of southern France. It is painfully prickly to pick, but as both ripe and unripe berries grow on the bush at the same time, you can pick the ripe ones, which are dark purplish brown with a bloom like a plum, by hitting the bush with a stick so they fall to the ground. This recipe looks complicated but is, in fact, extremely easy.

Tomato, Onion, and Potato Gratin with Thyme and Juniper
CHARLOTTE DE POMMES D'AMOUR

Serves 4

1 lb. onions, peeled

¼ cup olive oil or goose fat

1 lb. tomatoes, peeled and thickly sliced

1 lb. 9 oz. potatoes, peeled and thinly sliced

2 sprigs fresh thyme, coarsely chopped

6 juniper berries, crushed

1 bay leaf

sea salt and freshly ground black pepper

Preheat the oven to 325°F.

Cut the onions in half down the middle and slice the two halves thinly. Heat 2 tablespoons of the olive oil or goose fat in a heavy, nonstick skillet. Add the onions, season with salt and black pepper, then soften for 30–40 minutes over a low heat. Stir frequently to prevent them from sticking or becoming too brown; they should soften and almost caramelize in their own juice. Drain well.

Meanwhile, soften the tomatoes gently in a similar pan with a tablespoon of the oil or goose fat, and a little salt and black pepper. Cook over low heat for about 5 minutes or until all the juices have thickened; the pieces should remain fairly whole. Stir gently from time to time.

Put the slices of potato in a bowl, mix them with the remaining goose fat or oil, and season well. Add the thyme and juniper berries and mix the potatoes around with your hands to coat them all over.

Lightly grease an oval gratin dish and layer the vegetables; first some potato, then some onion, then some tomatoes. Place the bay leaf on top of the tomatoes, then put in more potato, onions, and tomatoes, and finish with a layer of potato.

Bake in the preheated oven for 1 hour. It should be brown and crunchy on the top and soft and succulent inside.

A similar gratin was served in its grizzled little earthenware dish to accompany grilled andouillette at the Hotel des Puits in Souillac on a winter pig-market day. Such a dish, with a carafe of dark Cahors wine, makes you feel you could go out and herd pigs for hours on end. The original recipe used blette (Swiss chard) rather than spinach and had extra garlic. The great thing about this dish is that it can all be made ahead, ready to put into the oven. It is succulent and goes well with roast meat, poultry, or game, or with simple grilled chops or steaks.

Spinach Gratin
PAIN D'ÉPINARDS Ⓥ

Serves 4–6

¼ **cup butter**

2 **lb. chard or spinach, washed and dried**

2 **tbsp. all-purpose flour**

1¼ **cups milk**

pinch of grated nutmeg

2 **free-range eggs**

2 **tbsp. crème fraîche**

¾ **cup fresh bread crumbs**

1 **tbsp. olive oil**

sea salt and coarsely ground black pepper

Heat half of the butter in a huge saucepan and throw in the spinach. Stir it around until it wilts, then season very lightly with salt and cover the pan. Cook for 5–10 minutes, stirring it around from time to time, then drain off the excess liquid and allow to cool.

Preheat the oven to 300°F.

Make a béchamel sauce by melting the remaining butter in a saucepan, stirring in the flour, and letting it cook for a few minutes over low heat. Then gradually stir in the milk and season with salt, black pepper, and nutmeg. Bring to a boil and simmer for 2–3 minutes, then allow to cool. Once cooled, stir in the eggs, one at a time, and the crème fraîche.

Mix the béchamel sauce with the cooled spinach and taste for seasoning, adding more salt, pepper, or nutmeg as you prefer. Transfer the mixture to a gratin dish and cover with the bread crumbs, just a thin layer. Sprinkle with olive oil—this is as much for the taste as anything, so do not use any other oil. Bake for 30 minutes.

Meanwhile, preheat the broiler. Once the gratin comes out of the oven, finish it off under the broiler so that it is slightly puffed, crusty, and sizzling on the top.

Asparagus is one of the most glorious vegetables in the Landes, and can be found in all its different colors. We were seduced by violet asparagus in the markets of St.-Jean-de-Luz, in the Pays Basque, alongside pearly, ivory, lilac, rose, and pale lemon; they also grow the less orchid-hued green, which is perfect for this dish. The asparagus season happily coincides with hens laying their best eggs in profusion, so this need not be considered an extravagant dish. Serve it on its own as a lunch or dinner dish, or as a side with broiled chicken.

Green Asparagus Gratin
PAIN D'ASPERGES Ⓥ

Serves 4

1 lb. green asparagus, cut into
1½-in. lengths, tough parts
trimmed off

2 tbsp. butter

2 tbsp. all-purpose flour

1¼ cups milk

1½ cups Cantal or Gruyère
cheese, finely grated

pinch of grated nutmeg

3 free-range eggs, separated

sea salt and freshly ground
black pepper

You will also need softened butter
for the gratin dish

Preheat the oven to 325°F. Lightly spread a large oval gratin dish with some softened butter.

Bring a large pan of well-salted water to a boil, throw in the asparagus, and simmer gently for 10 minutes. Drain it well on a flat wire rack.

Make a béchamel sauce by melting the butter in a saucepan, stirring in the flour, and letting it cook for a few minutes over a low heat. Gradually stir in the milk, then bring to a boil and simmer for 2–3 minutes. Remove from the heat, stir in the cheese, and season with salt, black pepper, and nutmeg. Allow to cool a little, then stir in the egg yolks.

Whisk the egg whites until they will stand up in soft peaks, then fold them gently into the cheese sauce.

Lay the asparagus in the greased gratin dish and pour the cheese mixture all over the top, spreading it to cover the whole dish. Bake in the preheated oven for 25–30 minutes, until it forms a golden brown, puffy crust and the center is still slightly runny. If you prefer the center to be firmer, bake for 40 minutes.

The Landaise version of pipérade *is a simple mixture of onion, garlic, tomatoes, and the local peppers, which are narrow, 6–8 inches long, green, with thin brittle flesh and a fresh taste; they do not need peeling. You can, of course, use ordinary bell peppers, either green or red, or, better still, red and yellow, to make this dish. However it is sometimes possible to buy long, sweet, green peppers from Italy, which are almost identical to the* piments du pays *of Southwest France, and these will give an authentic flavor to the dish. Serve* pipérade *like a sauce, with broiled fish, grilled or roast chicken, or with fried eggs, in omelettes, or in scrambled eggs.*

Braised Bell Peppers from the Landes
PIPÉRADE LANDAISE Ⓥ

Serves 6

3 tbsp. olive oil

1 large onion, thinly sliced

2 cloves garlic, finely chopped

10 *piments du pays*, cut lengthwise, seeded and cut into thin strips, or 4 green, red, or yellow bell peppers, peeled, seeded, and cut into strips (see p. 64)

4–5 tomatoes, peeled, squeezed, and coarsely chopped

sea salt and pimenton or cayenne pepper

Heat the oil in a sauté pan or small casserole and soften the onion and garlic over a moderate heat until they are wilted and transparent. Add the strips of bell peppers or piments du pays and sauté them gently until they, too, are soft, approximately 10–15 minutes. If using ordinary peppers that have already been roasted, sauté for 5 minutes only.

Add the tomatoes, season with salt and pimenton or cayenne pepper, cover, and braise gently for 20–25 minutes, until you have a soft mixture and all the liquid has been absorbed. If the mixture is still too wet, remove the lid and cook for an additional 5 minutes or until the vegetables have reached a jamlike consistency.

This is an early summer dish, to be made when fresh peas flood the markets. The main variety on sale in the Southwest are the tiny, pale-colored petits pois, *but any fresh peas, or even frozen peas, will give a good result; a wonderful succulent sort of vegetable ragoût for dinner, or as an appetizer for a simple meal.*

Braised Peas with Ham and Lettuce
PETITS POIS AU JAMBON

Serves 6

For the braised peas:

2 tbsp. olive oil or goose fat

¾ cup lardons from *jambon cru* or *ventrêche* bacon

2¼ lb. fresh peas in pods, shelled

8 pearl onions, peeled (and quartered if large)

3 baby lettuce heads, cut in half lengthwise and outer leaves removed

a few sprigs of parsley

a few sprigs of savory

1 bay leaf

12 asparagus spears, cut into short lengths (discard all tough parts)

12 small new potatoes

sea salt and freshly ground black pepper

For the fried bread:

¼ cup olive oil

2 cloves garlic, sliced

6 slices thick French bread (known as *parisien* or *bâtard*), each cut into 2 triangles

Heat the olive oil or goose fat in a heavy-bottomed pan over a gentle heat. Add the lardons and let them cook for a few minutes until the fat starts to run, then throw in the peas, the pearl onions, and the lettuces. Stir them around for a few minutes, then add 2 cups water. Throw in the parsley, savory, and bay leaf, season well, and simmer for 10 minutes.

Add the asparagus and potatoes, arranging the vegetables so that the potatoes sit in the cooking liquid (add a little more water if necessary). Cover the pan and continue simmering for 10–15 minutes, or until the potatoes are tender.

Meanwhile, prepare the bread by heating 2 tablespoons of the olive oil in a skillet. Add the slices of garlic and cook for a minute or so, then remove with a slotted spoon and discard. Fry the triangles of bread in the garlic-flavored oil, until they are golden brown on both sides. Fry a few pieces at a time and use the remainder of the oil as necessary. Once golden, drain on a piece of paper towel, sprinkle with a little salt, and keep warm.

When the vegetables are ready, strain off the cooking liquid and reduce it down over a fairly high heat; I often do this with all sorts of dishes and it makes a huge difference to the end result. As well as improving the texture of the sauce and the look of the dish, it concentrates the flavors.

Return the juices to the vegetables in the pan and remove the parsley, savory, and bay leaf. Serve with the slices of fried bread and perhaps some slices of fried ham, if you like.

We first came across la truffade *in La Roquebrou, in the foothills of the Cantal mountains, on our way to visit a cheesemaker. It was lunchtime in the town and the place looked deserted. The hotel L'Etoile, a fine art-deco building, seemed empty and shut. In disappointment we climbed the dusty stairs . . . and to our delight found a vine-covered balcony overlooking a river and a vast dining room full of happy diners. We thankfully sat down with them and were offered this wonderful potato dish. When we originally ate it, it was cooked in goose fat, but a shopper in Martel market, where we were buying the soft new Cantal cheese that is traditional for this dish, insisted that people prefer it lighter now, using olive or sunflower oil. She suggested half the amount of cheese to potatoes, but this is extremely rich, and I find one-third is a good proportion.*

Truffade
LA TRUFFADE Ⓥ

Serves 4–6

10 oz. *Tome* (fresh Cantal), Raclette, or Tilsiter, or a mixture of Gouda and Edam cheese

2¼ lb. firm, waxy potatoes, peeled

3 tbsp. olive oil, sunflower oil, or goose fat

2 large cloves garlic, minced

sea salt and plenty of freshly ground black pepper

Cut the cheese into small, thin, manageable slices about 1½ inches in length. Slice the potatoes thinly (approximately ⅛ inch thick) on a mandolin, or with the slicing blade of a food processor, then pat them dry with a cloth.

Heat the olive oil in a large skillet, together with the garlic, and slide in the sliced potatoes. Season them well and let them cook very gently, without browning, for 30–40 minutes, or until they are tender. Turn them fairly often with a wooden spatula, but be careful not to break the potatoes up too much.

Once the potatoes are tender, start adding the cheese, a quarter at a time, turning it in with the potatoes. As it melts, add another bunch and continue doing this until all the cheese is mixed in and melted. This will take about 10 minutes.

Turn up the heat a little and brown the bottom to give a golden crust. Turn this crust into the mixture, then repeat this once or twice more. Spoon or pour off any fat that runs out, and serve either on its own or with broiled, coarse-cut pork sausages.

Pumpkins are found on autumn market stalls all over southwest France and throughout Provence. They come in all shapes and sizes, although the large orange, ribbed pumpkins are the most common and the best for roasting. Also good are the blue-skinned pumpkins, which almost appear to be sculpted from stone or oxidized copper. They have the required firm, fine-textured, sweet flesh, particularly if they are on the smaller side; the larger, coarser pumpkins tend to go mushy when cooked. Otherwise, squashes such as butternut, acorn, and Hubbard can be used instead.

Roasted Pumpkin with Sage
POTIRON RÔTI AU FOUR Ⓥ

Serves 4

four 1½-in. slices of pumpkin or squash, unpeeled, seeded

1 tbsp. olive oil

½ cup olive oil

16 sage leaves

sea salt and coarsely ground black pepper

Preheat the oven to 375°F.

Place the pumpkin slices on a baking sheet and sprinkle with the olive oil, salt, and black pepper. Rub the pumpkin slices well with the oil and seasonings, then roast in the preheated oven for 30–40 minutes, turning them over once. The center of the pumpkin should be tender.

Meanwhile, heat the remaining olive oil in a very small saucepan. Deep-fry the sage leaves, a few at a time, until they are crisp. This takes about 10–20 seconds. Drain them on a paper towel and sprinkle with a little salt.

Transfer the pumpkins carefully to a warmed dish, sprinkle the sage leaves over the top, and serve on its own or as an accompaniment to roast veal or pork.

You can add chopped sage or chives to these small, orange pancakes for a more complex taste. The plain pumpkin flavor contrasts well with fried ham or bacon; in the Languedoc they are eaten with broiled oysters wrapped in bacon.

Pumpkin Galettes
GALETTES DE POTIRON Ⓥ

Serves 6

1 lb. 10 oz. firm, fine-textured pumpkin

4 tbsp. olive oil

1 heaping tbsp. all-purpose flour

2–3 free-range eggs, lightly beaten

3 tbsp. butter

sea salt and freshly ground black pepper

Preheat the oven to 375°F.

Cut the pumpkin into slices approximately 1½ inches thick. Remove the seeds but do not peel. Place on a baking sheet and sprinkle with one tablespoon of olive oil, and the salt and black pepper. Rub the pumpkin slices well with the oil and seasonings, then cover the tray with a large sheet of foil. Bake for 30–40 minutes, turning them over once, until tender. Once cooked, peel the pumpkin and place the flesh in a large bowl. Mash and leave to cool.

Once cooled, mix in the flour and 2 eggs for a very light mixture (this can be tricky), or 3 eggs for a firmer pancake. Season and add some herbs if you like.

Heat a little olive oil and butter in a skillet, and drop tablespoons of the pumpkin mixture into the hot fat. Fry to a golden color on each side and drain carefully on paper towels. Continue frying the rest with oil and butter.

If possible, use blue pumpkin or small pumpkins, as they are less watery than the large ones and have a concentrated flavor. American food writer Paula Wolfert's recipe uses the deep-frying method, but I shallow-fry instead.

Fried Pumpkin Sticks
FRITES DE POTIRON Ⓥ

Serves 4–6

1 pumpkin, weighing approximately 2¼ lb.

1 cup milk

¾ cup all-purpose flour

1 cup olive oil

sea salt

1½ tbsp. olive oil; 4 cloves garlic, finely chopped; and 2 tbsp. Italian parsley, finely chopped, to serve

Slice the pumpkin into thick wedges and peel them. Scoop out the seeds, then cut the flesh into batons the size of french fries, approximately 2½ x ¼ inches. Dip the pumpkin sticks into the milk, shake, and dip them into the flour.

Meanwhile, heat the olive oil in a large skillet so that the oil is about ½ inch deep. Fry the pumpkin sticks, in batches, on all sides, for about 5 minutes, or until the outside is crisp and golden brown and the inside soft and tender. Do not allow the oil to become too hot or the outside will cook first.

When ready, lift out with a slotted spoon and place on a paper towel. Sprinkle with a little sea salt to keep the sticks crisp.

Heat 1½ tablespoons of olive oil in a small skillet and briefly fry the garlic and parsley. Using a slotted spoon, sprinkle them over the pumpkin to serve.

Crisp, sticky, and melting, potatoes from Périgord, cooked in goose or duck fat in the Sarladaise way, can hardly be improved on, but they can be made more luxurious by the addition of black truffles. If you have a truffle, slice it up and throw it in as if it were a normal thing to be doing. But if you do this, leave out the parsley, or people may not know the expensive little tuber is there.

Sarladaise Potatoes
POMMES SARLADAISES

Serves 4–6

3 lb. 5 oz. firm, waxy potatoes, peeled

¼ cup goose or duck fat or butter

1 tbsp. olive oil

3 large cloves garlic, finely chopped

3 tbsp. Italian parsley, finely chopped

sea salt and freshly ground black pepper

Slice the potatoes thinly (approximately ⅛ inch thick) on a mandolin, or with the slicing blade of a food processor, then pat them dry with a cloth.

In a large skillet, heat 3 tablespoons of goose fat, duck fat, or butter, and the olive oil until it is just starting to smoke. Add the potatoes, season them generously with salt and pepper, and begin to brown them. Cook until the bottom layer is golden, then turn the potatoes over gently with a wooden spatula and brown another layer. (Avoid breaking the potatoes up; they should stay in slices as much as possible.) Continue doing this for approximately 15 minutes, by which time about half of the potatoes should be golden brown.

Turn the heat down, cover with a lid, and cook gently for 10 minutes. Then sprinkle with the garlic and parsley and continue cooking, covered, for another 10 minutes or until the potatoes are evenly cooked and tender.

Lastly, turn up the heat again and add the remaining tablespoon of goose fat, duck fat, or butter. Cook until the underside is crisp and golden brown; the inside of the potatoes should be almost caramelized and like jam, the bottom a crunchy crust.

In the rose-red city of Toulouse, it is exciting to find tender green beans smaller and thinner than fork prongs. This recipe works well with any small, fresh, French, or green beans; they become both crisp and succulent at the same time.

Extra-Fine Green Beans from Toulouse
HARICOT VERTS EXTRA-FIN DE TOULOUSE

Serves 4

9 oz. small, thin, green beans (*haricots verts*), trimmed

¼ cup butter

1 shallot, finely chopped

1 large clove garlic, finely chopped

1 tbsp. parsley, finely chopped

1 tbsp. all-purpose flour

¾ cup chicken stock

1 free-range egg yolk

2 tsp. white wine vinegar (you can also use tarragon vinegar)

sea salt and freshly ground black pepper

Bring a pan of lightly salted water to a boil and blanch the beans for about 1–2 minutes, according to their size. Drain thoroughly.

Heat the butter in a large skillet and sauté the beans over medium heat, together with the shallot, garlic, and parsley. Cook gently without browning for 5 minutes, then stir in the flour and cook for an additional 2 minutes. Pour in the stock and simmer gently for 5–10 minutes, depending on the size of the beans (they should retain some firmness). Season with salt and black pepper.

Meanwhile, mix the egg yolk and the vinegar together in a small bowl. Take the beans off the heat, and stir a tablespoon of the hot bean cooking liquid into the egg and vinegar mixture, then return the mixture to the beans and shake it to make a little sauce.

Serve very hot with roast chicken, roast lamb, beef, or ham.

People tend to think Bordelaise means cooked in red wine, but this is often not the case; in this recipe garlic and parsley are the main ingredients. The attraction of this dish is the slippery smoothness of the caps of the ceps and the sweet nuttiness of the chopped stalks. If the ceps are too moist, broil the caps gently to extract some of the moisture before sautéing them.

Ceps Cooked in a Bordelaise Way
CÈPES À LA BORDELAISE Ⓥ

Serves 4

12 small or 8 large ceps

4 cloves garlic

a large handful of Italian parsley

2–3 tbsp. olive oil

sea salt and freshly ground black pepper

Take the ceps and separate the caps from the stalks. Wipe the caps carefully and if the spongy part underneath seems slimy, remove it. Peel or scrape the stalks with a small knife to remove the dirt.

Place the stalks on a large chopping board with the garlic and parsley, and make a hachis (see p. 281) by chopping everything fairly coarsely.

Heat 2 tablespoons of olive oil in a large skillet and brown the caps on both sides until they are golden. Season judiciously with salt and black pepper, then throw in the hachis and cook briskly for 4–5 minutes, adding another tablespoon of olive oil if necessary.

This is an overwhelmingly rich and exquisite way to cook precious chanterelles. It comes from the Cantal mountains, where it is traditionally made with the local mountain cheese. However, any mountain cheese, such as unpasteurized Gruyère or tome de vache of any sort, would be almost as good.

Chanterelles with Melted Cheese
CHANTERELLES POÊLÉES AU CANTAL

Serves 4

9 oz. chanterelles

2 tbsp. goose fat or butter

³/₄ cup lardons, cut from *poitrine fumée* or pancetta

1 shallot, finely chopped

2 tbsp. crème fraîche

1 cup Cantal or other mountain cheese, cut into thin flakes

3 tbsp. parsley, finely chopped

sea salt and freshly ground black pepper

Clean the mushrooms carefully, without soaking them; a quick rinse in a sieve is enough and the rest can be done with a small knife.

Heat the goose fat or butter in a pan and cook the lardons until lightly browned, then remove them from the pan and set aside. In the same pan, cook the shallot and mushrooms for 10 minutes or until any liquid that has been released has evaporated.

Return the lardons to the pan and add the crème fraîche. Season well with pepper but add very little salt; the lardons are salty and so is the cheese. Cover the pan and cook gently for 5 minutes.

Take the pan off the heat and stir in the flakes of cheese. Replace the lid and let the cheese melt. Sprinkle generously with parsley and serve hot.

I ate a wonderful dish called étuvée de légumes oubliées *in Aix-en-Provence. It was winter, and Jean-Marc Banzo, cooking at Le Clos de la Violette, had produced an eclectic selection of vegetables to serve with a wonderful dish of raviolis stuffed with* pieds de veau. *His "forgotten vegetables" included salsify and cardoons, which add yet more to what a friend describes as a jewel box of a dish; Banzo served his with* trompettes de mort *mushrooms. The black fungi look wonderful with the white and gold vegetables, but brown or yellow chanterelles are also excellent with this dish. Or, leave out the mushrooms and serve the sautéed leaves of the turnips instead. These vegetables are perfect with roast partridge (see p. 169).*

Roasted Forgotten Vegetables
LÉGUMES OUBLIÉES Ⓥ

Serves 4

8 Jerusalem artichokes, peeled

3 parsnips, peeled

1 small kohlrabi, peeled

12 baby turnips, peeled

12 precooked chestnuts, vacuum-packed or fresh, boiled and peeled

8 fat cloves garlic, peeled

12 small shallots or baby onions, peeled

¼ cup butter or goose fat

3 tbsp. olive oil

sea salt and freshly ground black pepper

1 tbsp. butter; 4 oz. trompettes de mort or brown or yellow chanterelles, carefully trimmed; and sea salt and freshly ground black pepper, to serve

Preheat the oven to 375°F.

Cut the Jerusalem artichokes, parsnips, kohlrabi, and turnips into chunks so that they are a little larger than the size of the chestnuts, about 1 inch square.

Bring a large pan of salted water to a boil and blanch all these vegetables, together with the chestnuts, garlic, and shallots, for 3 minutes from the time the water returns to a boil. Drain them well. (But note that if you have chestnuts that have already been cooked, do not blanch them, just roast for 30 minutes.)

Meanwhile, put the butter or goose fat, and the oil in a roasting pan and heat in the oven for a few minutes. Add the blanched vegetables, season with salt and black pepper, then stir them around to get a good coating of the hot fat. Roast for 1 hour, turning them over gently from time to time.

When the vegetables are almost ready, heat 1 tablespoon of butter in a skillet and gently cook the mushrooms. Season them carefully.

Remove the roasted vegetables from the pan with a slotted spoon and transfer them to a warmed dish. Serve the mushrooms sprinkled over the vegetables.

Alternatives

Celeriac and sweet potatoes can also be used in this dish. If you have the young leaves of the turnips, you can serve these with the roasted vegetables instead of the mushrooms. Wash them, and while they are still wet, cook them in 1 tablespoon of olive oil, together with a minced clove of garlic. Once the leaves have wilted, sprinkle them with 1 tablespoon of water and cook gently until the water has evaporated. Sprinkle the leaves over the roasted vegetables.

Breads

People may say that French baking is in decline, and succumbing to a modern inclination toward softness, which is the unfortunate result of fast, modern baking methods (think of the steam-baked loaf and the burger bun made in the shape of a baguette). But most French villages larger than a hamlet will have at least one baker with a deep-rooted knowledge of traditional baking, who will still offer a range of hand-made breads, proved, as always, on ridged cloths or in baskets lined with canvas, and often cooked in wood-fired ovens, whose smoke pervades the streets outside. As well as traditonal French sticks, *baguettes de tradition*, *bâtards*, *flutes*, *ficelles*, and *Parisiens*, which have to be eaten fresh and do not last a day, there may be enormous round loaves of long-keeping *pain de levain*,

sourdough bread, with the holey, chewy, and satisfying interior and thick, almost caramel-flavored crust. Then there are the *fougasses*, some made with pork fat, walnut oil, or olive oil and slashed into palm-leaf shapes, the twists of sugary, deep-fried pastry called *oreilles* because they resemble pigs' ears, seductive twisted loaves, and soft, cylindrical *pain de mie*. On market stalls today there are also hefty whole-wheat loaves, *pain complet*, and rye loaves, *pain de seigle*, big, rustic, long-fermented loaves made with a mixture of rye and wheat flours, called *pain de campagne* or *campaillou*, and little loaves baked with nuts or raisins for eating with cheese.

Some enriched breads, such as *coques* and fougasses, sweetened and flavored with aniseed, lemon, and orange flower water or crystallized fruit, or with savory toppings (see p. 246) are still made to celebrate saints' days. Those from Beziers, which are eaten on the birthday of the town's patron saint, Saint Aphrodise, and sold in batches of six, are oval, while the Christmas *fougasses* of Aigues-Mortes are square-shaped. *Pompe à l'huile*, which, literally translated, means "oil pump," bread with walnut oil (see p. 244), and *brioche anisée*, aniseed-flavored brioche (see p. 247), can also be eaten at Christmas.

So although in restaurants the bread may often be disappointing, the skills for making a decent loaf are still alive in the Midi, and I would say, particularly in the Lot and the Dordogne, where a loaf is really a loaf and can be too big to go comfortably under the arm or in a bicycle basket, the two traditional places for carrying bread.

This is not a pizza, but a Niçoise dish that combines fantastic quantities of onions, melted to a succulent, sticky jam, with anchovies and black olives on a bread dough or pastry base. Make it as large as possible. In the past, the dough was spread with a paste made with salted and sun-fermented tiny fish, such as sardines and anchovies. This was called pissalat, *hence the name* pissaladière.

Onion Tart with Anchovies and Black Olives
PISSALADIÈRE

Makes a 13-inch square pissaladière

For the topping:

¼ cup olive oil

2¼ lb. onions, peeled and thinly sliced

4 large cloves garlic, unpeeled

1 tsp. dried marjoram or thyme

a few sprigs of fresh thyme

18 black olives

18 anchovy fillets

sea salt and freshly ground black pepper

For the dough:

3¼ cups all-purpose flour, plus extra for kneading

2 tsp. active dry yeast

1 tsp. salt

1 tsp. superfine sugar

3 tbsp. olive oil

1¼–1½ cups warm water

1 cookie sheet measuring at least 12 x 12 in.

olive oil, for greasing

For the topping, heat the olive oil in a large, heavy casserole and put in the onions, garlic, and dried marjoram or thyme. Season with a little salt and plenty of black pepper, then cover and cook over a moderate heat for one hour, stirring from time to time. Then remove and reserve the cloves of garlic and allow the onions to cool.

In a large bowl, mix together the flour, yeast, salt, and sugar. Stir in the olive oil and enough of the warm water to form a soft, almost sticky dough. Gather the dough up with your hands, form it into a ball, then knead on a floured surface for 10 minutes or until smooth and elastic. Pour a teaspoon of olive oil into a large bowl, shape the dough into a ball again, and roll it around the bowl to get a good coating of oil. Cover the bowl with plastic wrap and leave the dough to rise in a warm place for one hour or until it has doubled in size.

Preheat the oven to 400°F.

When the dough is ready, punch it down. With a floured rolling pin, roll the dough out into a 12-inch square. Place this on a lightly greased cookie sheet and prick all over with a fork. Pile on the onions and spread them out evenly, almost to the edge of the dough. Sprinkle with the fresh thyme leaves, stick the unpeeled cloves of garlic in here and there, then decorate the top with olives and anchovies.

Leave to prove (rise for a second time) for 15 minutes, then bake in the preheated oven for 20–25 minutes. The crust should be golden brown and the underside of the pissaladière cooked through. Serve cut into squares; it is nicest hot or warm, and reheats well.

This is an excellent bread from the Lot, whose name means "oil pump." It is rich, with a flaky crust the color of toasted hazelnuts, and it belongs to the same family as fougasse. All over the Midi, these rich breads were baked for fête days, weddings, and funerals. They varied enormously from village to village; round or oval, oblong or crown-shaped, sweet or salty, sometimes with grattons (bits of crispy fat), sometimes with crystallized citrus peel and orange-flower water. The dough could be made with pork fat, eggs, and butter, and as rich as croissant dough. This fine version uses walnut oil. It keeps well and is good toasted for breakfast.

Walnut Oil Bread
POMPE À L'HUILE Ⓥ

Makes 1 loaf

1¾ cups strong bread flour, plus extra for kneading

1 tsp. active dry yeast

1 tsp. salt

¾ cup warm water

1 tbsp. walnut oil, plus extra for drizzling

¼ cup unsalted butter, softened

Mix the flour, yeast, and salt together in a large bowl. Stir in the water and the tablespoon of walnut oil, then gather up the dough with floured hands, forming it into a ball. Knead the dough on a well-floured board for 10 minutes. At first it will be sticky and must be sprinkled fairly often with a little flour, but it will soon turn smooth, silky, and elastic.

Roll the dough into a ball, coat it with a little walnut oil, and place it in a clean, lightly oiled bowl. Cover the bowl with plastic wrap, then leave in a warm place to rise for an hour or until doubled in size.

Punch the dough down and roll it out into a ½-inch-thick rectangle. Spread the butter over the dough with the palm of your hand, leaving a ¾-inch margin around the edge. Fold the rectangle into three and give it a half turn (180 degrees), then do another roll and fold. Return the dough to the greased bowl, cover, and allow to rise for an additional hour or until doubled in size.

Again, punch the dough down and do another roll and fold as before, then roll the dough out into a rectangle measuring 12 x 6 inches. Lightly grease a long cookie sheet and place the dough on it. Cover and leave to rest for an hour.

Preheat the oven to 375°F.

Prick the dough all over with a fork and bake for approximately 30 minutes. The bread is ready if it sounds hollow when tapped on the bottom. Place on a cooling rack and drizzle the top with 1–2 teaspoons of walnut oil. It can be eaten warm or cold.

Based on a recipe for traditional bread, sold in bakers' shops and street markets as Coque Catalane, *this is a rustic, oval brioche baked either as a loaf or as flat rolls, with a variety of toppings. A light bread, best eaten hot, it makes the perfect start to a meal, served with soup, or on its own, or a good snack any time. For anyone who has ever made bread, the basic brioche is incredibly easy and quick to make, and versatile; use it to improvise any amount of different breads. It keeps extremely well for three days, and reheats perfectly. There are a range of extra ingredients and flavorings that can be added, as shown in the following recipes.*

Hot Red-and-Green Cheese Brioche
COQUE DE FROMAGE AUX POIVRONS ⓥ

Serves 6

For the dough:

3 cups strong bread flour, plus extra for kneading

2 tsp. active dry yeast

1½ tsp. salt

6 tbsp. unsalted butter, softened

3 large eggs, lightly beaten

⅓ cup plus 1 tbsp. warm water

For the topping:

2 peppers, preferably 1 red bell and 1 pale yellow-green pepper, roasted, peeled, and cut into thin strips (see p. 64)

8 chili-flavored black olives, halved

1½ cups melting cheese, such as Raclette, Cantal, or Fontina, coarsely grated

oil, for the cookie sheets

To make the brioche, put all the dough ingredients into a food processor and process briefly, until they form a mass. Remove the dough and knead for 10 minutes, using extra flour if necessary to prevent it from getting too sticky. Alternatively, put everything into an electric mixer fitted with a dough hook for 15 minutes, or mix and knead by hand.

Once the dough is smooth and silky, roll it into a ball and place in a lightly oiled bowl. Cover and allow to rest until the dough has doubled in size. Punch it down, form into two small oval, flat loaves, about 1¼ inches deep (the loaves will rise to about 2 inches deep), and place on two oiled cookie sheets.

Lightly dry the strips of pepper with paper towels, then place them on top of the loaves, together with the olives and the grated cheese. Allow to rise, covered, in a warm place until thick and puffy. Preheat the oven to 375°F.

Bake in the preheated oven for 20 minutes, then cover loosely with foil to prevent the cheese from overcooking. Continue baking for an additional 5–10 minutes or until the brioche sounds hollow when tapped on the bottom, then transfer to a cooling rack. Serve warm. Wrap in foil to reheat.

Alternatives

For Anchovy and Pepper Brioche, after shaping the brioche, cover the top with 2 bell peppers, roasted, peeled, and cut or torn into pieces (see p. 64); 20 anchovy fillets; and 8 black olives cut into pieces. Sprinkle with a little fresh thyme and olive oil, and continue as before.

For Country Brioche with Toulouse Sausage, skin a 100 percent pure pork Toulouse sausage and cook it in a little olive oil, breaking it up into lumps with a fork. Drain on paper towels, then sprinkle over the shaped brioche prior to rising, and continue as before. This is irresistible.

This brioche loaf is perfect for breakfast. In the Aude, it is eaten at the Feast of Saint Roch, an interesting character who was cured of the plague by his dog, who brought him a stealthily obtained loaf of moldy bread every day as he lay racked with fever. Roch survived to become a protector against all plagues and maladies. On August 16, these breads, made in a rectangular shape, are offered, sprinkled with holy water, to those who take mass, and are also eaten as a snack or dessert.

Sweet Aniseed Brioche
BRIOCHE ANISÉE ⓥ

Makes one loaf

For the dough:

3 cups strong bread flour, plus extra for kneading

2 tsp. active dry yeast

1 tsp. salt

¼ tsp. aniseed seeds

¼ cup superfine sugar

6 tbsp. unsalted butter, softened

3 large eggs, lightly beaten

⅓ cup plus 1 tbsp. warm water

For the top;

aniseed seeds

1 egg yolk (optional)

1 tbsp. milk or cream (optional)

2 tsp. turbinado sugar or crushed sugar cubes

oil, for the cookie sheet

Put all the dough ingredients into a food processor and process briefly, until they form a mass. Remove the dough and knead for 10 minutes, using extra flour if necessary to prevent it from getting too sticky. Alternatively, put everything into an electric mixer fitted with a dough hook and mix for 15 minutes, or mix and knead by hand.

Once the dough is smooth and silky, roll it into a ball and place in a lightly oiled bowl. Cover and allow to rest until the dough has doubled in size. Punch it down and form into a round loaf with a flattened top. Place on a lightly oiled cookie sheet, then sprinkle with a few more seeds of aniseed and roll these in with a rolling pin. Allow to rise in a warm place, covered, until it looks puffy and taut, approximately 30–60 minutes. Preheat the oven to 375°F.

Bake in the preheated oven for 15 minutes, then cover the top loosely with foil and reduce the oven temperature to 350°F. Bake for an additional 30 minutes or until the brioche sounds hollow when tapped on the bottom, then transfer to a cooling rack. Mix the egg yolk and the milk or cream together, and glaze the brioche while it is still hot. Finally, sprinkle with the sugar.

Note
For a festive loaf, double the quantities and shape the dough into a ring, or *couronne*, before letting it rise.

Fougasse is usually an enriched bread, but this version comes from the Languedoc and is made with flaky pastry. It has the intriguing Catalan mixture of sweet and salty flavors. It makes a good amuse bouche (canapé) with a glass of chilled wine.

Fougasse with Bacon
FOUGASSE DE LARDONS CATALANES

Serves 4–6

4 oz. *lard maigre*, bacon, or pancetta, cut into slices

7 oz. flaky or puff pastry

1 tsp. superfine sugar

finely grated zest of 1 lemon

oil, for the cookie sheet

Preheat the broiler to its highest setting.

Place the bacon slices on a wire rack and broil them until they are crisp and golden, but do not allow them to get too brown. Transfer them to a paper towel and allow to cool, then cut or break into small pieces.

Lightly grease a cookie sheet with a little oil. Roll the pastry out so that it is approximately ⅛ inch thick, then cut out an 8½-inch circle, using a plate as a template, and place it on the cookie sheet. Sprinkle the pieces of bacon evenly over the top and press them into the pastry with your fingertips. Chill in the refrigerator for 20 minutes.

Preheat the oven to 425°F.

Using a very sharp knife, divide the fougasse into twelve wedges, cutting through the bacon and the pastry. Mix the sugar and the lemon zest together, and sprinkle evenly over the fougasse.

Bake in the preheated oven for 15 minutes, or until the pastry is crisp. If necessary, loosely cover the fougasse with a sheet of aluminum foil after 10 minutes to prevent it from becoming too brown. Serve warm.

Desserts

From Bordeaux to Nice, each region still has its own special traditional treats in the way of candies, confectionery, and desserts. In St. Emilion, a noble little wine town east of Bordeaux, almond macaroons are a specialty, while the Landes provides pine nuts—the kernels of umbrella pines that grow so happily in the sandy soil—and these are used in the making of *pignola*—pine nut cakes. The celebration-loving French Basques serve the *gâteau Basque*, a sort of covered tart with a filling of cherries, prunes, or cream, and in Gascony the specialty is the *croustade* (see p. 272) or *tourtière*, another covered tart, this time skillfully made with veils of paper-thin, amber-colored pastry filled with apples. Another version, from Lot-et-Garonne, uses the same pastry, sprinkled between the layers with sugar and Armagnac.

In Perigord they favor greengage tart, *gâteau au noix*, tender walnut tart (see p. 268), various chestnut puddings and cakes, and a thick, set batter filled with cherries, called *clafoutis*, which can also be made with the sumptuous prunes from Agen.

Crème caramel, flan, crème brûlée, and other egg custards have crossed the Spanish border to the Pays Catalan, together with the elaborate nougats called *turon*, and brilliant green figs made with marzipan, while in Provence there are the *calaissons d'Aix*, soft little lozenges of paste of crystallized melon rinds, covered with icing, and *berlingots*, little boiled candies made from the sugar syrup left over from making crystallized fruits. As for the Mediterranean coast, as far as desserts are concerned, they tend to favor cheese and fresh fruit— eaten separately in the summer season of fruits such as strawberries, peaches, and apricots, or with the cheese in winter if it is apples or pears. They also like sorbets and ice creams in the heat of summer, particularly an orange or lemon, hollowed out and filled with the appropriate-flavored ice, or grand concoctions of locally made ice cream in every possible color and flavor, with fruit, nuts and cream, chocolate, and crystallized violets, all piled into a deep sundae glass.

As well as in cafés, ices are also sold in the many pâtisseries, still flourishing in the tradition of turning out exquisite pastries and desserts. On Sunday mornings, a family member will arrive at the shop, look in the window, ready to pick out his chosen tart or cake, which will be lovingly stowed in a pretty box on a scalloped mat or gilded cardboard plate. Swinging it by its dashing ribbon, he sets off for home with the feeling of doing something nice for everyone. The dessert is ready.

It is astonishing what a few spoonfuls of red wine can do to the flavor and color of raspberries. Floc de Gascogne is, in fact, a sweet wine fortified with Armagnac found in the Gers, which is superb with raspberries, strawberries, or ripe peaches, particularly vine-peaches, which are already a deep hollyhock pink. But, since it is difficult to find, red wine and sugar make a good substitute.

Raspberry Floc
FRAMBOISES AU FLOC Ⓥ

Serves 4–6

1 lb. 9 oz. ripe raspberries

½ cup superfine sugar

juice of 1 lemon

3 tbsp. red wine

1 tbsp. Armagnac (optional)

Put the raspberries in a bowl and sprinkle them with the sugar and lemon juice. Turn them very lightly for a moment, then leave them to steep in their own juices for an hour or more.

Sprinkle with the wine and Armagnac and chill for an hour or two, or leave overnight.

In Provence, I found all the fruit for this salad growing in the garden. If you can't find pomegranates, use small melons, halved, filled with blackberries, and topped with figs, opened out like a flower. Languedoc is the fig center, but Provence also grows wonderful figs—emerald, brown, violet, and black. For this salad, choose black figs that are soft when pressed and have a small split in them.

Salad of Figs, Blackberries, and Pomegranate
SALADE DE FIGUES, MÛRES ET GRENADINES Ⓥ

Serves 4

1 lb. 5 oz. sweet, ripe blackberries

juice of 2 limes, or 3 tbsp. sweet wine, such as Rivesaltes or Banyuls

4 tbsp. superfine sugar

4 ripe figs

1 pomegranate

Put the blackberries on four dessert plates and sprinkle with lime juice and sugar. Make crisscross incisions at the stalk ends of the figs, without cutting right through, so that you can open them like a four-petaled flower to reveal the beautiful interior. Place a fig in the middle of each plate.

Cut the pomegranate in half and remove the seeds, peeling off every scrap of yellow membrane, which is bitter. Sprinkle the ruby seeds on and around the figs, and chill.

Early autumn in Lot-et-Garonne is when people exchange their recipes for fig jam. This one was recommended by a friend. The fennel—a traditional flavoring for figs in the Southwest—gives it a rich, subtle taste, and the lemons add sharpness.

Green Fig Jam
CONFITURE DE FIGUES VERTES Ⓥ

Makes two 1-pound jars

2 small lemons

3¼ cups sugar

2 lb. soft but slightly underripe green figs, stalks removed, quartered

a pinch of fennel seeds

You will also need paper circles

Pare the zest from the lemons and cut it into tiny, thin shreds. Remove the pith from the lemons, segment them, and cut the flesh into small cubes.

Pour 1¾ cups of water into a large preserving pan, add the sugar, and let it dissolve over a low heat; do not allow the water to boil. When the sugar crystals have completely disappeared, add the quartered figs, the lemon flesh and zest, and the fennel seeds. Turn the heat up and bring to a boil, then simmer gently for approximately 1½ hours or until the jam reaches the light-set stage.

While the jam is cooking, put one or two small plates in the freezer to use for testing later on. Wash and oven-dry two 1-pound jars; the best are French with faceted sides and plastic lids. The old-fashioned covers, with paper held on by rubber bands, do not keep the jam airtight, so it eventually dries out.

To check if the jam is ready, put a teaspoon of it on a chilled plate. Leave for a moment or two to cool, then slowly push the jam with your finger. If the jam forms a skin that wrinkles when you push it, it is ready.

Pour into the clean, warm jars, cover with paper circles, allow to cool, and seal.

These Provençal meringues, from La Cuisinière Provençale *by J. B. Reboul, the nineteenth-century Provençal chef, are exquisite if made with good-quality pine nuts (*pignons*). These seeds of the umbrella or stone pine, that quintessential coastal tree, fall to the ground in summer. Fresh and creamy in texture when young, they dry, darken, and harden with age, eventually becoming rancid unless kept in the refrigerator. Pignons are encased in a hard, beige shell covered with patches of blackish, sooty powder. Once shelled, they are used as an alternative to almonds in the hard, long-keeping round or oval cookies that are so good with sweet wine, and which can be found on the markets of the Midi. In this much lighter and more luxurious recipe, there is some strange alchemy between the meringue mixture and the pine nuts, so that they end up almost roasted and covered in a thin coat of crisp sugar inside the meringue. Dark blueberries,* myrtilles, *look enticing with the white meringue.*

Pine Nut Meringues with Cream and Blueberries
MERINGUES AUX PIGNONS ET AUX MYRTILLES Ⓥ

Serves 4–6

For the meringues:

3 egg whites

1 cup superfine sugar

³/₄ cup pine nuts

oil for greasing, and wax paper

1¼ cups whipping or heavy cream (*crème fleurette*); 2 tbsp. confectioner's sugar, sifted; and 1⅓ cups blueberries, to serve

Preheat the oven to 275°F. Lightly grease two cookie sheets and cover them with wax paper.

Whisk the egg whites to stiff peaks, then gradually whisk in the sugar, one third at a time. Continue until all the sugar is incorporated into the egg whites and the meringue is glossy and fairly stiff, holding soft peaks.

Using a large spoon, carefully fold the pine nuts into the meringue. Spoon heaping tablespoons of the meringue onto the baking trays, spaced apart. The mixture should make approximately twelve meringues. Bake for an hour, then turn off the oven and leave the meringues there until the oven is cool.

Lightly whip the cream and mix in the confectioners' sugar. Serve the meringues with the sweetened cream and the blueberries.

Note

You can, if you prefer, make one large round meringue, in a nest shape, and serve it covered with blueberries and whipped cream (see recipe for *Marrons Mont Blanc*, p. 261). It is much messier to serve, but it looks and tastes glorious.

Some Provençal bakers make giant meringues, almost the size of a football, and bake them with pine nuts sprinkled over the top for decoration.

This pudding, popular in the chestnut-growing areas of the Dordogne and the Lot, is meant to look like Mont Blanc covered in snow, but it is much easier to serve if it is not precipitously steep. You will need a large, flat, round plate or board to serve it on. In the Lot-et-Garonne, they drink bourru—*freshly pressed, fizzing golden grape juice*—*with chestnuts.*

Meringue with Chestnut Puree and Whipped Cream
MARRONS MONT BLANC Ⓥ

Serves 6–8

For the meringue:

half a lemon

6 egg whites

1³/₄ cups superfine sugar

oil for greasing, and wax paper

For the filling:

one 1-lb. can sweetened chestnut puree

1 tbsp. superfine sugar

2 cups crème fraîche (low-fat is good for this)

2 tsp. lemon juice or Armagnac

one 1-lb. can whole chestnuts, drained

³/₄ cup pitted, semidried prunes (optional)

Armagnac (optional)

For the chestnut puree:

12 oz. fresh chestnuts, peeled and sliced finely

1¹/₂ cups milk

3 tsp. superfine sugar

2 tbsp. unsalted butter

Preheat the oven to 300°F. Cover a lightly oiled cookie sheet with wax paper.

Rub a large bowl with the cut side of half a lemon to remove any grease, then add the egg whites and whisk them to stiff peaks. Whisk in the sugar, one third at a time, and continue until the mixture is stiff again.

Spread the meringue into a large circle (approximately 10 inches across) on the wax paper, hollowing out the center a little to make a nest shape. Put into the oven, turn down the heat to 275°F, and bake for an hour. Turn off the oven and leave the meringue inside to cool, preferably overnight.

Make the chestnut puree. Put the chestnuts into a small pan with the milk and simmer until they are soft and the milk has reduced considerably. While the chestnuts are still hot, stir in the sugar and butter, and allow them to dissolve. Finally, puree the chestnuts in a *moulin légumes* (food mill) or food processor.

Put the chestnut puree into a bowl and stir in the tablespoon of sugar and 2 tablespoons of the crème fraîche. Add the lemon juice and stir in all of the whole chestnuts.

When you are more or less ready to serve the Mont Blanc, or up to an hour in advance, transfer the meringue carefully to a flat dish, pile the chestnut puree into the middle of it, and spoon the crème fraîche over the top. Decorate with the prunes, sprinkled lightly with Armagnac, if you wish, chill and serve.

Peeling chestnuts—the Bordeaux method

Make a cut around chestnuts a few days old (they are more difficult to peel if they are perfectly fresh or if they are dried out). This cut should be fairly deep, about ¹/₄ inch, and all the way around the circumference of the nuts. Bring a pan of water to a boil, drop in the chestnuts, let them cook until the upper and lower halves of the shells are separating and you can see the white of the nut showing; fish them out with a slotted spoon and press and roll them in a cloth, one at a time, which should remove the skins and shells all in one go. Some nuts have to be peeled by hand, which I do with a knife, as it is quicker.

I was delighted to find this version of bread-and-butter pudding in Languedoc, where desserts are few. Instead, people tend to eat cakes and cookies, often with one of the golden dessert wines for which this region is well known, such as Banyuls, Rivesaltes, Muscat de Rivesaltes, or Maury. However, proximity to the land of flan means the frequent appearance of crème caramel and other egg custard–based puddings, of which this is a good example. It comes from L'inventaire du Patrimoine Culinaire de la France, *a useful sourcebook on the Languedoc published by Editions Albin Michel.*

Bread-and-Butter Pudding from the Languedoc
COUPETADE Ⓥ

Serves 4

6 slices of stale white bread, approximately ¹/₂ in. thick, with crusts removed

3 cups milk

1 vanilla bean, cut in half lengthwise

1³/₄ cups confectioners' sugar

6 medium eggs

12 pitted, ready-soaked prunes

³/₄ cup seedless raisins

Soak the slices of bread in ³/₄ cup of the milk for an hour. At the same time, put the vanilla bean and its seeds in a saucepan, pour over the remainder of the milk, and leave to infuse for an hour.

Preheat the oven to 325°F and prepare a hot *bain marie* by placing a baking or roasting pan half-filled with water in the oven to warm.

Put the sugar into a large bowl, add the eggs, and lightly beat together. Bring the milk and the vanilla bean to boiling point, then remove them from the heat and allow to cool slightly. Slowly, in a steady stream, pour the milk onto the egg mixture, stirring as you do so. Remove the vanilla bean.

Quarter the soaked slices of bread and place them in a large terrine or baking or pudding dish (7-cup capacity). Arrange the prunes and raisins on top, then pour over the egg mixture.

Place the dish in the hot bain marie; the water should come halfway up the side of the dish. Bake in the preheated oven for 1¹/₄–1¹/₂ hours or until the center of the pudding has just set. (The pudding will take less time if you are using a terrine.) Serve warm.

Jars of Armagnac-saturated prunes are a great temptation in the kitchen cupboard before Christmas, particularly if made with the new season's pruneaux d'Agen, rich, fat, and juicy, with a complex plum-pit flavor. In the autumn, you can buy these along the roadsides and in the markets of the Gers and the Lot-et-Garonne. Eat prunes in Armagnac at the end of a meal, instead of dessert, and spoon some of their liquid over them, or use them to make ice cream (see p. 267).

Prunes in Armagnac
PRUNEAUX À L'ARMAGNAC Ⓥ

Makes 2 jars

¼ cup soft brown sugar

1¼ cups hot, weak tea

1½ cups Agen prunes or large, good-quality dried prunes

1¼ cups Armagnac

two 1-lb. airtight jars, cleaned thoroughly

Dissolve the sugar in the weak tea and allow to cool. Once cooled, pour it over the prunes and leave them to soak overnight.

Pour the prunes into a sieve, placed over a bowl, and drain thoroughly. Pour the liquid into a saucepan and boil on a fairly low heat until it turns syrupy. This will take approximately 5–8 minutes and you should end up with about 4 tablespoons of syrup. Allow the syrup to cool.

Divide the prunes and their syrup between the two clean jars. Pour in the Armagnac, dividing it equally between the jars. Seal the prunes and store them in a cool place, turning a few times during the first two weeks. Keep for at least a month before eating.

Prune ice cream is a specialty of the Lot-et-Garonne, whose plum orchards are so ravishing in the spring. This is an opportunity to use the prunes in Armagnac (see p. 264), together with one of the special honeys found in the Midi, such as lavender honey from Provence, acacia honey from the Midi-Pyrénées, or chestnut honey, dark and strong, from the Languedoc. You can replace the prunes with large Malaga raisins, pitted and then soaked in the same way.

Honey Ice Cream with Prunes
GLACE DE MIEL AUX PRUNEAUX ⓥ

Serves 6

1⅓ cups pitted, semidried prunes (vacuum-packed if possible)

6 tbsp. Armagnac or Cognac

2½ cups milk, or a mixture of heavy cream and milk

2 tbsp. confectioners' sugar

4 egg yolks

⅓ cup liquid flower honey such as lavender, acacia, or chestnut

Soak the prunes in the Armagnac or Cognac overnight, stirring them around occasionally. Drain thoroughly and cut them into small pieces.

Put the milk into the top half of a double boiler. Stir in the sugar, bring to a boil, and remove from the heat. Let it cool a little before adding the egg yolks, stirring them in completely.

Return the mixture to the double boiler, over a very low heat, and keep stirring until you have a custard that coats the back of a wooden spoon. People with strong arms can do this custard-making directly over the heat, without the double boiler, but it can go wrong. Pour the custard through a sieve into a bowl, and allow it to cool.

Once cool, stir in the prunes and the honey, then churn in an ice cream maker and freeze. If you do not have an ice cream maker, pour the mixture into a shallow plastic container and half-freeze it. Remove from the freezer, transfer to a bowl, and whisk until the ice crystals are completely broken up. Pour back into the container and refreeze.

In the Lot-et-Garonne, although the pâtisseries are top quality, it is considered the height of hospitality to offer a homemade tart or cake, and this is one of the favorites. Fresh walnuts in damp, cool shells are best for this. Crack them and shell them if you can bear it. If not, store-bought walnut halves will do quite well, and you will still end up with a tart that is succulent and crisp at the same time, with a honeyed flavor.

Tender Walnut Tart
TARTE AUX NOIX Ⓥ

Serves 6

For the pastry:

1¼ cups all-purpose flour, plus extra for rolling

¼ cup superfine sugar

2 tbsp. ground walnuts

½ cup (1 stick) unsalted butter, cut into small pieces and softened to room temperature

½ tsp. vanilla sugar, or a few drops of vanilla extract

2 tbsp. lightly beaten egg

For the filling:

½ cup superfine sugar

2 eggs, separated

1 tbsp. Armagnac

2 tbsp. butter, melted

1⅓ cups walnut halves, 6 kept for decoration, the rest coarsely chopped

1 tbsp. heavy cream

2 tsp. lemon juice

For the pastry, place the flour, sugar, ground walnuts, and butter in a food processor and blend for 20 seconds. Add the vanilla sugar or extract and the beaten egg, then blend for an additional 20 seconds or until the ingredients begin to form a mass. Transfer to a lightly floured work surface and gently bring the pastry together with your hands, kneading lightly for a few moments to get the dough smooth. Gently flatten the pastry into a circle, cover with plastic wrap, and chill for 1 hour.

Line the base of a metal tart pan with a circle of wax paper. The pan should measure 9½ inches across by ¾ inch deep, and preferably have a loose bottom.

Dust a work surface and a rolling pin with flour, then carefully roll the pastry out; it is quite sticky so the work surface needs to be kept well-floured. If the pastry does stick, loosen it with a palette knife. Line the tart pan with the pastry and neaten the edges. If the pastry breaks in places, just press it together with your fingers. Chill in the refrigerator for an additional 30 minutes.

Preheat the oven to 375°F.

Prick the pastry base with a fork and line with wax paper and baking beans or pie weights. Bake in the preheated oven for 15 minutes, remove the paper and baking beans, and bake for an additional 5 minutes. Take the pastry case out of the oven and increase the oven temperature to 400°F.

While the pastry case is baking, prepare the filling. With an electric beater, beat together the sugar and the egg yolks until they are pale and creamy. Add the Armagnac and continue beating for 3 minutes. Next, with a large metal spoon, carefully fold in the melted butter, the chopped walnuts, the cream, and the lemon juice.

Lastly, whisk the egg whites to a soft peak and gently fold them into the walnut mixture. Carefully pour the filling into the pastry case and decorate with the six walnut halves. Bake in the preheated oven for 15 minutes, until pale golden and set.

This stunning covered tart is one of a family of sweet, scented breads, cakes, and tarts eaten around Christmas Eve in Provence, often as one of the Treize Desserts. These thirteen desserts are not complicated but may include: dried fruit and nuts of all kinds; dates; crystallized apricots; black nougat; golden raisins; almonds; quince paste; the special almond-shaped petits fours from Arles called calaissons, *made with peach kernels and crystallized melon;* marrons glacé; and pompe a l'huile *(walnut oil bread, see p. 244). Glacé fruits are also often one of the thirteen desserts. These jewel-like crystallized fruits, a local specialty, shine from Christmas windows and are a glory, especially when they include whole pineapples or whole melons like huge pieces of carved amber.*

Orange and Almond Tart
TARTE DE NÖEL Ⓥ

Serves 8

For the filling:

½ cup (1 stick) unsalted butter, softened

⅔ cup superfine sugar

4 free-range egg yolks

2¼ cups ground almonds

⅓ cup heavy cream, lightly whipped

2 tsp. Cointreau

finely grated zest of 1 orange

juice of half an orange, approximately ¼ cup

1 tsp. lemon juice

For the tart:

1 lb. 2 oz. flaky or puff pastry

1 egg

1 tbsp. milk

First make the filling. Cream the butter and sugar together in a mixer or food processor until pale and creamy. Gradually beat in the egg yolks, mixing thoroughly between each addition. Using a large spoon, fold in the ground almonds, cream, Cointreau, orange zest and juice, and lemon juice.

Divide the pastry into two and roll each piece out. Cut out two rounds, one measuring 11 inches across, and the other 12 inches across. Place the smaller round on a lightly greased cookie sheet—I use a large pizza pan. Carefully spread the almond mixture over the center of the pastry, in a layer approximately ¾ inch deep, leaving a margin of 1 inch around the edge. Brush the margin lightly with water, then place the second round of pastry accurately on top. Press the edges very carefully to seal them all the way around, removing any air pockets as you do so. Neaten the edges, then chill the tart in the refrigerator for 30 minutes.

Preheat the oven to 400°F.

Mix together the egg and milk and brush this glaze over the top of the tart. Next, make a pattern by drawing parallel lines ¼ inch apart with a knife tip; draw quite firmly but do not pierce the pastry. Rotate the tart by sixty degrees and draw another set of lines so that you have a crisscross pattern.

Bake in the preheated oven for 10 minutes, then turn the temperature down to 375°F and bake for an additional 20–25 minutes. If necessary, loosely cover the tart with a piece of foil once it has turned a good golden color, to prevent it from becoming too brown. Serve hot or warm, with or without cream. This exquisite tart keeps for several days.

This is a Gascon apple pie, but the amazing crust is so unbelievably thin that they call it the "wedding veil." Originally it was rolled out by hand, but phyllo pastry makes a very good croustade *and is easy to use. This spectacular pie keeps well for a day, or even two, and can be reheated.*

Apple Pastis
CROUSTADE OR PASTIS GASCOGNE ⓥ

Serves 6–8

2¼ lb. Golden Delicious apples, peeled, quartered, cored, and thinly sliced

⅓ cup Armagnac

¼ cup unsalted butter, melted

9½ oz. packet of phyllo pastry, containing 6 sheets measuring 19¼ x 9½ in.

⅔ cup superfine sugar

1 tsp. vanilla sugar or a few drops of vanilla extract

finely grated zest of 1 lemon

Put the sliced apples in a bowl with the Armagnac, cover, and leave overnight in a cool place.

The following day, preheat the oven to 375°F. Prepare a metal tart pan, measuring 10 inches across and about 1¼ inches deep (preferably with a loose bottom), by brushing it with a little melted butter.

Brush one sheet of phyllo pastry with melted butter and place it across the base of the pan, draping the excess pastry over the sides. Sprinkle with half a teaspoon of sugar. Brush a second sheet of pastry with butter, place it at right angles to the first sheet, and sprinkle with sugar. Repeat the process with two more sheets of pastry, this time laying them across diagonally. You should end up with four buttered and sugared layers of pastry.

Drain the apples, but not too thoroughly, as the Armagnac flavor is so good, and mix them with the remaining sugar, the vanilla sugar or extract, and the lemon zest. Pile the apples into the tart pan and spread them out evenly. Cover with the remaining sheets of pastry, brushed with melted butter and sprinkled with sugar as before, and placed at right angles to each other.

Draw the overhanging ends of the pastry lightly over the top, arranging them so that they stick up as much as possible, like crumpled tissue paper. They should completely cover the top of the pie, forming a light and airy crust. Brush lightly with butter.

Bake in the preheated oven for 20 minutes, then cover loosely with a sheet of aluminum foil. Continue baking for an additional 20–25 minutes. Allow to cool slightly in the pan before transferring to a serving plate. If you feel nervous about this, serve it from the pan.

Although this is not a traditional Gascon cake, I have included it because their version has improved radically on the basic carrot cake by the inclusion of almonds.

Carrot and Almond Cake

GÂTEAU AUX CAROTTES ET AUX AMANDES Ⓥ

Serves 8

For the cake:

3 cups sliced almonds

3 medium eggs, separated

1¾ cups confectioners' sugar

juice and finely grated zest of an organic lemon

pinch of salt

10 oz. carrots, peeled and finely grated

½ cup self-rising flour, sifted

For the pan:

oil, superfine sugar, all-purpose flour, and wax paper

To decorate:

confectioners' sugar

You will need a cake pan measuring 9 inches across and about 2½ inches deep, preferably a springform pan. Lightly brush the pan with oil, then line the base with a circle of wax paper. Grease the paper lightly, then give the pan a dusting of superfine sugar, and then all-purpose flour. Turn the pan upside down and give it a sharp tap to remove any excess sugar and flour.

Preheat the oven to 375°F and preheat the broiler to its highest setting.

Put the sliced almonds in a food processor and grind them until they are the consistency of fine bread crumbs; some will be coarser than others and that will add a good texture to the cake.

Put half of them on a cookie sheet and toast them under the broiler to a pale brown color. Keep an eye on them and stir them around once or twice. Allow to cool.

Using an electric beater, beat together the egg yolks, sugar, lemon juice and zest, and salt. After 5–10 minutes, when the mixture is pale and mousselike, carefully fold in the carrots, flour, and all the almonds.

Whisk the egg whites until they form soft peaks and then gently fold them into the carrot and almond mixture.

Transfer the mixture to the prepared pan and bake in the preheated oven for 30–40 minutes or until the center of the cake is cooked. Test by inserting a knife into the middle of the cake; it should come out clean. Allow to cool for 5 minutes in the pan, then transfer to a cooling rack. Once cooled, dust the top with confectioners' sugar, shaken through a sieve.

Note

This is a very moist cake and can be served rather like a dessert, with crème fraîche or vanilla ice cream.

Sauces, Marinades, and Basic T

echniques

These recipes and techniques will help your cooking move south, to taste as if your food was grown and cooked under the sun. Do not look here for smooth, soothing sauces based on flour, butter, and cream—look, rather, for a jolt to the senses. Laden with garlic, strong flavors of vinegar and bitter fresh herbs, chilies, mustard, capers, and scallions, these are intense, oil-based sauces from the South of France. Strong, too, are the marinades with their high seasoning; think about cooking and eating out of doors, grilling over a barbecue or a wood fire, and think of quite primitive flavors.

The marinades are followed by a few basic methods of starting a great many dishes, and also of finishing them. These, again, help to move all dishes into the rougher, brighter zone of concentrated tastes and smells that is the Midi.

Sauces

This collection of sauces covers some of the essential and common ones that are regularly used in southern French cooking.

TOMATO SAUCE
La Sauce Tomate Ⓥ

A basic tomato sauce is useful in thousands of ways in the Provençal kitchen. This one is both simple and rich.

Serves 2–3
3 tbsp. olive oil
3 cloves garlic, peeled and lightly minced
2 lb. red, ripe tomatoes, peeled, seeded, and coarsely chopped, or use canned tomatoes, drained and lightly chopped
pinch of sugar
½ tsp. tomato paste (optional)
1 tbsp. fresh basil, shredded
sea salt and freshly ground black pepper

Heat the olive oil in a large skillet with the cloves of garlic. When the garlic cloves are golden brown, remove them and put in all the tomatoes. Season lightly with salt, black pepper, and sugar, then bring to a boil and simmer gently for about 40 minutes.

If you feel the sauce could do with a little more color or flavor, add ½ teaspoon of tomato paste. Sprinkle in the shredded basil, check the seasoning, and serve.

MIDI MAYONNAISE
Mayonnaise du Midi Ⓥ

This mayonnaise, which I first came across in the Lot, is quick to make. It takes three minutes. Note that it has no vinegar or lemon juice; it simply is not needed, and the mayonnaise tastes unusually fresh without strong acid notes. Because it is light in flavor and texture, it is the perfect companion to cooked spring vegetables, artichokes, fava beans, and, in particular, asparagus. Or eat it for a simple lunch with last night's roast chicken, or fish poached and cooled to room temperature, some small potatoes, boiled in their skins, cooled and served whole, and a herb-strewn salad.

Serves 4
1 heaping tsp. Dijon mustard
1 egg yolk
½ cup fresh sunflower oil
sea salt

Stir the mustard into the egg yolk, then whisk in the oil as usual, with a small whisk or a fork, but have no fear, the mustard helps to prevent the mayonnaise from splitting. Season with sea salt.

SOFT-BOILED EGG SAUCE
Sauce à l'Oeuf à la Coque Ⓥ

This cold, summery sauce is a beautiful compromise between hollandaise sauce and mayonnaise. The first time I made this was on a scorching August day in the Lot and I didn't want to go shopping, so I went out and picked any wild herbs I could find in the meadow outside. I found two kinds of mint, marjoram, fennel, and burnet, which gave it a fierce, harsh, aromatic flavor that was wonderful with the cold roast chicken I had prepared. It also goes well with warm or cold poached farm chicken, hard-boiled eggs, or a cool lobster or baked sea bass.

Serves 2
2 fresh free-range eggs
1 large or 2 small shallots, finely chopped
1 tbsp. white wine vinegar
¼ cup olive oil
1 heaping tbsp. fresh herbs (preferably wild), marjoram, mint, salad burnet, fennel, or 1 heaped tbsp. cultivated herbs, mint, chives, chervil, Italian parsley, dill

Boil the eggs for 4 minutes, cool a little, and cut the tops off as if you were eating a boiled egg. Spoon the yolks into a bowl, crush them finely with a fork, add the shallots, and gradually stir in the vinegar and olive oil. Lastly, add the herbs.

GAZTE GREEN SAUCE
Sauce Gazte Ⓥ

This excellent fresh-tasting sauce makes a fine change from mayonnaise, with fish. Serve cold with sea bass or John Dory, steamed or baked, and cooled to room temperature.

Serves 4–6
10½ oz. young spinach
2 handfuls sorrel, or more to taste
3 scallions, finely chopped
3 hard-boiled egg yolks
1 tsp. pale Dijon mustard
¼ cup olive oil
1 tbsp. white wine vinegar
sea salt and freshly ground black pepper

Wash the spinach and sorrel thoroughly, remove any coarse stalks, and chop roughly.

Bring 1¼ cups of water to a boil, then add some salt and drop in the spinach, sorrel, and scallions. After 5 minutes drain the vegetables, reserving their cooking liquid, and puree in a food processor.

Crush the egg yolks in a bowl with a stainless-steel fork. Stir in the mustard, then add the olive oil, drop by drop. Add the white wine vinegar, and the pureed spinach and sorrel, and enough cooking liquid to make a soft sauce. Season well.

VERJUICE
Verjus Ⓥ

Made from green, unripe grapes, this sour juice is between lemon juice and vinegar and can be used in salad dressings. First pick bunches of green grapes before they ripen, *avant la vernaison*. (A Martel cook told me they should be picked in June, but I made it in August with very small grapes, and it was a great success, having a much mellower flavor than either vinegar or lemon.)

Take the grapes off their bunches and throw away the stems. Weigh 2¼ pounds of grapes and liquidize them for a minute or so. A beautiful, deep green liquid emerges from the mush of skins and pale green seeds.

Strain this through a sieve to extract about 2 cups of green juice, or, better still, let it drip through a jelly-bag or cloth into a bowl. Decant the liquid into a jug and it will clear, leaving a sediment at the bottom. Pour it off, leaving the sediment behind, add a pinch of salt, stir to dissolve it, and transfer to a bottle with a lid. If possible, keep it in the refrigerator for a week before using it in cooking, or freeze.

AÏOLI Ⓥ

A mayonnaise-like emulsion of oil, raw garlic pounded to a paste, and usually egg yolks, although some purists make it without. Traditionally it is eaten in a Friday dish named *le grand aïoli*, with boiled snails, salt cod, boiled carrots, potatoes, green beans, and hard-boiled eggs or stirred into the broth of a fish or squid soup to make *bourride* (see p. 119). Small fried squid are exquisite eaten with this sauce, as are boiled chicken and young vegetables. Try it with just-cooked green or fava beans, artichokes, or aparagus.

Serves 4
2–3 large cloves garlic (or more, up to two heads of garlic)
2 egg yolks
1⅓ cups olive oil
a few drops lemon juice
sea salt

Crush the garlic to a fine pulp with a mortar and pestle, adding a little salt, then mix in the egg yolks. Gradually add the oil, a few drops at a time, working it in with the pestle or a whisk, as if you were making mayonnaise. When the aïoli becomes very thick, add half a teaspoon of hot water, then continue adding the oil, and continue adding a few drops of lemon juice and more oil, until it is all used up.

LA ROUILLE Ⓥ

Bright orangey-red *rouille* is one of the more potent sauces, being almost solid with raw garlic and hot peppers. It is eaten spread on pieces of fried or toasted baguettes, with fish soup and bouillabaisse, and is guaranteed to bring you out in a sweat, so is best eaten outdoors.

To make it, follow the recipe below, or pound together the peeled cloves from two heads of garlic and up to eight red chilies, seeds removed. Add 3 tablespoons of olive oil, and keep the fiery mixture in a jar in the refrigerator. Dilute it with chicken or fish stock, or mix it into mayonnaise.

Another way to make rouille is to make an aïoli and stir in a quantity of harissa, the hot paste used in couscous, which comes in small cans or in tubes.

Serves 4–6
3–4 cloves garlic, crushed
2 large, dried dark red Spanish chilies called *choriceros* (see p. 186), or other large, fairly hot, dried chilies, soaked until soft and scraped to obtain the pulp
1 small potato, boiled in its skin and peeled
2 egg yolks
1⅓ cups olive oil
sea salt

Pound the garlic and salt with a mortar and pestle, add the chili pulp and crushed potato and pound to a smooth paste. Stir in the egg yolks and then gradually add the oil, little by little, as if making a mayonnaise. It should be rather thick, but if it is too thick, add a teaspoon of fish stock from the bouillabaisse. Serve the sauce spread on diagonally cut rounds of toasted pain de campagne (country bread), floated on top of the bouillabaissse, or stir the rouille into the soup.

PISTOU Ⓥ

Unlike Italian pesto, Provençal pistou contains nothing but garlic, basil, and olive oil and perhaps raw chopped tomato— no pine nuts and no Parmesan cheese. However, it is often accompanied with grated Gruyère cheese served separately. It contains plenty of freshly pounded basil and is used to flavor a summer vegetable soup, well known in the Var, called *soupe au pistou* (see p. 99).

The simplest marinades

Familiar flavors of lamb, good-quality free-range chicken, young farm-reared rabbit, and top-quality beef can be extraordinarily heightened by wood-grilling. And one of the best ways to flavor meat for wood-grilling is simply to rub it with freshly minced cloves of garlic and sprinkle it with lemon juice or white wine, coarsely ground pepper, and perhaps robust herbs. Thyme, rosemary, marjoram, or *herbes de Provence* are classics, but fennel or crumbled bay leaves, *serpolet*, the wild thyme smelling of lemon, or *sariette*, which is winter savory, make good alternatives. Lastly, a moderate quantity of olive oil is sprinkled or massaged over the surface. This can be done an hour or so in advance. Salt is added just before the food goes onto the fire.

More complex marinades may be needed for dry, fatless meat like venison, wild squab, or some older game birds. These can be marinated overnight with red wine, vinegar, onions, and so forth, together with oil; the acid element breaks down fibers, while the oil prevents the food from drying out too quickly. Normally, though, food only benefits from a complex marinade if you feel it needs extra flavor.

There are plenty of bottled marinades around but it is far better to make your own. Here are some suggestions.

DRY, SPICED MARINADE FOR LAMB KABOBS
Marinade Séche Pour Brochettes d'Agneau

A dry marinade is a spiced version of a broiler marinade, similar to one enjoyed by the Moroccan and Algerian community in and around Arles. The meat, usually lamb, cut in pieces ready to make *brochettes* (kabobs), is marinated with a blend of chopped or ground onions, chopped Italian parsley or dried or fresh mint, or fresh cilantro, and cumin, paprika, and turmeric. After a couple of hours the flavors have penetrated the meat. It is then seasoned with salt and pepper, threaded on skewers, sprinkled lightly with olive oil, and grilled.

SIMON HOPKINSON'S MARINADE FOR FARMED RABBIT OR ORGANIC CHICKEN
Marinade Pour Lapin d'Elevage ou Poulet de Grain Biologique

We often grill rabbit for lunch, accompanying it with slices of grilled bread rubbed with fresh tomato, garlic, and olive oil, grilled eggplants, and a chilled local rosé wine.

Serves 4

For the marinade:
4–5 cloves garlic, coarsely chopped
1–2 glasses white or rosé wine
several handfuls of coarsely chopped herbs such as Italian parsley, rosemary, savory, tarragon, thyme, basil, sage, chives, sweet marjoram, and fennel
2–3 bay leaves, torn in pieces
2–3 tbsp. olive oil
sea salt and coarsely ground black pepper

You will also need 1 rabbit cut into 6–8 pieces (2 forelegs, 2 pieces saddle, and 2 hind legs, which can each be cut into two pieces).

Mix all the marinade ingredients in a bowl or gratin dish, put in the pieces of rabbit, and let them soak in the marinade overnight, or for up to 2 days, in the refrigerator. Drain the rabbit pieces for a few minutes before grilling them slowly on a rack, turning them from time to time. Baste them with the marinade as they cook, but let them become golden brown. Chopped chilies can be added to the marinade, and also lemon juice and zest.

ZIRIKO FOR WHOLE SHOULDERS OR LEGS OF LAMB
Ziriko

This method of cooking is especially for larger pieces of lamb cooked over a wood fire, and it comes from the Pays Basque. The idea is that you build a fire outdoors (preferably with oak, as it keeps the heat so well) on which to cook the meat. The lamb itself should either be a whole young lamb cut into quarters, or a shoulder of lamb; these pieces are threaded onto pointed sticks of boxwood, or onto large steel skewers which are then driven into the ground around the fire. During the cooking, the meat is basted with the following mixture, which must be made earlier, so that the flavors can blend together.

The *pili-pili* marinade:
2 cups water
2 cups vinegar
6 cloves garlic, finely chopped
3 red chilies, finely chopped
¼ cup olive oil
2 tbsp. salt

Turn the skewers around from time to time to keep the meat roasting evenly.

A few basic techniques

Here are some basic and necessary cooking techniques that are an essential feature of southern French cooking. They range from the basic techniques of making a fricassée, which is essential for some soups, to rendering pork fat, a vital flavoring for this region.

SOFRITO, SOFREGIT ⓥ

Since one of the most common acts, when starting to cook a dish, is to slice or chop an onion and then fry it, there are good reasons for having a name for the process. Each region has its own variation on the theme. In Languedoc, particularly toward the Spanish border, it is called the *sofrito*. This is onion, cooked very slowly in olive oil, to which tomato is usually added and reduced to the consistency of marmalade. It is used, like *picada* (see below), to flavor and thicken the sauce of many dishes. When eggplants and bell peppers are added, it is called a *samfaïna*.

Sofregit is the Catalan word for a mixture of onions, garlic, parsley, and perhaps bell peppers and tomatoes, cooked in oil, and used at the start of sautéed and braised dishes, particularly those that include tomatoes.

LE HACHIS

In other parts of the Midi, *le hachis* is the name given to the onion-softening process, and here the mix often includes other vegetables such as carrots and tomatoes, garlic, shallots, herbs, salt pork, bacon, or spices, all cooked or softened in olive oil, duck or goose fat, or *graisse de porc* (pork fat). The word *hachis* also implies chopped meat, herbs, and vegetables for stuffing. The following hachis can be used for any braised vegetable dish, or with rabbit, chicken, or veal.

2 carrots, sliced or chopped (optional)
1 large Spanish onion, chopped
2 cloves garlic, chopped
2 large ripe tomatoes, peeled, seeded, and chopped (optional)
1 tbsp. chopped parsley, stalks removed
1 tbsp. olive oil
salt and freshly ground pepper

You will also need a splash of white wine

Put everything on a board and chop finely or coarsely, whichever you prefer, with a large knife. Heat the olive oil in a casserole, put in the onions, season, and soften over a low heat. Add the remaining ingredients. Place the chosen vegetables or piece of meat on top, moisten with white wine, cover the pan, and cook very gently until done.

PERSILLADE

Persillade is simply chopped parsley or, more usually in the Midi, a mixture of chopped garlic and parsley. It is added to a dish, usually toward the end of cooking, to lift the flavor. It is used frequently with mushrooms, such as ceps, and with potatoes. It is also added to fried goose or duck confit, to cut the richness.

LA FRICASSÉE 1

A fricassée in the Dordogne freshens the flavor and thickens the texture of soups toward the end of their long simmering. When making vegetable or meat soup, cook one or more of the following chopped vegetables, either raw or lifted from the soup, in goose fat, and add back to the soup pot toward the end of the cooking: onions, scallions, sorrel, pumpkin, marrow, zucchini, ceps (fresh or dried and soaked), celeriac, leek, carrots, turnips, garlic, and parsley.

If you wish to thicken the soup, cook the vegetables until they are golden, in goose, duck, or pork fat and then stir in a tablespoon of all-purpose flour. Stir this around until it is lightly browned, then gradually stir in some bouillon from the soup; transfer this vegetable roux to the soup.

LA FRICASSÉE 2

Cook chopped onion, garlic, and lardons of *poitrine fumé* or pancetta in goose fat, or olive oil, and add to the soup toward the end of the cooking.

LA PICADA

Catalans prefer to thicken and flavor some dishes with a picada, a mixture of pounded pine nuts, almonds, or walnuts, garlic, bread—either fried, toasted, or plain—and *saindoux* (lard). This can be combined with tomatoes and used, for example, to make a sauce for poultry or small game such as partridges or rabbit. A special picada for a Christmas goose cooked with quinces contains pine nuts, almonds, cinnamon, and bitter chocolate, an almost Baroque combination.

TAPENADE

We have come to think of tapenade as a paste made of olives, but it seems that it was originally made by an establishment in Marseille, called La Maison Dorée, who named it after the Provençal word for caper, *tapeno*. In addition to capers, this strong-flavored paste contained pounded anchovies, marinated tuna fish, English mustard, and black olives, all mixed with olive oil. It was used, among other things, for stuffing eggs. Today, olives, usually black but sometimes green, predominate in tapenade, which is eaten on *pain grillé* (grilled bread) with drinks, or with crudités of raw young carrots, tomatoes, fennel, asparagus, celery, fava beans, and cooked baby beets, green beans, bell peppers—in fact any raw or cooked vegetable that can be dipped into the sauce.

TABBOULEH Ⓥ

Tabbouleh is a fresh, minty salad made with cracked wheat (or couscous in and around Nice). It originated in Syria and Lebanon. To make it, first prepare the cracked wheat by soaking it in water until just tender, then draining it well. Then mix with olive oil, chopped onion, plenty of coarsely chopped fresh mint and parsley, and, if you like, either chopped raw tomato or pieces of cucumber, or both. Season with salt and pepper, and lots of fresh lemon juice. Serve it on lettuce leaves.

POUDRE FRIANDE (POUDRO AGRELADO) Ⓥ

This mushroom powder can give an exquisite flavor to omelettes, scrambled eggs, and *civets* (stews). It can also be used with chicken and for sauces for fish.

To make it, take a quantity of dried mushrooms and pound them to a powder with a mortar and pestle. The nineteenth-century Provençal chef J. B. Reboul suggests a mixture of cultivated mushrooms, morels, *mousserons*, and if possible, the dried shavings of black truffles. The last can, of course, be left out, and the powder made with any mushrooms, provided they are completely dry.

CHAPONADE Ⓥ

These crusty, fragrant pieces of crisp, toasted bread are floated in bowls of soup to add crunch and flavor. In the Languedoc, the *chaponade* is also added to salads. Toast slices of bread—the best bread to use is pain de campagne (country bread) but baguettes are also good—in a warm oven. When they are crisp and dry all the way through, rub with garlic cloves and drizzle with a mixture of half walnut and olive oil or white wine vinegar.

LES ESCARGOTS

To cook snails you must first cleanse them as they may have eaten poisonous plants. To do this, hang them up in a cool place (such as a dark, airy basement) in a salad-shaker with a lid, or put them in a bucket with small holes in it, covered so they cannot escape, and let them fast for at least a week.

Then make a court-bouillon with thyme, basil, peppercorns, bay leaves, and perhaps a clove or two. Cook the snails in this for 30 minutes. Remove them and wipe the shells to cleanse them. Hook out the snails with a fork and remove the curly gut from the fleshy body. Boil the shells and then rinse them and dry them. Put the snails back into their shells—what a nuisance it all is, resolve to buy them ready-prepared next time!—then stuff in some snail butter made with chopped garlic and parsley, and perhaps some Bayonne or other uncooked ham. Lastly, put the snails into a very hot oven, and when they are bubbling, serve with plenty of bread.

In a *cargolada*, the snails, after being cleansed by fasting for a week, are rubbed with salt and vinegar and left to froth, then washed in plenty of cold water. They are then grilled over a fire of charcoal or embers and served with large slices of toast, spread with aïoli, and pins to pry them out of their shells. A little melted pork fat can be drizzled into each snail before eating for extra flavor.

FOIE GRAS

This is how I was shown to cook fresh foie gras by Madame Bonomi of Martel, in the Lot. She made it seem the easiest thing in the world to cook—it took her only about four minutes to prepare the foie gras and push it into its terrine (always the same earthenware terrine, although I prefer porcelain). Black smoke poured from the oven (probably because we were both more interested in cooking in it than cleaning it) and I was often anxious for the foie gras, but it always came out perfect. For me there is only one way to eat foie gras and that is this, the simplest way.

FOIE GRAS DE CANARD

Choose a fine raw, but vacuum-packed, fattened duck liver weighing 1 pound 5 ounces. As already mentioned, these are available in any market in southwestern France before Christmas and throughout the autumn and winter. Outside France, they can be found in good grocers in December.

At first the foie gras will be cold and hard, so it must be brought to a temperature where you can open it out and remove any tissues and nerves from between the two lobes. To do this, bring it to room temperature and then leave in a bowl of lukewarm water for half an hour. With a tiny knife, remove the sinews in between the two lobes, handling the liver with great care so as not to crush it. Open it out and sprinkle lightly with salt and pepper and a drop or two of Armagnac, *Vieille Prune*, or Port, then put the two lobes back together and place in a bowl covered with foil. You can let the liver marinate in the refrigerator for an hour, or even overnight for a stronger flavor.

When you are ready to cook the foie gras, mix 3 ounces of duck fat with a teaspoon of the same alcohol used in the marinade, and keep it alongside. Preheat a bain marie using an oval earthenware gratin dish containing 1 inch water in the oven at 300°F.

Put the liver in a small terrine, into which it just fits, and cover it with the prepared fat. Put the lid on and place the terrine in the bain marie in the oven and cook for 45 minutes. Turn off the oven and allow it to cool for two hours. Then place it in the refrigerator and, if possible, allow to mature for two days before eating.

Before serving the foie gras, place it in the freezer for 15 to 20 minutes. This makes it easier to slice. Serve in quite thick slices with hot, toasted pain de campagne (country bread), brioche, or raisin bread and a glass of good Barsac, Sauternes, or other dessert wine.

RENDERING PORK FAT

Pork fat (*graisse*) is a good substitute for goose fat or butter, and was traditionally the main cooking medium in the kitchens of Gascony.

Makes 5–6 ounces of rendered pork fat

1 lb. pork fat, cut into small pieces

Preheat the oven to 275°F.

Place the pork fat in an ovenproof dish and pour in enough warm water to come halfway up the pieces.

Bake in the preheated oven, occasionally straining off the fat through a sieve into a clean bowl. Continue doing this for 3½–4 hours or until the pork pieces have released all their fat. Allow the rendered fat to cool, then keep in the refrigerator until required.

PRESERVED PORK RIND

The *couenne* is pork rind or skin; it is cut in strips, seasoned, rolled, tied with string, and gently cooked in water or in pork fat until tender. These rolls, *les couennes*, are used in long-cooked dishes such as daubes, and other stews, to add body, a velvety texture, and extra flavor to the juices, and to help prevent the meat from drying out.

If you should buy a piece of pork with the rind intact, ask the butcher to remove the skin in one piece (with ¼ inch of fat attached), or do it yourself. Cut it into rough rectangular shapes, measuring approximately 1½ x 4 inches. Sprinkle these couennes with salt and leave them for several hours in the refrigerator. Brush off the excess salt, roll them up like little jelly rolls, and secure with string. Cook in fat and water like the pork (see recipe on page 191).

Couennes can be preserved in fat in exactly the same way as the *confit de porc* and will keep for two weeks in the refrigerator. Use one when you are cooking a daube or, better still, use two or three; they will add a velvety succulence to the stew, as well as an excellent flavor. They will also help to prevent the meat from becoming dry as it cooks.

Index

Bibliography

Anonymous
La Cuisine à l'Anchois
(Repro-Dupli, 1996)

Bertholle, Louisette
Secrets of the Great French Restaurants
(Opera Mundi, 1972, translated by
George Weidenfeld and Nicholson, 1973)

Bontou, Alcide
Traité de Cuisine Bourgeoise Bordelaise
(Feret et Fils, 1921)

Brown, Michael and Sybil
Food and Wine of South-West France
(Batsford Books, 1980)

Cabanau, Laurent
Connaître la Chasse au Sanglier
(Éditions Sud-Ouest, 1994)

Claustres, Francine
Connaître La Cuisine Gasconne
(Éditions Sud-Ouest, 1990)

Comelade, Eliane Thibaut-
Les Coques Catalanes
Portet-sur-Garonne,
(Éditions Loubatières, 1991)

Comelade, Eliane Thibaut-
Ma Cuisine Catalane au Fils des Saisons
(Edisud, 1998)

Comelade, Eliane Thibaut- and
Pierre Torres
Cuisine Catalane & Vins du Roussillon
Portet-sur-Garonne,
(Éditions Loubatières, 1995)

Coulon, Christian
Le Cuisinier Médoquin
(Éditions Confluences, 2000)

Cowl, Jean
Gastronomic Tour de France
(George Allen and Clarin, 1959)

Crewe, Quentin
Foods from France
(Ebury Press, 1993)

Davidson, Alan
North Atlantic Seafood
(Macmillan, 1997)

Davidson, Alan
Mediterranean Seafood
(Penguin Books, 1987)

De Croze, Austin
Les Plats Régionaux de France
(Éditions Montaigne, 1928)

Duluat, Claudine, et Jeanine Pouget
Recettes du Quercy
(Les Éditions du Laquet, 1991)

Escurignan, Maïté
Manuel de Cuisine Basque
(Les Éditions Harriet, 1982)

Galé, Anne-Marie
La Cuisine Basque
(Éditions Sud Ouest, 1994)

Guérard, Michel
Le Sud-Ouest Gourmand
(Éditions Albin Michel, 1993)

Hussenot, Xavier Domingo Pierre
Le Goût d'Espagne
(Flammarion, 1992)

Koffman, Pierre, and Timothy Shaw
Memories of Gascony
(Headline Book Publishing, 1990)

Kurlansky, Mark
*Cod: A Biography of the Fish That
Changed the World*
(Jonathan Cape, 1997)

La Maison Corcellet
*Les Belles Recettes des
Provinces Françaises*
(Librairie Ernest Flammarion)

Marty, Albin
*Fourmiguetto, Souvenirs et Recettes
du Languedoc*
(Éditions Creer, 1978)

La Mazille
La Bonne Cuisine du Périgord
(Flammarion, 1929)

Montagné, Prosper (revised and
introduced by) Le Trésor de la Bassin
*Méditerranéen par 70 Médecins de
France, Offert par les Laboratoires
du Dr Zizine*
(Les Imprimeries Lainé et Tantet)

Olney, Richard
Simple French Food
(Penguin Books, 1974)

Pardies, Françoise
Manuel de Cuisine Landaise
(Jean Curuchet, les Editions
Harriet, 1987)

Penton, Anne
*Customs and Cookery in the Périgord
and Quercy*
(David and Charles, 1973)

Le Président du Conseil Régional de
Languedoc-Roussillon
*Languedoc-Roussillon, Produits du
Terroir et Recettes Traditionelles*
(Éditions Albin Michel, 1998)

Raimes, Helen
A Taste of Périgord
(Robert Hale, 1991)

Reboul, J. B.
La Cuisinière Provençale
(A. Volleyre et Cie)

Recettes de France
La Cuisine Périgourdine
(Créalivres, 1987)

Robinson, Jancis
The Oxford Companion to Wine
(Oxford University Press,
2nd Edition, 1999)

Rouanet, Marie
Petit Traité Romanesque de Cuisine
(Édition J'ai Lu, 1999)

Rouré, Jacques
Table Mise en Pays Catalan
(Éditions Equinoxe, 1998)

Sevilla, Maria José
Life and Food in the Basque Country
(New Amsterdam Books, 1990)

Strang, Jeanne
*Goose Fat and Garlic, Country Recipes
from South-West France*
(Kyle Cathie, 1991)

Wells, Patricia
La France Gourmande
(Flammarion, 1988)

For Michael

Laurel Glen Publishing
An imprint of the Advantage Publishers Group
5880 Oberlin Drive, San Diego, CA 92121-4794
www.laurelglenbooks.com

First published in Great Britain in
2002 by PAVILION BOOKS
(an imprint of Chrysalis Books)
64 Brewery Road
London N7 9NT, U.K.

ISBN 1-57145-949-9
Library of Congress Cataloging-in-Publication
Data available on request.

Printed in Hong Kong
1 2 3 4 5 07 06 05 04 03

**All recipes suitable for vegetarians are marked
with a** (V)

ACKNOWLEDGMENTS

The foundation of my culinary connection with
France stems from my translations of the series
of influential books published in the late
seventies and early eighties by Robert Laffont,
which were the foundation of all today's new
cooking, breathing new life into French food.
I translated, edited, and introduced a series
of seven books written by eight of the top
three-star chefs of the day: Michel Guerard,
Roger Vergé, Jean and Piere Troisgros, Alain
Chapel, Alain Senderens, Jacques Maximin, and
Georges Blanc. The series introduced to Britain
and America the concept of the Nouvelle
Cuisine—innovative food that was beautiful,
light, fresh, fast, and delicate, emphasizing the
quality and fresh ingredients, as opposed to the
rich, elaborate, long-cooked food that preceded
it. For the first time, chefs came out of their
hellish hot kitchens and became media
celebrities, a status they have enjoyed ever
since. These innovative books sold well, but
became overimitated and fell out of fashion,
although this was where it all started.

My new book was inspired by the years of
associating with those *maîtres*—masters of their
profession. Each of them loved what they called
la cuisine de grandmère or *cuisine du terroir*.
Their real affection was for the peasant dishes,
the long-cooked simple dishes of home, and it is
this that my book celebrates, although my
cooking is infused with the knowledge that I
gained from associating with the masters.

I started this book in the Lot and finished it in
the Languedoc. In between I traveled all over
the South of France, and I should like to thank
the many people whose brains I picked along
the way. But most of all I should like to thank
all the friends who helped me so generously
and made it such a pleasure to write this book
and to cook the food for the photography,
particularly Stafford Cliff, Gilles de Chabaneix,
Michele and Bruno Viard, Luc and Jean-Claude
Sarrazin, Faith Evans, Susan Campbell, Jasper
Conran, Avril Giacobbi, Chantal at
Puiserampion, Sandra Purkess, Phillipa
Theophinides, Suzanne Lowrie, Michael Seifert,
Helen Hamlyn, and Denis Maurey. I also thank
my editors, Vivien James and Zoe Antoniou, for
their patience, encouragement, and enthusiasm.

SUPPLIERS

Chef's
P.O. Box 620048
Dallas, TX 75262
(800) 884-CHEF
www.chefscatalog.com

Cooking.com
2850 Ocean Park Blvd., Suite 310
Santa Monica, CA 90405
(800) 663-8810
www.cooking.com

Dean & Deluca
2526 East 36th Street North Circle
Wichita, KS 67219
(877) 826-9246
www.deandeluca.com

Kitchen Etc.
32 Industrial Drive
Exeter, NH 03833
(800) 232-4070
www.kitchenetc.com

Peppercorn
1235 Pearl Street
Boulder, CO 80302
(800) 447-6905
www.peppercorn.com

Sur La Table
1765 Sixth Avenue South
Seattle, WA 98134-1608
(800) 243-0852
www.surlatable.com

Williams-Sonoma
3250 Van Ness Ave.
San Francisco, CA 94109
(877) 812-6235
www.williams-sonoma.com

Zabar's
2245 Broadway
New York, NY 10024
(800) 697-6301
www.zabars.com